EVER AFTER

Lost Love Series, Book 2

Two couples torn apart—one by war between countries, one by war within.

In this moving sequel to *Even Now*, Emily Anderson, now twenty, is attending college on a soccer scholarship when she meets the man who changes everything for her: Army reservist Justin Baker. Their tender relationship, founded on a mutual faith in God and nurtured by their trust and love for each other, proves to be a shining inspiration to everyone they know, especially Emily's reunited birth parents, Lauren Gibbs and Shane Galanter.

Lauren and Shane still struggle to move past their opposing beliefs about war, politics, and faith. Shane believes it's possible but Lauren doesn't. So she says a painful good-bye to her long-ago love and returns to her job as a war correspondent in Afghanistan.

Both hearts are shattered, and Lauren and Shane believe that this time their relationship has truly ended forever. Then tragedy sends shock waves through all their lives. Can Lauren and Shane set aside their opposing views so that love—God's love—might win, no matter how great the odds?

 **ZONDERVAN®**

Visit us on Facebook & Twitter!

 TNZFiction

 @TNZFiction

What Readers Are Saying about Karen Kingsbury's Books

"Karen Kingsbury's books inspire me to be a stronger follower of Jesus Christ, to be a better wife, mother, sister, and friend. Thank you, Karen, for your faithfulness to the Lord's gentle whisper." —Tamara B.

"It's as simple as this: God's heart comes off these pages—every line, every word. You can feel the love and redemption of Christ through every character's life in each book. The message is a message of hope, hope in the One who has saved us and reigns victorious!" —Brenae D.

"Karen's books are like a personal Bible study—there are so many situations that can be applied directly to the truths found in God's Word to help strengthen and encourage me . . ." —Laura G.

"I have read many of Karen's books, and I cry with everyone. I feel like I actually know the people in the story, and my heart goes out to all of them when something happens!" —Kathy N.

"Novels are mini-vacations, and Karen Kingsbury's novels are my favorite destinations." —Rachel S.

"Karen Kingsbury's books are amazing! They are inspirational, encouraging, heart-touching, and definitely life-changing. Thank you, Karen, for sharing your gift with us." —Lisa M. P.

"The best author in the country." —Mary H.

"Karen's books are like chocolate—very addicting! You can't just eat one piece at a time, you have to eat the whole thing—you can't just read one chapter at a time, you have to read the whole book!" —Sarah M.

"Karen truly has a God-given talent . . . I have laughed, cried, and rejoiced with your characters as if they were real people! Please keep writing, Karen . . . I can't put your books down! God bless you!" —Rebekah H.

"The stories are fiction; their impact is real." —Debbie L.R.

"It was my lucky day when a friend introduced me to Karen Kingsbury's books! A day without K. K. isn't complete . . ." —Bette O. J.

"My daughter and I 'fight' to read Karen's books first. She has even said, 'Mom, I'll do dishes. *You* go read the latest Karen Kingsbury book!'" —Terry S.

"Karen Kingsbury books are like my best friends. They make me cry, laugh, and give me encouragement. God Bless you, Karen, for using your talent for Him." —Tammy G.

"Every time I read one of Karen's books I think 'it's the best one yet.' Then the next one comes out and I think, 'No, this is the best one.'" —April B. M.

"Karen's Kingbury's books are fantastic! She always makes me feel like I'm living the story along with the characters!" —Courtney M. G.

"Karen's books speak to the heart. They are timely, entertaining, but, more important, they speak God's love into hungry souls." —Debbie P. K.

"Whenever I pick up a new K. K. book, two things are consistent: tissues and finishing the whole book in one day." —Nel L.

"When I was in Iraq, Mrs. Kingsbury's books were like a cool breeze on a hot summer day, and they made the hard days a bit easier to bear. By the end of my tour, all the ladies in my tent were hooked!" —Olivia G.

"These books are the *best*! I have bought every one of them. I love getting my friends 'hooked' on Karen Kingsbury!" —Dana T. C.

"Not only do Karen Kingsbury books make you laugh and make you cry . . . they will leave you begging for more . . . I stay awake all night when a new one comes out, reading by flashlight while my family sleeps!" —Hellen H.

www.KarenKingsbury.com

Other Life-Changing Fiction™ by Karen Kingsbury

KAREN KINGSBURY

ZONDERVAN®

ZONDERVAN

Ever After
Copyright © 2007 by Karen Kingsbury

This title is also available as a Zondervan ebook.
Visit www.zondervan.com/ebooks.

This title is also available in a Zondervan audio edition.
Visit www.zondervan.fm.

Requests for information should be addressed to:
Zondervan, *Grand Rapids, Michigan 49530*

Library of Congress Cataloging-in-Publication Data

Kingsbury, Karen.
        Ever after / Karen Kingsbury.
            p. cm.
        Sequel to: Even Now.
        ISBN 978-0-310-24756-2
        1. Life change events — Fiction. 2. Women college students — Fiction.
    3. United States — Armed Forces — Reserves — Fiction. 4. Iraq War, 2003 — Fiction.
    I. Title.
    PS3561.I4873E945   2006
    813'.54 — dc22   2006025081

Published in association with the literary agency of Alive Communications, Inc., 7680
Goddard Street, Suite 200, Colorado Springs, CO 80920 www.alivecommunications.com

ISBN 978-0-3103-3784-3 (2013 repackage)

Printed in the United States of America

13 14 15 16 17 /QG/ 21 20 19 18 17 16 15 14 13 12 11 10 9 8 7 6 5 4 3 2 1

In Memory of Joshua Dingler

I bring you this book in honor of the memory of Joshua Dingler, age nineteen.

At the final stages of editing *Ever After*, I received a letter from one of my readers—Karen Dingler. She said God had used one of my books to help her understand that her son, Joshua Dingler of the First Battalion, the 108th Armor Regiment of the U.S. Army in Calhoun, Georgia, had not died in vain.

What defined Joshua was his life, how he lived. Joshua was the son of a pastor, Tommy Dingler. His mother had just taken on the role of his army unit's family support group leader when his family learned of his death. Joshua left behind a younger brother, Samuel.

When he was a young boy, Joshua played Little League baseball. He was a Boy Scout who earned the rank Life Scout, and in middle school, he went to Australia and New Zealand as a student ambassador for People 2 People. He helped out at church and volunteered at the sound booth. He was in JROTC at East Paulding High School in Hiram, Georgia, where he was known and loved by everyone he came in contact with. He would defend NASCAR to anyone who questioned it as a sport. Joshua planned to come home and marry his high school love and wanted to be a history teacher.

In honor of Joshua, I am starting two new links on my website, *www.KarenKingsbury.com*. The first is for Active Military

Heroes. The second is for Fallen Military Heroes. If you have a friend or loved one serving our country, please send me a photo and a brief description of that person—name, rank, where they are serving, and how we can pray for them. The Active Military Heroes page will honor these men and women. It will be a place where readers can see the face on the fight for freedom, a place where readers can visit to pray for each other. If you've lost a loved one or a friend in military action, please send that photo and a brief description also. This will be posted on my Fallen Military Heroes page. Joshua Dingler's photo will be at the top of that page. If you are sending a photo and information, please put the word "SOLDIER" in the subject line and send it to *Kingsburydesk@aol.com.*

As you read the pages of *Ever After*, think about Joshua Dingler. The sacrifice for freedom is a real one. And please pray for and support the families and members of the U.S. Military. Pray every day.

In His light and love,
Karen Kingsbury

Joshua Dingler, 1986–2005

Dedicated To ...

Donald, my prince charming. In this season of life, with you working as full-time teacher here at home for our boys, I am maybe more proud of you than ever. I'm amazed at the way you blend love and laughter, tenderness and tough standards, to bring out the best in our boys. A second season of homeschooling? Wow! Don't for a minute think that your role in all this is somehow smaller. You have the greatest responsibility of all. Not only with our children, but in praying for me as I write and speak and go about this crazy, fun job God has given me. I couldn't do it without you. Thanks for loving me, for being my best friend, and for finding "date moments" amidst even the most maniacal or mundane times. My favorite times are with you by my side. I love you always, forever.

Kelsey, my precious daughter. You are just newly seventeen, and somehow that sounds more serious than the other ages. As if we jumped four years over the past twelve months. Seventeen brings with it the screeching of brakes on a childhood that has gone along full speed until now. Seventeen? Seventeen years since I held you in the nursery, feeling a sort of love I'd never felt before? Seventeen sounds like bunches of lasts all lined up ready to take the stage—and college counselors making plans to take my little girl from home into a brand-new big world. Seventeen tells me it won't be much longer. Sometimes I find myself barely able to exhale. The ride is so fast, I can only try not to blink so I won't miss a minute. Like the most beautiful springtime flower, I see you growing and unfolding, becoming interested in current events and formulating godly viewpoints that are yours alone. The same is true in dance, where you are simply breathtaking on stage. I believe in you, honey. Keep your eyes on Jesus and the path will be easy to follow. Don't ever stop dancing. I love you.

Tyler, my beautiful song. Can it be that you are fourteen and helping me bring down the dishes from the top shelf? Just yesterday, people who called confused you with Kelsey. Now they confuse you with your dad—in more ways than one. You are on the bridge, dear son, making the transition between Neverland and Tomorrowland, and becoming a strong, godly young man in the process. Keep giving Jesus your very best and always remember that you're in a battle. In today's world, Ty, you need His armor every day, every minute. Don't forget … when you're up there on stage, no matter how bright the lights, I'll be watching from the front row, cheering you on. I love you.

Sean, my wonder boy. Your sweet nature continues to be a bright light in our home. It seems a lifetime ago that we first brought you—our precious son—home from Haiti. It's been my great joy to watch you grow and develop this past year, learning more about reading and writing and, of course, animals. You're a walking encyclopedia of animal facts, and that too brings a smile to my face. Recently a cold passed through the family, and you handled it better than any of us. Smiling through your fever, eyes shining even when you felt your worst. Sometimes I try to imagine if everyone, everywhere had your outlook—what a sunny place the world would be. Your hugs are something I look forward to, Sean. Keep close to Jesus. I love you.

Josh, my tender tough guy. You continue to excel at everything you do, but my favorite time is late at night when I poke my head into your room and see that—once again—your nose is buried in your Bible. You really get it, Josh. I loved hearing you talk about baptism the other day, how you feel ready to make that decision, that commitment to Jesus. At almost twelve, I can only say that every choice you make for Christ will take you closer to the plans He has for your life. By being strong in the Lord, first and foremost, you'll be strong at everything else. Keep winning for Him, dear son. You make me so proud. I love you.

EJ, my chosen one. You amaze me, Emmanuel Jean! The other day you told me you pray often, and I asked you what about. "I thank God a lot," you told me. "I thank Him for my health and my life and my home." Your normally dancing eyes grew serious. "And for letting me be adopted into the right family." Well. I still feel the sting of tears when I imagine you praying that way. I'm glad God let you be adopted into the right family too. One of my secret pleasures is watching you and Daddy becoming so close. I'll glance over at the family room during a playoff basketball game on TV, and there you'll be, snuggled up close to him, his arm around your shoulders. As long as Daddy's your hero, you have nothing to worry about. You couldn't have a better role model. I know that Jesus is leading the way, and that you are excited to learn the plans He has for you. But for you, this year will always stand out as a turning point. Congratulations, honey! I love you.

Austin, my miracle child. Can my little boy really be nine years old? Even when you're twenty-nine, you'll be my youngest, my baby. I guess that's how it is with the last child, but there's no denying what my eyes tell me. You're not little anymore. Even so, I love that — once in a while — you wake up and scurry down the hall to our room so you can sleep in the middle. I still see the blond-haired infant who lay in intensive care, barely breathing, awaiting emergency heart surgery. I'm grateful for your health, precious son; grateful God gave you back to us at the end of that long ago day. Your heart remains the most amazing part of you, not only physically, miraculously, but because you have such kindness and compassion for people. One minute, tough boy hunting frogs and snakes out back, pretending you're an Army Ranger, and then getting teary-eyed when Horton the Elephant nearly loses his dust speck full of little Who people. Be safe, baby boy. I love you.

And to God Almighty, the Author of life, who has, for now, blessed me with these.

ONE

Two blue and gray fighter jets raced low over the neighborhood and looped toward the barren mountains in the west. Lauren Gibbs heard the vibration in the subtle rattle of picture frames on the mantel, sensed it in the wood floor of the old house, felt it all the way to her soul. Training drills, same as most days. She froze long enough to watch them, long enough to catch her fiancé's attention.

"They still bug you."

It wasn't a question. Shane Galanter doled out the stack of plates in his hand one at a time onto the white linen tablecloth.

"Not really." Lauren grabbed the napkins and followed behind him, setting one at each place. She caught his eye and hesitated. No fooling him, not when he knew all the back roads of her heart. She released a slow breath. "Okay, yes." She set a napkin down on the next plate. "They bother me."

Shane didn't ask if her frustration was with the noise of the jets, or with the fact that they flew training maneuvers over the neighborhood where he lived, a few blocks from the navy's Top Gun facility in Fallon, Nevada. Or if it was something bigger. Like the fact that these were the very jets and pilots that would be used in battle if necessary.

He didn't have to ask. He already knew.

Because long ago he'd learned to know her mind, back when they first fell in love as kids. Yes, time and circumstances had separated them for nearly two decades, and now that they were in their midthirties, they'd both changed. But even so, ever since

1

they'd found each other again, Shane could still look into her eyes and know what she was thinking.

"Sometimes, Lauren." He crooked his finger and placed it gently beneath her chin. His eyes looked more tired than usual. "Sometimes I wonder about us."

Panic stirred and she felt her world tilt. She shouldn't have hesitated at the noise, shouldn't have looked out the window. "It's no big deal." An anxious laugh sounded in her throat. "This is your life. I can handle it."

He didn't look away. "It's about to be your life too." His tone was kind, careful. "Remember?"

"I know." She put her hand alongside his cheek and kissed him. "By then I'll be used to it."

He searched her eyes. "It's been six months, Lauren."

She refused to give fear a foothold. Instead she kissed him again, slower this time. "I'm trying." She breathed the words against his lips. "Give me that, at least."

The wedding was set for Christmas Eve — not by her choosing. She would've had them married by now. Every conflict resolved and nothing but a bright future ahead of them. Their nineteen-year-old daughter Emily felt the same, especially since her fall figured to be crazy-busy. She had accepted a soccer scholarship to Pacific Lutheran University in Tacoma, Washington, and she was about to start work in the public information office of the army base at nearby Fort Lewis. Following in her father's footsteps. "Make it a summer wedding," Emily had pleaded with them. "Before school starts."

But Lauren figured Emily wasn't worried about her schedule as much as she was worried about her parents working things out. Even so, Shane wouldn't budge. He wanted to wait and work through some of the issues that stood in their way. Faith, his career choice, their politics, and nearly twenty years between the first time they fell in love and this second chance ...

That was fine. Lauren would wait. She'd do whatever it took to prove to Shane that she could deal with all this. The smallness of Fallon, Nevada; the hour's drive west to the Fallon Airport every time her editors at *Time* magazine sent her on an assignment. And the incessant sound of fighter jets overhead. She could learn to deal with all of it, right? Even if there were days when being so close to a military base threatened her sanity.

Shane set the plates down and turned into her arms. "So you're saying—" he wove his fingers through her straight blonde hair—"I have nothing to wonder about."

At his touch, the warm tone in his voice, Lauren's world righted itself. She relaxed in his embrace. "Nothing."

"Alright, then." He kissed the tip of her nose. "I'll get the lasagna."

As long as Shane responded to her this way, as long as it took only her kiss to send him into her arms, then she could find a way to live here. She had to find a way. Yes, she was still writing military features for the magazine and flying around the country for interviews several times each month. Most of the time that was enough. So what if some days she wanted to jump on a plane and head back to Afghanistan, to her work as a *Time* magazine war correspondent. Never mind that she still mistrusted the government and the military and their roles in the Iraqi war. Never mind that her fiancé's political views were on the other end of the hemisphere from hers …

As long as she had Shane, she could look past all of it.

The doorbell rang, and Lauren took a step back from the table. Their company had arrived. Three couples, none of whom she knew. Not really. Two of the guys worked with Shane in the training department, and the third was a pilot they were considering as an addition to the instruction staff. Each was bringing his wife.

Lauren took a deep breath. The conversation would be predictable, but she would smile through every minute. She headed for the door, glancing over her shoulder. "I'll get it."

"Thanks." Shane didn't sound at all concerned. His opinionated fiancée was about to share an evening with three couples whose viewpoints didn't line up with hers, but he wasn't uptight. He trusted her.

The thought eased her tension. She smiled, opened the door, and found all three couples waiting. One of the guys was small and compact, with bright, laughing eyes. His exaggerated shrug was full of good humor. "We all showed up at the same time." He looked at the others. "Imagine that."

The others laughed, and a beat later, Lauren did too. "Yes. Imagine that." When everyone was inside, she shut the door and introduced herself. One of the guys—the heavyset one—she'd seen before. But she hadn't met the smaller guy, nor the pilot, nor any of their wives. Lauren felt better once they were past the introductions. The wives—Becky, a redhead; Sally, a blonde; and Ann, a petite brunette—seemed friendly enough. Becky noticed Lauren's colorful beaded necklace.

"I haven't seen anything like it." The woman looked a little too well put together. She moved in closer and studied the beads. "Macy's?"

"No." Lauren kept her tone even. She paused. "Afghanistan." She measured their reaction. "A local woman made it for me."

"Oh—" Becky smiled—"How interesting."

"Yes." Ann, the brunette wife of the shorter pilot nodded. "When we've spent time overseas I always buy from the locals." She looked at the others. "Very vogue."

"The economy in Afghanistan is in a shambles." Lauren touched her necklace. "I try to support the people as much as possible." As soon as she said the words, she chided herself. The explanation wasn't necessary. The redhead was only trying to be kind, trying to find common ground by giving her the compliment.

A silence fell over the group, an awkward silence. Buying a necklace overseas was one thing, but from Afghanistan? As a way of supporting the country's economy? Suddenly it was as if all of them were remembering that Lauren was different. Certainly one or another of them had heard about her, Shane Galanter's liberal fiancée. The one person in their midst who didn't feel a sense of pride and purpose every time she passed a military base, who made her living writing for *Time* magazine.

Finally Ann smiled. "Those Afghani women must cherish the freedom to make and sell their wares."

Touché. Lauren gritted her teeth and kept herself from responding. The brunette was right. If Afghanistan hadn't been liberated, the women couldn't have presented themselves or their jewelry in public. But there were other problems, life-threatening issues that faced the Afghani people and the Iraqis. What was the United States doing about that?

Shane found them in the entryway. He seemed to sense that things were a bit tense. "Well—" he clapped his hands—"Lauren and I made our best lasagna." He gestured down the hall toward the dining room and kitchen. "Let's move in and we can get started."

The others were happy to follow him. As he walked down the hall, Shane grinned at the guys and nodded at their wives. "I'll tell you what," he shook the pilot's hand, "that was some fancy flying you did the other day."

"No doubt." The heavier guy took the spot on the other side of Shane. "Best flying I've seen in years."

The women formed a small cluster as they headed into the dining room. "Speaking of Macy's," Becky tossed her red hair, "It's their big sale this week."

"I *thought* it was coming up." Ann eased her designer purse onto her shoulder and laughed. "Sounds like a date night, ladies."

They rounded the corner and spilled into the dining room. Country music played from the living room, something slow and crooning. Shane took the pitcher of iced tea and held it up. "Anyone thirsty?"

The guys each reached for a glass, but the women kept talking. Lauren hung back in the hallway, pretending to arrange the vase of flowers Shane had bought for the evening.

"Any night but Wednesday." Sally pulled a face that made the other women smile. "Youth group meets at our house on Wednesdays."

"And Chad wouldn't miss that." Ann poked her finger in the air. "The kid hated church until high school. Now you can't keep him away from youth group."

"I think maybe Chad's noticing the girls more than the gospel." Becky raised an eyebrow.

"Whatever." Ann moved toward the guys and the iced tea. "As long as he's going."

"Okay, so Macy's any night but Wednesday." Becky pretended to jot a note. "Let's aim for Tuesday."

Nods of approval followed, and the plan seemed set.

Lauren was still in the hallway, staring at the women. Was this what Shane wanted her to be? Someone whose greatest challenge in a given week was whether Tuesday or Wednesday would be better for shopping at Macy's? Whether the kids liked youth group because of the gospel or the girls?

Then, as if a switch had been flipped, she caught herself. What was she doing, being silently critical of these women? Critical and judgmental and mean-spirited? Were her views against the war so entrenched that she would dislike a group of military wives simply for who they married? Regret and sorrow came over her in a rush. She had no right to judge these women or challenge them. They played both father and mother to their kids much of the time, and during wartime, they faced losses other people couldn't understand.

She drew a slow breath. She would change her mood now, before they thought she was a terrible person. Before Shane saw how she was acting. She could hardly be a supporter of peace and then hurry into conflict right here in Shane's living room. At that moment, Sally tucked a piece of her blonde hair behind her ears, turned toward Lauren, and came a few steps closer. Her slim shoulders lifted in a dainty shrug. "Anything I can do to help?"

Lauren looked across the room. Ann and Becky were lost in another conversation. In addition to everything else they thought about her, now they would think she was rude. She'd have to make it up to them later. She turned her attention to Sally. The woman had compassionate eyes. Lauren gave her a sheepish smile and nodded toward the kitchen. "Help me slice the bread?"

"Sure." When they reached the counter where two hot loaves were sitting on separate cutting boards, Sally tilted her head. "Ann and Becky don't mean any harm."

"I know." Lauren reached into the nearest drawer for a couple knives and handed one to Sally. "I need to remember that everyone isn't an enemy. Just because my views are different from everyone else's in Fallon."

"I know you think so, but you're not that different." Sally shrugged. "War's complicated." Sally washed her hands and dried them on a nearby towel. "We might be married to military guys, but we wonder, we question." She reached for one of the loaves of bread and began slicing it. "We believe in the cause of the war in the Middle East, and we support our troops and the president. But we wouldn't be breathing if we didn't have concerns." Something deep and sad filled her eyes. "Our husbands' lives are at stake."

Lauren washed and dried her hands too and reached for one of the loaves of bread. She hadn't thought about that. Even military people might not see things in entirely black and white. Something stirred in her heart, an unsettling thought that if she'd been wrong about the women she was sharing dinner with, maybe she'd been wrong about other aspects of the war. Maybe some of the things military information officers had told her hadn't been so exaggerated or distorted after all. She ran the knife through her loaf and banished the thought. She could be wrong on some things. Tonight she was, and she was sorry. But she wasn't wrong in her passion to see the war ended, to have the president admit that the loss of life and resources was all for naught and that nothing had been gained in the process.

Sally finished slicing her loaf. She lifted her eyes to Lauren. "I'm a Christian." She looked across the room at Becky and Ann. "We moved here from the Northwest. Most of the women I've met here, navy or married to navy, are Christians too. That defines them more than their politics." She was quiet for a minute. "Seems that peace is a lot more about kindness and sacrifice than any kind of international political paradise."

Peace. There it was again. The idea that peace could come through more than one course of action. Shane had tried to convince her of that since they reunited just after Christmas, back in Illinois. Peace comes from the inside, he would tell her. Lauren wanted to believe it was true, but she couldn't. Not yet, anyway. Sally was waiting for a response. Lauren moved the sliced bread from the cutting board to a wooden bowl. "Peace is complicated, I guess." She kept her eyes on the bread. "Just like war."

"Hmm." Sally added in her bread. "I guess."

Lauren wanted to let the subject go. Talking to Sally — to someone who didn't see her as a freak of nature — was nice. If she stopped now, they could at least have the beginning of a friendship. But she couldn't let it go. "What I want is a peace that'll send our kids home where they belong." Her tone was gentle, with a subtle pleading. Maybe if she explained herself well enough, they could be friends despite their fundamental differences. She sighed. "I keep thinking of all those young people who've lost their lives. That's why I'm against the war." Lauren looked over her shoulder at the chatty women in the dining room. "If any of you lost a husband or brother or daughter, you'd switch sides in a heartbeat, don't you think, Sally?"

"No." The blonde woman covered Lauren's hand with her own. She exuded patience and her eyes shone in a way that Lauren had seen before—with Shane and their daughter Emily. "That's not how it works."

Something tightened in Lauren's gut. She didn't want to hear about patriotism and courage. Patriotic, why? Courageous over what? Sacrifice for whom? Dying for the sake of dying? Wasn't that all any of them could say about a convoy of American kids being killed by a roadside bomb? Or being struck down by an insurgent sniper?

Lauren sighed. "I'm sorry, Sally. I sort of have my mind made up on all that." She smiled. "But tell me about the Northwest. Our daughter's moving to Tacoma to play soccer for Pacific Lutheran University. I've always wanted to visit."

A sad smile tugged at the corners of Sally's lips. "We lived in the Portland area." She breathed in. "It's beautiful. Water runs through much of the city, and the trees are ..."

Lauren felt herself drift. In her mind's eye, she was no longer in her kitchen, but standing among the orphans in a dusty, hot little structure where forty kids lived. She could almost feel herself handing out lollipops and then being called out into the courtyard. Hear someone say her name and then the sound of children running out behind her, following her ...

Hear the scream of bullets spraying from snipers' guns a dozen yards behind the building ... hear the little girl crying out as she hit the ground ...

No!

Heart pounding, Lauren tried to focus on Sally's words, to let her description of Portland push the ugly images from her mind.

She succeeded for a while, but during dinner, when the guys discussed the Fallon base and upkeep of older fighter jets, her mind drifted again. Back to the orphanage, the attack. The little boy and girl who lost their lives. The women wailing as they knelt over their bodies, crying out for an answer, a reason.

Midway through dinner, Dan, the heavier guy, set down his fork and looked at her. "You and Shane grew up together, is that right?"

Lauren was caught off guard, but she smiled. Maybe this was when she could show them she was capable of compassion. "Yes. Our families were friends."

Dan pointed at her and then at Shane. "You were apart for twenty years, Shane told me."

"Right." Shane wiped his mouth with a napkin. He had a take-charge tone, as if he wanted to protect her from whatever direction the conversation might go. "Our daughter Emily brought us back together."

Lauren's heart warmed. She loved that Shane was quick to come to her defense. Even before there was any actual need. "I decided to move from Afghanistan to Fallon." She looked at Shane, and for a moment there seemed to be no differences between them whatsoever. Just her and Shane and a love that would stay between them until they died.

"So you're not covering the war anymore?" Becky adjusted her chair so that she could see to the far end of the table where Lauren was sitting.

"Not as much." Lauren fought the uneasiness that rose within her. *Come on. Just because they're asking about my writing doesn't mean they're ready to attack.* She forced herself to relax. "Most of my stories still involve some aspect of the war, but usually with interviews of politicians in Washington, D.C., or some other major city."

"I wanted to be a writer when I was in college," Sally took a sip of her water. "I still do sometimes. The travel must be hard for you and Shane."

"It is." She thought about her last trip, how she had dreaded coming home to Fallon but missed Shane all at the same time.

"Bet you were surprised when you heard about Shane studying world issues and peace in college." Dan leaned back and pushed his empty plate aside. "If anyone understands this war, it's Shane Galanter."

Shane straightened and reached for the salad bowl. "Lauren understands it too." He smiled, his tone a little strained. "Just from a different angle."

The conversation switched gears, but Lauren's heart was dizzy with wonder. No matter what their struggles privately, Shane would defend her to the ground in public. Just the way he'd done here. Dan had tried to make a point that Shane's opinions were based on years of education. But Shane was more concerned with how people saw Lauren.

With that kind of love, how could they have any problems at all?

Later, when dinner was over and the guests had gone home, Shane found her on the back patio. He came up behind her, eased his hands beneath her arms and slipped them around her waist. "Tonight was hard?"

"No." The stars shone from every corner of the sky — the one thing she loved about Fallon. She leaned her head back against his chest. "Not after I stopped being a jerk."

"You mean that was the *nice* you?" He took hold of her shoulders and gently turned her around so she was facing him. His voice held a hint of humor, but his eyes showed his frustration. "It was hard. For both of us. For everyone at the table. We're talking about renovating the naval fleet, and you ask if anyone has any idea how many homeless people could find housing for that kind of taxpayer money?"

"I was curious." She searched his eyes, willing him to see her sincerity. "I smiled, I was pleasant. I'm not trying to be difficult, Shane. Really."

"Okay, but Lauren, have you ever considered how you sound to these people? These women's husbands ... their lives are on the line." His voice was low and so sad. Sadder than she'd heard him in a long time.

"Yes. I've thought about it." She winced and brushed her knuckles against his cheeks. "Shane ..." She groaned. "I'm sorry. I don't want to be mean or critical. Sometimes I just can't help what I say."

He studied her. "Yes, you can. You meant everything you said tonight. It drove you crazy to sit at the same table with those women."

"I liked Sally." She bit her lip. "But the other two treated me like I was from a different planet."

"Because you act like you are." He linked fingers with hers. "Because you want to be different."

"Shane ..."

"No, it's true." Again his tone was kind, but his eyes told her he was serious. "One of the guys pulled me aside in the kitchen after dinner." Shane sighed, and the sound seemed to come from deep in his heart. "He said you were very interesting, intelligent, but he wondered how we'd ever work out together." Shane's tone grew resigned. "He was worried for me, Lauren."

"So ..." Her heart pounded. She hated when their conversations went this way—which they did more and more often. "I love you." She took a step closer and brought her lips to his. "Did you tell him that?"

"He knows." Shane looked like he wanted to kiss her longer, but he resisted. "I told him the whole story a few weeks ago. About our early years and how we just found each other again."

"Exactly. And that's enough, Shane. We found each other again for a reason. We both believe that. We don't need to agree about everything." She looped her arms up around his neck. "Every couple has differences."

"But ours define us. Not just our politics, but our faith."

Lauren stiffened. He was more than a little troubled if he was bringing up faith again. "I said I'm trying." Her words were small and quiet, but they were the truth. Their daughter Emily was doing everything she could to help Lauren understand the faith she and her father shared. But something deep inside held Lauren back. *What's wrong with me? Why can't I think like everyone else? Why do I have to make everything so hard?*

She turned and walked out into the yard, her back to Shane. He didn't follow.

Lauren sank into a lawn chair. She and Emily talked at least twice a week. At nineteen, with her second year of college on the horizon, there was so much for Emily to talk about. Still, the conversation always turned to faith. Lauren agreed with everything her daughter said — in theory anyway. Since reconnecting with Shane and with her family, it only felt right to reconnect with the beliefs she'd held as a child.

But believing in God and having a relationship with Him were two different things. When her thoughts turned to her Creator, she couldn't bring herself to ask the questions Emily wanted her to ask. *What is my purpose, God, what are the plans You have for me? What do You want from me?* No, instead she found herself asking more practical questions. *Why do You allow wars? And how could so many Christians support the U.S. involvement in the Middle East? Didn't fighting go against the very principles of the Christian faith? And why did so many soldiers have to die?*

So far she wasn't hearing much response from God, but that was understandable. The questions were hard, and Emily had said that some things won't make sense this side of heaven.

Period. No, what Lauren really hated was when anyone questioned her faith. When they wanted some kind of simplistic capitulation from her, as though the entire issue weren't painfully complicated. She sighed. Like everything else about her new life.

Footsteps sounded from behind her, and Shane came up by her side. "I'm sorry." He leaned close and kissed her cheek. "I love you, Lauren."

Her anger dissipated. She stood and turned into his arms, exhaling long and slow. "I spent all my growing up years looking for you, Shane." Her voice was a desperate whisper. "You're the only one I've ever loved."

"So—" he brushed aside a stray lock of her hair—"why does it seem so hard, right?"

"Right." They held each other for a long time, swaying as the high desert breeze whistled through the nearby canyons. The temperature had dropped into the fifties, and Lauren would've been cold if not for Shane's arms. She eased back and kissed him. "I have to go."

"I know." He took her hand and led her inside, his steps slow and measured. "We don't need all the answers today."

She hugged him once more before she left, but the moment she climbed into her car and started the engine, fury assaulted her. Not at Shane, but at herself. She was the one making their relationship so difficult. Why couldn't she look the other way or just put her questions aside? Did every discussion have to be a platform for her politics? And what was the point, anyway? She wasn't going to change anything with her attitude.

She kept the radio off, rolled down the window, and let the cool air wash across her face. Her thoughts blew around the car in the breeze. She tried to picture Him—the God Emily talked about, the One who wanted a friendship with her. But all she could sense as she turned onto the main highway was His enormity.

God the Creator. Too big to be involved in the trivialities of her life. *God ... are You there?* She waited. Emily talked about hearing from God, sensing His voice and His response deep within her. Lauren stared straight out the windshield and tried again. *God, I need to know ... are You there?* She hesitated, but again, nothing. No, as she set out toward her apartment, she couldn't tell whether God was with her or not. But that only figured.

Just one more question He wasn't answering.

TWO

[faded text from previous page showing through]

S hane listened as Lauren's car drove away, but he didn't go back inside.

Watching her leave stirred a memory. Once, when he was twelve years old, he and a friend were playing catch in the house. His mother was at the store, and the last thing she'd told him was to keep the baseball outside. "Too many things to break indoors," she'd said.

But it was hot and humid outside that day, so Shane chose to do things his way. He was a good catcher, and so was his friend. They spread out on opposite sides of the living room and tossed the ball carefully. At first. But after a few minutes, they were whizzing it at each other. He was just about to tell his friend to cool it, slow it down, when the ball came firing at him and tipped his glove.

Shane willed it to hit the wall, but instead it smacked with a thud against a decorative vase, something his mother had gotten from one of her trips to Europe. Both boys fell silent, and Shane took slow steps toward the three-foot-high vase. It still looked intact, still stood right where it had always stood.

But as he went to take hold of it, the glass container fell apart in his hands. He remembered trying to hold it in place, to keep the pieces together as if he could somehow will it whole again.

He squinted at the night sky.

That's how it feels now, Lord. About Lauren. Things *looked* whole and good. They were together, after all. Engaged to be married on Christmas Eve. But he had the feeling, if he didn't hold onto her just right, everything would fall apart. He gripped the railing and tried to remember when he'd first noticed the cracks.

That was obvious, wasn't it? From the beginning.

Emily worked so hard to bring them together last winter, but it had only taken him and Lauren one evening to figure out that they stood on opposite sides of a political chasm. Only God could bridge such an abyss.

They began by talking about the article she'd written for *Time*, the one slamming fighter pilots. He could still hear her voice that night in her parents' house, after everyone was asleep. Snow fell outside and bright flames crackled in the fireplace.

She'd let her head fall back against the sofa. "Shane ... how did you wind up on the wrong side of this war?"

He took her hand, worked his fingers between hers. "The question is ..." his voice held no accusation, "how did you?"

Talk of the war seemed to place a wall between them, one they volleyed over the rest of the night. She asked him to consider the fact that Jesus came to bring peace, and that no one could call himself a Christian without also wanting peace.

"I want peace, Lauren. We all do. The question is how we find it." Passion filled Shane's words. Passion and an anger that she hadn't seen in him before. "And just so you know, Jesus didn't come to bring peace, He came to bring us life. Life to the fullest measure."

"Okay, good." She kept her intensity. "If He came to bring us life, then how can you be part of a war that kills people?"

The debate raged the rest of the evening. She used arguments in favor of pacifism, and he tried to explain peace through strength. But at the end of the night, they were no closer to bridging the distance between them. They might never even have tried, except that week, they watched her father die.

After his death, Shane asked Lauren not to leave, not to return to her post as a war correspondent in Afghanistan. Their differences could be worked out, especially if she could find the faith she'd been raised with. When her father died, his loss struck a nerve deep inside her. She'd missed her father's last two decades because of her anger and stubborn pride. The thought of leaving Shane, of missing a life with him, was enough to shake her convictions.

Even so, it wasn't until she was on the plane, flying away from him, that Lauren finally changed her mind. At her connecting destination, she called her editor, asked for a stateside job in Fallon, and flew to meet Shane. He smiled at the memory. No matter how long he lived, he would always see her the way she looked that day. As she walked up, he lost his breath and his heart all in the same instant. She'd come back to him! She cared enough to come! And for a while, everything was sunshine and laughter. She rented an apartment and they spent hours together every available evening.

The first cracks came about eight weeks later, in early spring.

Lauren attended a series of parties on the base with Shane, and each time she seemed to slip a notch backward, back to the person she'd been when they talked near the fireplace that first night. Instead of being patient and understanding toward the military and its efforts, she was uptight and sarcastic, her thoughts running in direct contrast to his.

Several times he'd reminded her that he too had studied the topic of peace, that he'd researched past civilizations and wars in order to form his conclusion. And what he'd learned was that peace could only come through strength. They talked again about September 11, and the plans the terrorists had, to make the events of that day seem minimal in contrast.

"Yes, we're at war," Shane said one night, "but terrorists haven't taken the life of one single U.S. citizen on American soil since we began fighting back."

Sometimes Lauren listened more intently, as if maybe she was finally seeing his way of thinking. But always she came back to one of her own sticking points. How could the U.S. send young men — boys, really — into battle? Did they understand what was at stake, and the risk they were taking? Wasn't there another way to protect the United States through diplomacy and international peace treaties — without sacrificing lives?

Lauren's ideas sounded so wonderful, so idealistic. Peace conferences, discussions with leaders of terrorist groups, diversity and tolerance training for children, an antihate program designed to help cultures learn to accept and respect each other.

"Educating the next generation *has* to be better than putting their lives in danger." Every time she said this, she searched his eyes, desperate for him to understand.

Those were the most frustrating moments of all. Times when he wanted to take her by the shoulders and shake her. Education? *Tolerance* training? Anyone who understood the terrorist mindset knew such an approach was utterly ludicrous.

They'd gotten into it again a week ago, and finally he'd had enough. "Terrorists have one goal, Lauren. One goal. To kill people who don't agree with them. And more often than not, that means people who live in or agree with the thinking of Western civilization. Terrorists are honored to die for the cause, so there's no reasoning with them, no educating them." He gathered his emotions and found a level of control. "The only option is to protect ourselves by weeding them out, arresting them or eliminating them."

"And now that we're fighting back, the attacks have stopped, right?" She could be so cutting at times, so sarcastic.

He fixed her with a hard stare. "On American soil, yes."

She turned away. "It's just a matter of time, and you know it. We're more vulnerable than anyone likes to think. And we just keep getting in deeper over there."

"Lauren, everyone wants a quick and easy war, but passing the reigns of freedom on to a region formerly run by dictators and terrorists is not a quick and easy job."

Shane rubbed his hand over his face, as though to erase the memories of their struggles. The entire topic made him feel sick and tired. His shoulders slumped a little and he turned back toward the house. Normally he'd put on some music, something to keep him company while he cleared the table and loaded the dishwasher. But this time he worked in silence. Even his thoughts weren't allowed to make noise. Not now. He'd done all the thinking he could for the moment.

Even though the thoughts didn't surface then, he wrestled with them all night and went to work the next day feeling unsettled and anxious. Dan Barber, one of the guys who'd been over for dinner, spotted him in the lunch room and moved to his table.

Dan was always laughing, and today was no exception. He plopped his burger down and rested his forearms on the table. "I was sitting across the room, and I see my best buddy over here eating a spinach salad by himself and looking like he maybe has a few days left to live, and I ask myself, 'Self, what could be eating my buddy that way?'" He rapped his knuckles a few times on the table. "So I told myself it could only be one thing." His smile faded. "Lauren Gibbs."

Shane sighed. He dragged his fork through his salad and tried to sort through the feelings pounding his heart. Anger and sorrow, and frustration and defeat. "What am I going to do with her?"

Dan crossed his arms and looked down at the table for a moment. "Girl's more liberal than Ted Kennedy. Thank goodness she's a lot better looking." When he looked up, all traces of the teasing were gone. "You love her, don't you?"

Shane pushed his salad plate back and stared at his friend. "Since I was a boy."

"Man." He shook his head. "I'm not sure you'll ever see eye-to-eye with her."

"Me either." The words jabbed at Shane's heart. But the truth remained. "And maybe we don't have to. Maybe we can at least learn to respect each other. Couples don't have to have the same political views, right?"

"Right." He didn't sound convinced. "But most couples don't make a living defending their politics." Dan straightened and found his familiar chuckle. "Or maybe one of those surgeries, a partial lobotomy. Remove that part of her brain that's been so conditioned it can't think for itself."

"Hey—" Shane could hear a mix of anger and hurt in his voice. Dan didn't mean harm, but his flip comment hurt. "Lauren's entitled to her way of thinking. She cares deeply for people." He pushed back from the table. "Maybe I need to work harder to see her point of view." The idea felt freeing. After all, he couldn't change Lauren's opinions, but he could certainly work on his own so that she would feel more of his support. He felt his anger fade. "You're a praying man."

"I am." Again the laughter was missing from Dan's voice. "You don't have to ask, buddy. Becky and I are praying for the two of you every night. Even got the little ones in on the action." He paused and looked as if he might wrap up his bit of dialogue there. But instead, he pushed on, his tone more tentative. "Ever thought that maybe, just maybe, the two of you aren't right for each other? That maybe you'll never find happily ever after?"

Shane shifted his gaze toward the wall of windows overlooking the airfield. He breathed in sharply through his nose and steeled himself. For a long while he said nothing, memories of another day, another decade playing again in his mind. "Life's been hard on her, Dan." He looked at his friend, but his mind was filled with images of Lauren. He loved her so much, but was love enough? He sighed. "Life changed us both."

"Then maybe it's time to let go."

His frustration crowded his throat, coming out in a choked growl. "I keep thinking that if life could change her once, it could change her again, expand her views so she could see more than her own. The same way maybe I need to broaden mine." His eyes found the window once more. "And then we'd be okay again, the way we were back when we were kids."

"Maybe that's all you were meant to be together. Just kids. Finding out about love. Maybe you were never meant to be together as adults." Dan shrugged. "Just a thought."

They fell silent, and though Dan didn't say anything else, his concern was clear. Shane's mouth felt dry. Could Dan be right? Were his and Lauren's good days behind them? If they hadn't been separated, they might have had a chance. Might have grown up seeing things the same way. But now ...

Shane looked at his food, dragged his napkin across his mouth, and tossed it on the plate.

Dan dug into his burger and motioned to Shane's spinach salad. "Better hurry and eat before it wilts."

"That's okay—" he picked up his plate and threw it into a trash can a few feet away—"I'm not hungry." He saluted his friend. "Catch you later."

As he walked out of the cafeteria, he passed a table of young pilots. All of them nodded toward him, but he was almost certain he heard one of them say something about Lauren. Shane picked up his pace. Of course they were talking about Lauren. She was one of the most well-known war correspondents, and while her reporting was intelligent and deep, it was also overtly critical of the war. Of course everyone was talking about them. They probably thought Shane had experienced one too many g-forces.

Outside, he slowed his pace and, as he'd done every day since finding Lauren, he lifted his eyes to the endless Nevada sky and wondered what she was doing, what she was thinking. *Lord, is everyone else right? Are we too different to share love and a life to-gether?* His questions lined up like so many sections of a barbed wire fence, separating him and the woman he loved.

At that moment, in the distance, a fighter plane roared down the runway and lifted off the ground. In seconds it was rushing toward the heavens, blazing fast and unstoppable.

Just like Lauren.

No matter what he wanted for the two of them, she was determined to go her own way, do her own thing. She continued to write for *Time*, surrounding herself with a way of thinking that left her suspicious of the U.S. military, and often downright antagonistic. He sighed and looked at the nearby mountains. *God ... only You can help us now. With You, something could soften her views, help her become less suspicious. Or maybe soften mine. Whatever it takes to help us find our way together. Make it a miraculous change. Help us both see the truth.*

His prayer ended, and he felt a blanket of peace settle around his shoulders. He wasn't going to give up yet, not when he'd asked God for a miraculous change. Because with the Lord working in their lives, anything could happen. She could finally understand why he believed so strongly in peace through strength, and he could find compassion toward the articles she wrote.

Yes, with God, all things were possible. Wasn't that what the Bible said in the book of Matthew? And if all things were possible with God, then a relationship with Lauren could still be real and right and good. The changes could happen a little more every day. Or all at once, if God willed it. Then they might discover the happiness and love they both wanted. A life together was possible, it had to be. God wouldn't have brought them back together only to have everything end in misery and frustration. Shane smiled to himself and began walking once more toward his office. He would keep praying, and one day they would find common ground.

Why, with God they might even find happily ever after.

THREE

E mily couldn't believe so much could happen in a single week. She finished classes and finals at Wheaton College, confirmed her scholarship and housing at Pacific Lutheran University, packed her things into two suitcases and four boxes, and finally set off for the Northwest. Now she was at her new university in Tacoma, about thirty miles south of Seattle, unpacking her box of photos in a new residence hall on a new campus, and wondering if she was crazy for agreeing to the change.

The photograph at the top of the box was surrounded by two layers of bubble wrap, and Emily eased it open. She looked down at the image of her grandparents, the two people who had raised her and loved her and encouraged every dream she ever had—whether it was excelling on the soccer field or finding her parents. Because of her grandparents' support, she'd seen all her dreams become realities—even this one. The goal of spreading her wings and trying life on her own.

She studied the picture for a moment. No surprise that so much had taken place in a week, not when she remembered all that had gone on in the past six months. Her papa was diagnosed with cancer, and at almost the same time, she'd done the impossible: found her parents. Her dad had been working as an instructor at the Top Gun facility in Fallon, and her mother was a writer for *Time* magazine. Their reunion had taken place in January, the same week Papa lost his battle to cancer.

Emily sat the photograph on the small nightstand near her narrow bed. The residence halls at PLU were not much bigger than her walk-in closet back at her grandparents' home. She removed the next picture from the box—a more recent shot of her parents taken at the airport after her grandfather's funeral.

"I still can't believe it, God." She dusted the frame and set it on the nightstand next to the other. "You amaze me."

Her roommate already had her things set up. Pam King was one of the best goalies in collegiate soccer, a transfer student, same as Emily. The two had been assigned the same residence hall, but they hadn't met until yesterday at the soccer orientation meeting. They sat next to each other and snickered at the same bits of sarcasm from the coach. By the time they realized they were in the same "res," as the others called the residence halls, they were on their way to becoming fast friends.

Emily finished unpacking and sat back on her bed. The summer would be a full one. She had chosen PLU for two reasons. First, the scholarship included tuition, room, and board—entirely based on her soccer ability. Second, it put her on the West Coast, closer to her parents and her grandmother—who was selling the house she'd grown up in and moving to Southern California to be near Emily's dad's parents—people who had been best friends with her grandparents until twenty years earlier.

A cool breeze drifted through a small window screen, bent and dirty from age. Between the gentle wind and the photographs she was unpacking, Emily's thoughts drifted back in time. Twenty years earlier, her parents were teenagers, juniors in high school in Illinois. When they came to *their* parents and told them they were expecting a baby, life as they'd known it completely fell apart. The adults—Emily's two sets of grandparents—grew angry and distrustful, pointing fingers of blame for the scandal. Her dad's parents thought they solved the problem by moving to Southern California.

Of course, the move solved nothing. Emily's mother tried every day to locate her boyfriend, and a month after Emily was born, her mother set off for California. Only after Emily came down with a dangerous case of pneumonia did her mother turn around and head back to Illinois. The next day, after holding vigil at her bedside all night and finally going home for a few hours of sleep, her mother called the hospital to check on her. But something went terribly wrong. Emily's mother was connected to another patient's nurse, who informed her that her infant daughter was already gone. Her mother figured that meant Emily was dead.

Overtired, riddled with guilt, her mother determined never to forgive either set of parents for separating her from the boy she loved. So once again—this time alone—she set out for California and never looked back. Not until Emily finally tracked Lauren down and contacted her in Afghanistan last winter, did she know her baby girl hadn't died from pneumonia that day, but rather had lived.

The reunion took place last January in the days before Emily's papa's death. The Galanters came to Illinois, and they and Emily's other grandparents finally made peace with each other.

The scent of lavender mixed with the breeze and filled the room. Emily smiled. The fact that her grandparents' friendships had been restored was one more part of the miracle. And now, in what could've been her grandmother's most lonely days, she was living just down the street from the friends she'd spent two decades missing.

Everyone was back together, and in just a few short months, Emily would stand up at her parents' wedding. The event would be the culmination of a lifelong dream, something Emily had prayed and wished for all her life. Ever since the wedding plans were in order, her schoolwork had come easier and her soccer playing was better than it had ever been.

She took hold of her foot and stretched the muscles along the front of her leg. It was as if now that her life was whole, now that her parents and grandparents were at peace, she could finally focus all her energy on her own life, on the gifts God gave her.

Emily checked the clock on her dresser. Nine-thirty already. Practice was in half an hour. Though the season wouldn't officially start until fall, they had six weekend tournaments scheduled between now and then. Practices were from 10 a.m. to 1 p.m. every day. Then, when she'd cleaned up, this afternoon was her first shift as an assistant public information officer at nearby Fort Lewis.

She'd seen the army base a few times from the freeway, but today would be her first time through the gates. She hadn't gotten the job the usual way—by walking in and applying. Instead, she mentioned to her father that she'd like to work there. The base was only a short drive from PLU, and working there would give her a better understanding of the military and whether she'd like that sort of career one day.

Her dad wasted no time making calls on her behalf to one of his friends—a high-up official at the base. As it turned out, the public affairs office needed an assistant, and the details were worked out in a single day. Emily was a journalism major, about to start her sophomore year. Working as a public information officer so early in her college career would look fantastic on her résumé.

She could hardly wait to start.

With a final glance at the photos of her parents and grandparents, she dressed in her practice clothes, clipped her iPod to her shorts, and stuck in her earbuds. The soccer field wasn't far from the residence hall, so it made for a good jog. By the time practice started, Emily was already warmed up.

Pam had gone to breakfast with another teammate, and she was already at the field when Emily arrived. The two waved to each other, but over the next three hours, Emily didn't think about anything but what was being asked of her by the coach.

He was a demanding man, a person whose sarcasm was his only comic relief. Otherwise, he ran practice like a drill sergeant.

Emily didn't mind. She needed someone to push her, to help her find the limits of her abilities.

When practice was over, she jogged back to the room, showered, ate a grilled chicken salad at the cafeteria, then set out for the school parking lot. She arrived at Fort Lewis twenty minutes before her scheduled shift.

The base was bigger than it looked from the road, taking up acres of land on both sides of the I-5 freeway. Emily liked the feel of it, the American flags that flew proudly from a number of the buildings, and the armored tank on display near the main entrance. Never mind that the area was known for its rainy gray skies; in the few days she'd been there, the weather had been nothing but sunshine. Now as she studied the complex and the blue sky that framed it, the picture was almost surreal.

She'd lived most of her life not knowing that her father was involved in the military, and still she'd always felt a sense of pride when she'd seen an officer or a convoy of army vehicles. After September 11, though she'd only been fourteen, she made a beaded flag pin and wore it every day for a year. When the announcements came in that the U.S. had launched a retaliatory attack on Afghanistan, and then on Iraq, she was one of the few kids she knew who rushed home from school to watch the footage.

Papa used to tease her that her blood wasn't red. It was red, white, and blue. Patriotic Polly, he'd called her. "That's my girl, giving us old folks hope for the next generation."

Her pride in America, in its military strength, was almost instinctive. War was a tough subject, and she had as many friends in support of it as against it. Emily didn't like war, but on her own she could see some benefits. For instance, the way the country seemed so much safer since the military took action against countries harboring terrorists.

But the war aside, there was something admirable about people who devoted their lives to serving their country. Emily might not work for the military after she earned her degree, but then again, she might make it a career—the way her dad had done. She would never know unless she tried.

She straightened her shoulders and headed toward the front doors of the main building on the base.

She'd had a conversation with a nice woman the day before, and now she knew that her first stop was the personnel office. She found it, no trouble, and smiled at the older man working behind the counter.

"I'm Emily Anderson. I start work here today."

"Ah, yes. Emily." The man looked beneath the counter for a moment and brought up a packet with her name on it. "Your father is Shane Galanter, isn't that right?"

"Yes, sir." Pride warmed her chest. "He arranged the job for me."

"Well—" he tapped the packet—"you let him know we're all happy to have his daughter here. Shane Galanter is a fine instructor, one of this country's best."

"Thank you, sir. I'll tell him."

She was going to like this job, she could already tell. If only her mom hadn't taken the news so hard.

"The military, Emily?" She hadn't exactly sighed, but her tone hinted at her frustration. "Isn't it enough that your father works for the navy without you bringing another branch into the picture?"

"Mom..." Emily tried to conceal her surprise. "I thought you and Dad were more on the same page about all that now."

Her mom's hesitation had been enough to stir a flicker of concern in Emily, but then her mother's voice relaxed. "We are, it's just ... I pictured you working for a newspaper, not the military."

Those words were the only grains of sand in an otherwise smooth transition to Tacoma and PLU—and now here, to the job at Fort Lewis. Emily dismissed the memory. Her mother's questions and concerns about the military would only lead her to a deeper understanding of the man she loved: Emily's father.

Emily took the packet of paperwork and moved to a nearby table. Ten minutes later she had filled out the necessary forms and signed all the documents. When she returned it to the man, he directed her to a place against a partition. He took her picture and after a few minutes, gave her an ID badge.

She was on her way down the hall to the public affairs office when two young uniformed soldiers turned into the same hallway and headed toward her. A smile played on her lips and she nodded at them in passing. Both were nice looking, but the tall one closest to her held her gaze longer than necessary.

A rush of warmth moved across her cheeks. *Get a grip, Emily.* She kept walking, but a sudden realization hit her. Until now, she hadn't considered that the base would be swarming with guys her age. Though she'd dated back at Wheaton, she'd always been too busy with school and soccer and the search for her parents for any kind of serious relationship. Besides, she'd learned something from her parents. Relationships were better when they happened later in life—certainly not a few months shy of her twentieth birthday.

No, she wasn't looking for a boyfriend. Not when she owed it to the soccer team and to her boss at Fort Lewis to give them everything she had.

Boys could come later. It was that simple.

Still … there *was* something about a guy in a uniform.

The public information office was just ahead on her right, and as she opened the door and went inside, she had the instant feeling she was home. A staff of people in cubicle spaces tapped away at keyboards. Two of them were sharing an easy conversation as they worked.

"Here's one the papers haven't pounced on." The comment came from a woman in her mid-thirties or so. "The number of guys enlisting is up — not just here, but across the country."

"Of course they haven't run that story." The man sitting across from her leaned back in his chair and grinned. "Doesn't support their notion of disillusionment."

"I guess."

Emily chuckled under her breath and made her way to the counter. A pretty, slender black woman was typing and staring at her computer screen. "Be with you in a minute." Her voice was pleasant. She finished whatever she was working on, then stood and held out her hand. "You must be Emily Anderson."

"Yes, ma'am. Reporting for duty."

"Good." The woman smiled. "I'm Vonda. I've got about three dozen press releases that need copyediting. Ten need to be twice as long, and twenty need to be cut in half. I think I'll start you on that."

She was upbeat and energetic, and between her and the few other people, the office had a wonderful feel to it. The woman showed her to a seat in front of another computer. "This will be your station for now. Let's go over a few things."

Emily tucked her purse beneath the desk and listened while the woman went over the operating system and how to access the press release files. She was fifteen minutes into the training when the door to the office opened and a soldier walked in.

Emily's eyes widened as heat tickled her cheeks again. It was the tall soldier from the hallway.

"Justin, thank goodness." The black woman threw her hands in the air. "This is our new girl, Emily Anderson." She put her hand on Emily's shoulder. "I need you to get her up to speed on the process of editing releases." She looked down at Emily. "And this is Justin Baker. He puts in three shifts a week here because he's got *big dreams.*" She raised her eyebrows at Emily. "Hotshot officer. Wants to run the place one day."

"Not for a few years, Vonda." Justin grinned and looked at Emily. His eyes were a shade of green that almost looked airbrushed in. "And sure, I'd be happy to help."

"Thanks." Emily forced the word and tried to exhale.

Justin had short light-brown hair. He was so handsome that her heart stumbled into double time. Even so, this wasn't the time to act weak at the knees. This was a job, her role here a professional one. She needed to act accordingly.

She gave him the same smile she'd given Vonda a few minutes earlier. "It shouldn't take much." She looked at the computer screen. "I think I've just about got it."

A phone rang on Vonda's desk, and she made an exaggerated wipe across her forehead, as if Justin had rescued her in the nick of time. As Vonda went to answer her phone, Justin pulled a chair next to Emily's. "Okay, the press releases are always in that file," he pointed to a folder on the computer desktop. "That way they're easy to access."

He walked her through the steps and even switched chairs with her so he could show her how to cut a release from the bottom while still keeping transitions and important details, and then how to lengthen a release. "You need to call up the interview file. Usually you can find enough quotes and details in the reporter's notes to double the size of any release. The reporter has to okay it afterwards."

She was listening, she really was. But her mind just couldn't seem to stay on task when everything about the guy next to her filled her senses. His cologne ... the subtle scent of soap and laundry detergent on his freshly starched uniform. And that wasn't all. His voice was kind and soothing, and she found herself wondering what it would be like to sit next to him at the movies or at a concert.

"Emily?"

She jumped and turned. He was looking at her, his expression blank.

"Did you hear me?"

Again her heart pounded. What was *wrong* with her? She almost never had this reaction around a guy. She straightened herself. "Sorry. I have a lot on my mind."

"I was just explaining that Mr. Williams makes the decisions on the length of releases. They're written at sort of a standard word length, and then the editing can cut that in half or double it—depending on where the release is being sent."

"Right." Good. She was recovering well. She would stay focused the rest of the afternoon.

Justin finished training her, then he sat back and smiled. "How's your dad?"

"My dad?" Emily hesitated, fingers poised over the keyboard. She lowered her brow. "You know him?"

"He and my dad spent time together in the Gulf War. I guess they were pretty good friends."

"We don't ..." She shook her head. "We don't have the same last name. So how did you figure it out?"

Justin laughed, and the sound was easy and genuine. "Your dad remembered that mine was stationed out here in the Northwest. Once you had the job here, the two of them talked." He shrugged. "My dad called me the next day and told me you were coming." He grinned at her. "Said you'd be brand-new and to look out for you. That sort of thing."

"Is that right?" She allowed a bit of teasing into her tone.

"Yeah." Justin crossed his ankle over his other knee. "But he didn't tell me you'd be gorgeous."

Again the air seemed to leave the room, as if some giant human vacuum was controlling the oxygen level, laughing at her and daring her to try and take a breath. She swallowed and willed her trembling heart to find its normal rhythm again. "Well, thanks." She looked at the computer. "And thanks for the training."

From the front counter, Vonda gave them both a look and brushed her hand in their direction. "Looks like we got us a pair of smitten youngsters." She shook her head. "Don't fight it, Emily. Once Justin sets his sights on a girl, it's all over." She smacked her lips together. "Mmmhmm. 'Mr. Smooth,' that's what we call him around the office."

Justin held his finger up and started to say something in response, but instead he let his hand fall to his side and gave Emily a lopsided smile. "Vonda doesn't hold back much."

She giggled. "I can see that." Ignoring the strange way she felt, she turned once more to the computer screen. "I better get to work."

The afternoon passed in a blur, and Emily did her best to stay wrapped up in the press releases. But every now and then, she'd look up and catch Justin watching her. To hear Vonda talk about him, he was a player. Someone who had the same smooth lines for every girl he met.

But his eyes told a different story. By the time Emily left the fort that day, she wondered if she'd ever get to hear that story. Either way, she was sure of one thing.

She would never step foot on the base without looking for the tall, green-eyed soldier with the honest smile that made her heart jump the way no other guy's ever had.

FOUR

Lauren was checking her email, reading a letter from her editor when the phone rang. Even after living in her Fallon apartment for half a year, the place was sparsely furnished. Just a kitchen table and two chairs, a sofa, a television, and a computer balanced on top of an old stand she'd picked up at a garage sale. Her bedroom held a simple double bed.

The phone sat on the edge of her computer stand, and she answered it on the second ring. "Hello?"

"Mom?" It was Emily. She sounded energetic and hopeful - — the way Lauren figured she must've sounded before running away to California all those years ago. "How are you?"

Lauren glanced at the email from her editor. It started out the same as the others he'd been sending every few days:

> Lauren, we understand your need for a stateside time of re-spite. But it's time to take your rightful place in the Middle East. No one can report the war like you can, Lauren. Your successors haven't been …

She closed her eyes and focused on her daughter. "Good, honey. I'm good." The email shouted at her, calling her a liar. She turned her back to the computer. "Working on another feature."

"Really? That's so cool." Emily was always easily impressed. She was a writer, after all, so every time Lauren talked about her job with *Time*, Emily seemed to hang on every word. "What's it about?"

"iPods and MP3 players, how they're causing a generation of kids to suffer early hearing loss." She chuckled. "Nothing too exciting."

"Oooh." There was worry in Emily's voice. "I listen to mine all the time."

"Just keep the volume down."

"Okay." Emily seemed in a hurry, as if she'd called for something other than just to chat. "So how's Dad?"

The question was rhetorical; Lauren could tell by their daughter's voice. She made regular attempts to help her parents find common ground, but she didn't really expect there to be trouble between the two of them—especially not troubles that loomed like a tidal wave over them and their plans for a future. Lauren tried to dismiss the memory of Shane's face from the night before, when once again they'd fought. She cleared her voice. "He's great."

"Good." Emily laughed. "Mom, you won't believe this."

"What?" It felt good to hear her daughter's enthusiasm. Maybe some of it would rub off, and Lauren could take a fresh look at the way her new life was falling apart. "You scored three goals in your scrimmage yesterday?"

"Well—" her laugh became a giggle, the way she must've sounded as a little girl—"okay, that too."

"Really?" Lauren stood and wandered across her apartment to the front door. "Seriously, Em? Three goals?"

"Four, but one was called back."

"The coach must be glad he signed you."

"I think I'm a little gladder than him, even." Her words danced with a new sort of joy. "'Cause guess what?"

Lauren chuckled. "I give up."

"Well," there was a definite smile in her voice, "you know I'm working at Fort Lewis, at the army base just outside of Tacoma?"

"Yes, I know." Lauren opened the door and stepped out onto her small porch. She sat in the webbed folding chair there and trained her eyes on the mountains. "Is it working out?"

"Definitely. I'm editing press releases and running errands and answering phones. It's great experience." She hesitated. "And I met a guy, Mom."

A guy ... so that was it. Lauren felt herself smile. "Well, well. My busy Emily wasn't supposed to have time for guys, remember?"

"I still don't." She laughed in a shy sort of way. "But it's the weirdest thing, Mom. I can't get him out of my head. I mean, every day I go to work and I'm like, you know, looking for him. But I don't really look for him because then he'd think I like him, and Vonda says he's Mr. Smooth to every girl he meets."

Lauren felt a rush of familiar feelings. What her daughter was describing was exactly how she'd felt about Shane once upon a yesterday. "Who's Vonda?"

"She runs the front desk at the public information office, remember?"

"That's right." Lauren wished she were with Emily in person. It'd be nice to hug her daughter and celebrate with her, but she needed to be a mother first. Especially after going so long without being one. "Vonda thinks the guy's a little too smooth, is that it?"

"He's not really." Emily giggled again. "I mean, I don't think so. I haven't seen a string of girls coming by to visit him at the office." She grabbed a quick breath. "And guess what else? His father is Dad's friend. They were together in the Gulf War."

So ... the boy was from a military family. Lauren tried to hide her concern. Emily sounded so smitten — something Lauren hadn't heard from her in the six months they'd been getting to know each other. She didn't want to dampen her daughter's excitement, even if she could feel herself being outnumbered.

In the distance, two fighter jets roared into the sky and circled wide over the tops of the mountains. She closed her eyes. "How interesting."

"It is interesting." Emily's voice lost some of its enthusiasm. "We haven't gone out or anything. But still ... I don't know, Mom. I'm tearing it up on the soccer field and I love my job, but at night when I talk to God, it's like I can't stop thinking about Justin."

"Be careful, Em. The smooth types can be the worst of all."

"I know." She was the sensible Emily again. "I just thought I'd tell you. And hey, I almost forgot. Can you and Dad come for a visit the first week of August?"

"A soccer game?" Lauren's heart soared. No matter what conflicts needed addressing in her own life, being reunited with her daughter was enough to make her smile.

"Yes. A tournament. Coach thinks we could win it."

Lauren did the math. The tournament was six weeks away. Truth was, there were times when she didn't think she'd survive that long before calling for a peaceful surrender with Shane and hightailing it back to the Middle East. But maybe a visit to see Emily would give them something to plan for, a reason to stay together and work things out. If that was possible.

"Mom ... how's that sound?" Emily's tone was slightly impatient. "Sorry, but I have to run. Soccer practice is in twenty minutes."

"Okay, well ... sure. I mean, yes, I'll definitely ask your dad. If he can get some time, I can too."

"Great. Okay, I gotta run, Mom. I'll call you in a few days. Love you."

"Love you too." Lauren hung up, then stared at the phone. It still didn't seem possible, that her daughter had been alive all these years—that she'd become such an accomplished, responsible, intelligent young woman—all while Lauren was busy trying to forget she'd ever given birth to a daughter—a daughter she thought long dead.

And now ... as if there was no harm done, Emily accepted her, welcoming her into every aspect of her life, inviting her to soccer tournaments and talking about her hopes and dreams. Even talking to her about this — her feelings for the young soldier.

It was more than Lauren dared hope for.

The sound of the fighter jets faded, and Lauren stood and moved back into the apartment, to her place at the computer. The email was still on the screen, and this time she read it through.

Lauren, we understand your need for a stateside time of respite. But it's time to take your rightful place in the Middle East. No one can report the war like you can, Lauren. Your successors haven't been hard-hitting enough, questioning enough. It's like they're buying into the notion that somehow good is going to come from the money and resources and people we're losing over in Iraq and Afghanistan. Anyway, we've arranged for you to step right back into your same position and carry on the way you were before. We have a ten percent pay hike waiting for you, and for Scanlon, of course. He's still shooting pictures for us, still waiting for his partner to join him. Won't you think about it, Lauren? The offer's open-ended. We'll be waiting for you. Just say the word. Bob Maine.

"Bob, Bob, Bob ..." Lauren sighed and read the letter over one more time. It was the same message he'd given her twice that month already. "What am I going to do with you?"

She tried to picture it, saying good-bye to Shane again, packing her things, and returning to the Middle East. She'd be put up in the media headquarters in Afghanistan at first, the same place Jeff Scanlon still lived. The two of them would reconnect, falling into the easy camaraderie they'd always shared. He was a good friend, and she missed him. Missed the work they did together.

Only Scanlon understood how the war had changed her, how reporting the casualties and destruction every day made an impression on one's mind that never went away — no matter how many stories a person might write on the dangers of MP3 players.

Everything about the offer sounded fantastic. She'd be out of Fallon, rid of the well-meaning military men and women who couldn't see past the flag, and she'd be doing something worthwhile with her life. All of it sounded wonderful, except one part. The part where she'd have to say good-bye to Shane.

He was the love of her life, wasn't he? How long had she looked for him, dreamed about him, pined for him after she left Illinois and headed to Los Angeles? She'd wept every mile of the way, broken over the loss of their daughter and angry at their parents for separating them.

Why hadn't someone—anyone—shown the sense to let them stay together? There was no telling what might've happened. The two of them would have stayed on the same page, certainly. They would've struggled financially, but they would've raised Emily in the faith they'd been brought up in. No taking opposite trails on the journey of life, because they would've walked every step together.

Lauren closed down her email program, stood, and wandered to her bedroom. If she were honest, she had to admit her apartment didn't look like it belonged to someone trying to put down roots in Nevada. Even her clothes were still in stacks on the floor against the wall. The only thing that gave the room any distinction was a framed photograph on the windowsill. A picture of her and Shane, not from this past year, but from her other life. Back when she was just seventeen and believed with all her heart that she and Shane would be together forever.

She went to the photograph, picked it up, and studied the people in the picture. Sometimes, when she was frustrated with the sound of fighter jets and idle military chat, she would look at the photo and convince herself that she'd been too young back then, too naïve to understand love.

Or she'd tell herself that Shane wasn't the same person, that the kindness in the young man's eyes was no longer there. He was a steely navy Veteran, an instructor with a bark that caused young pilots to stand a little straighter, fly a little sharper.

But as she stood there, she knew the truth. Shane hadn't changed. He'd always stood for what was right. No, he wasn't perfect, but he wanted so badly to be on the good side. And what he lacked, he made up for with a faith that knew no bounds.

No, Shane hadn't changed.

She dusted her finger over the glass, bringing their faces into clearer focus. They hadn't been too young to understand love. Their eyes told a story even she couldn't rewrite. The love they shared back then was pure and raw, uncomplicated by politics or differing viewpoints. It was enough to make her drive away from home and never look back. Enough to keep her searching for him years after it no longer made sense.

So ... what now?

She looked out the window and tried to picture Shane, dressed in his decorated white uniform, sitting at a desk that overlooked the entire Top Gun airfield. She would tell him about Emily's offer, about taking a trip to Tacoma and seeing where their daughter lived and played and worked. But she was kidding herself if she thought that was going to solve anything.

She'd been asking God what chance they had, and how she could ever become the sort of military wife Shane needed. She'd tried swallowing her opinions, muffling them, and banishing them altogether. But always they came back, and always she and Shane argued because of them.

She set the photograph back on the windowsill. She'd been looking for an answer to her prayers, searching her heart and Shane's eyes, and examining their relationship every time they'd been together lately. God's answer *had* to be somewhere—His will as clear as the love that once shone from their faces.

When she was around Shane, she still felt weak in the knees, her heart still responded the way it had when she was a girl. She loved him as she would never love another man. But their differences loomed larger every time they were together.

She looked out the window at the streets of Fallon, and slowly, gradually, it hit her. Maybe God had been trying to answer her prayers all along. Maybe he'd tried once, twice, three times. Nine times. But this time—finally—she was able to hear what He was telling her. The message hurt her heart even to consider it. It wasn't spoken with the voice of God, of course. But with one that was even more familiar.

The voice of her editor, Bob Maine.

$\mathcal{F}$IVE

The breakthrough happened that same afternoon, the day Emily shared her feelings with her mother. She'd been determined not to make the first move with Justin. There were countless reasons why. She was busy, she had to be dedicated to her team, she was still getting used to the Tacoma area, she didn't know him well enough.

The list was long.

But that didn't change the way she felt every time he walked into the room. He was broad shouldered with a rugged face and a quick sense of humor. Just like her dad. Already she knew that Justin's faith, his beliefs, mattered as much to him as hers did. Even so, she wouldn't make her feelings obvious. Especially after the Mr. Smooth comments from Vonda. If Justin Baker *was* a smooth talker, let some other girl fall for him. She was certainly too busy to be taken on a meaningless ride.

That afternoon, she was editing releases when he pulled a chair up beside her and waited for her to look at him. When she did, she couldn't stop her breath from catching in her throat. She kept her tone light. "More training?"

"If you need it." He gave her a look that made her laugh.

"Not really." She raised one eyebrow. "See, I had this teacher, and, well ... he was so talented, I don't have a single question."

"That's good." He ran his tongue along his lower lip and shifted in his seat. It was the first time he'd looked nervous. "Hey, Emily, I want to clear something up."

"Okay." She turned to face him.

"I hear you over there, Justin Baker, all flirty and everything." Vonda was a relentless teaser. She stood at her desk and winked in their direction. "Just go on ahead and get over yourself, Mr. Smooth. Ask the poor girl out, already. She's dying for you to do it." She made a loud exasperated sound and sat down hard on her seat. "Love is wasted on the youth, I tell you. Wasted!"

Justin looked at Emily for a beat, and then leaned his head back and groaned. "Thanks, Vonda."

"Anytime." Vonda picked up the phone, her attention mercifully off the two of them.

Emily gave him a sympathetic smile. "You were saying?"

"Right." He looked at her, and she noticed his cheeks were darker than before. He couldn't be any more irresistible. "About the Mr. Smooth part." He shook his head. "It isn't true."

"It isn't? How's that?"

"Well ..." He craned his neck and cast a quick look in Vonda's direction. His voice dropped a notch. "The thing is, if I were Mr. Smooth, I would've already done it."

"Done what?" Emily enjoyed the exchange, wherever it was leading.

His eyes found hers, and he looked beyond the surface to someplace deep inside her. "Asked you out."

And just like that, his feelings were on the table. She felt herself lifting off the floor, floating around the room. But when she looked down, she could see herself still in the computer chair, her feet still on the ground. She remembered first to smile, and second to breathe. "Really?"

"Yeah." He exhaled as if he'd been holding his breath. "Emily, you don't know how hard that was."

"Your turn, Miss Emily." Vonda was off the phone again. She smacked her hand down in a mock show of disgust. "Do I have to come over there and teach the two of you how to do this?"

Emily laughed. "That's okay." She looked at Justin and her insides felt all jumbled together. "I think we can figure it out."

Justin shielded his eyes with his hand and shook his head. "Thanks again, Vonda."

"Like I said, anytime."

"So?" Justin lowered his hand and winced. "Can I take you out to dinner? After work tonight?"

"Sure." Emily kept her tone light. She looked over her shoulder once more. "But I'm not sure how we'll get by without Vonda."

"Me either." He shrugged, and the gesture made him look adorable. "I guess we'll never know if we don't try."

They both laughed, and Justin snuck back to his work station—thankfully under Vonda's radar so they avoided any comments about how it went or whether Emily had made the boy's day by saying yes. The rest of the shift passed in a blur, and every few minutes Emily had to remind herself to focus.

What could it mean, Justin asking her out? Had he been feeling about her the way she'd been feeling about him? Like even the most beautiful summer day couldn't compare to the way it felt simply to sit in the same room together, working on press releases and breathing the same air?

When their shift finally ended, they decided he would follow her back to her residence hall, and they'd both ride in his car—a Jeep Cherokee his dad had given him. He opened the sunroof as they set out, and she settled into the spot beside him. The leather seats felt soft and inviting. "I like it."

"I had no idea Dad was giving it to me." Justin kept his eyes on the road. Now that Vonda wasn't around, he seemed relaxed, at ease. As if the two of them had known each other forever. "I came home from my first tour in Iraq and my parents met me at the airport. They drove me to the base, and there it was in the parking lot. Covered with yellow ribbons." He smiled. "My first car."

Emily studied him for a moment. So, he'd been to Iraq. The detail was proof that the two of them didn't know each other nearly as well as it might seem. She pressed her shoulder into the seat and faced him. "How long were you there?"

"A year, about the same as most guys." Something changed in his eyes.

"I thought ..." She remembered the first time she met him, "I thought you wanted to *run* the base."

"Vonda exaggerates." He grinned at her. The evening was still sunny and would be for another three hours, but the temperature had cooled. He looked up at the sunroof and back at her. "You cold?"

"No." She brushed her fingers over her long sleeves. "It feels good."

"It does." He pulled onto the freeway and merged into a heavy flow of traffic. "I wanna be career military. Like my dad." He shot her a quick smile. "Like yours." He shrugged. "If they let me run the base, I'll take it."

"So ..." She didn't want to ask, didn't even want to picture him in danger — this golden young man who had so easily taken up residence in her heart. "So what did you do in Iraq?"

"I'm trained for medic work, but that's not where I spent my time. I did the frontline stuff, kicking in doors, looking for insurgents." He made a face that suggested it was no big deal. "Traveling in convoys, that sort of thing."

Each bit of description hit her like a blow. He'd been in the most dangerous positions, she knew that much from her conversations with her father. Army guys who went looking for insurgents were the ones in the greatest danger. Certainly with his family's pull, he could've been worked off the front line, still serving without putting his life in imminent danger.

When she didn't say anything, he gave her another quick look. "Hey, it wasn't so bad. The people love us over there."

Emily was fascinated and frightened all at once. "Tell me about it."

"The truth isn't something you'll read in a newspaper article—" he winced—"or in a magazine piece your mother might write."

So he knew about her mother. Emily's expression must've changed, because he hurried to cover himself.

"My dad says your parents' story is complicated. I mean—" he changed lanes—"people are entitled to their opinions, Emily. Don't get me wrong."

"I'm not." They were already in Seattle, and ahead she could see the Sound and a hundred sailboats dotting the water. "I think ... I think a lot of people helped shape my mother's viewpoints."

He nodded toward the water. "Pike Place Market okay? They have some great seafood restaurants."

"Seriously?" She'd heard about the place from some of the girls on the soccer team, but she'd never been anywhere other than school and Fort Lewis. "I'd love it."

He took the next exit. Ten minutes later, he had a parking space near the water, and they climbed out and began walking toward the closest pier. Seattle had an eclectic feel about it, a mix of fast-paced business people in their suits and nice dresses, and urban earthy types with baggy clothes, long hair, backpacks, and sandals. Over all of it towered the Seattle Space Needle.

The sun was still high in the sky, and the smell of exhaust fumes and seawater mixed in the cool breezy air. When they'd settled into a comfortable pace, Justin took a slow breath. "Like I was saying, it's so different over there. I went expecting a battle, and I found one. The war is a long ways from over."

"That's what I hear." She kept her pace even with his, and every now and then, the smell of his cologne mixed with the evening wind.

"But the best part was the people." He smiled and his eyes took on an added depth. "They're so glad to be free, Emily. Men, women, and children—all of them so grateful. To most of them, we're the heroes." He gave a single laugh. "My mom made a scrapbook with all the pictures I took. Pictures of me and the people of Iraq. Especially the kids."

"So … so you weren't in a lot of danger?" They were walking down a hill now, along a cobblestone road, and just ahead, the sun cast a blanket of diamonds over the water of Elliott Bay and the distant Puget Sound.

"There was danger." His smile faded. He was quiet for a moment, and then he looked at her. "I lost two buddies, guys who were hit by a roadside bomb on a day when I stayed back to do weapons inventory."

She felt her heart sink. "I'm sorry." And she was. But at the same time, she breathed a prayer of thanks to God for sparing Justin, for allowing the soldier beside her the chance to live the life ahead of him.

"The majority of people here and over there support us, and that's a good thing." His words were slower now, thoughtful. "It's not like it was for the Vietnam guys. Not hardly. But still—" he looked up at the sky and squinted at the setting sun—"I wish more people knew the truth. We're getting a lot done over there, Emily. It's a good thing, even with our losses."

The conversation shifted to her and her role on the soccer team. "I've played midfield since I was a little girl, and it's more fun now than ever."

"Because you can see the light at the end of the tunnel?" His comment wasn't rude or flip, just an honest observation.

And an accurate one. "Yes." She felt her arm brush against his, and the sensation sent a shiver all the way to her feet. "I'm good, but I won't be on an Olympic team or trying out for the pros." She gave him a sad smile. "This is it, so I'm giving it everything I have."

"I'd love to see you play." They came to an intersection and crossed, stepping up onto a sidewalk that ran along the water's edge. "I played, back in high school."

"Really?" Again Emily had the sense that she'd always known him. If they'd been at the same high school, they would've been the best of friends. Or maybe they would've found the sort of teenage love her parents had shared. She blinked away her thoughts. "What position?"

"Midfielder. Same as you." They stopped and he looked out at the water. "I miss it sometimes. But it wasn't my passion." He cocked his head and met her eyes again. "Not like being in the army."

Emily's admiration grew. "When did you get back ... from Iraq?"

"In October. Right before the holidays." He leaned his forearms on the metal railing that separated the sidewalk from the embankment down to the water. "Made my parents happy."

"So now ... you're done?" She kept her tone light. The question dangling in her heart wasn't one she wanted to ask, but she had to know. She rested her arms on the same metal railing and turned her head so she could see him. "Now you work on other training and, you know, learning how to run the base, that sort of thing, right?"

He chuckled and—intentionally or not—slid his right arm over so that it was touching hers. "I have one more tour, if that's what you're asking."

Fear tightened her airways, and she stared out at the farthest bit of ocean she could find. No, he wasn't going back to Iraq, that couldn't be what he'd said. "But ... but you already did the dangerous stuff, right?"

"They're looking for guys to go twice." He stood a little straighter. There was no worry or concern in his voice. "I can't very well lead guys if I'm not willing to make sacrifices myself."

His answer was exactly what she would've expected him to say. "So you'll be back on the front lines?"

"Probably." He smiled at her and nudged her arm with his. "But that's where the people are, Emily. It's what makes me sure we're supposed to be there. Besides, God's got my back. I felt Him with me every minute last time I was there."

She had the sudden urge to run. What point was there in getting to know this wonderful guy beside her if he was going to leave for another year in Iraq, if nothing about his future was even a little bit sure? But before those feelings could take root, she stopped herself.

God knew the plans He had for Justin, same as He knew the plans He had for her. Neither of them was guaranteed their next breath. So why borrow worry from tomorrow? She breathed out and felt herself relax. "When, Justin?" She didn't move her arm, didn't break the connection between them. "When do you go?"

"End of September." He smiled and eased his fingers between hers. "Come on. Let's find some dinner."

They walked slower than before, and with her hand tucked in his, Emily had to keep telling herself she really was here, he really was beside her, walking with her hand in hand along the edge of Seattle's Puget Sound. And no, she wasn't floating ten feet off the ground, no matter how she felt.

For the rest of the evening, they avoided talk of his return to Iraq. Instead they found a restaurant and were seated near a window that overlooked the water. He took the spot across from her and told her about his younger sister.

"She's eighteen now, four years younger than I am." He unfolded his napkin across his lap, clearly at ease in the upscale dining room. "The whole family has a list of stories about her."

"Like what?"

He grinned. "Like the time she bought a new cell phone. She was all excited because it had a speed dial feature for up to thirty phone numbers." He planted his elbows on the table and rested his chin on his fist, his eyes on Emily. "So we're at dinner that night and she's going on about which numbers she's programmed in, and how one of them is 9-1-1." He changed his voice to sound like a ditzy girl. "'That way, if I have an emergency, I can just dial star-two-seven instead. Or was it star-two-eight?'" Justin's laugh was full of warmth and affection. "The rest of us rolled. Only my sister would think it could save time to dial star-two-seven instead of 9-1-1."

They ordered salmon and vegetables and a couple of lattes. When the waiter left, Justin asked her about her parents. "I know they were apart for a long time, but I don't know the whole story."

So she told him, told him how they'd been so in love, and how the things her mother had written about her father could still make any of the three of them teary eyed. She told him about the struggle of her mother's pregnancy, and how none of her grandparents had supported the young couple.

"The amazing thing is that I found them." She folded her hands in her lap and searched his face. "It was my dream, my daily prayer that God would bring them back to me and to each other." She took a sip of her coffee. "He did both. I can't ask for more than that."

The hour was relaxed and full of more stories. They finished eating and popped peppermint candies into their mouths as Justin paid the bill. When they were outside, he took her hand and led her once more to a spot along the railing. The sun was just dropping below the horizon. Nearly ten o'clock. Right on time for a Northwest summer night.

Pink and orange streaks mixed with deep blues as the sunset began leaving its mark on the sky. Again Justin stood close to her, his arm touching hers a little more than before. A smile tugged at the corners of his lips, and in the glow of the setting sun she could hardly take her eyes off him. "Why the smile?"

"Because—" he looked down and chuckled, soft and low—"I was thinking about Vonda."

"Crazy Vonda?" Emily felt a shiver run along her spine again, and she wasn't sure if it was from Justin's nearness or the cooling air.

"Yeah. I can almost hear what she'd say if she were standing behind us."

"What?" She angled herself to face him more than the water.

"She'd say, 'Enough already, Mr. Smooth. Do I have to come over there and tell you how to do it?'" He turned too, his shoulders squared to hers. Only a few inches separated them. His tone changed, and there was a pull between them that Emily couldn't resist. He swallowed, still imitating the office manager. "'Or will you just go ahead and … kiss the girl.'"

Emily had been kissed once before. After a prom date with a guy she had a crush on for most of her junior year. But here, now, she knew what was coming and she wanted it more than she wanted her next breath. She moved closer, so close she could smell the peppermint on his breath. "You know what I think?"

He brushed his cheek against hers and drew back enough to see her eyes. "What?"

"I'd hate to frustrate Vonda." Her words came out slow, breathy. The foot traffic on the sidewalk had tapered way off, but she wouldn't have cared if they'd been standing in a crowd of people.

"Yeah." He moved in, slowly, tenderly, and touched his lips to hers. "Me too." His hand moved to her waist and drew her close as he kissed her again, slower this time, longer. The tentative sweetness of his kiss told her more clearly than words that they stood together on the edge of a canyon of emotions and feelings. All they needed to do was find the courage to jump.

Emily could've stood there all night being kissed by Justin Baker, kissing him back. But after a few minutes, he touched his knuckles to her cheek and gave her a final kiss. "I need to get you back."

"Okay." At the seemingly abrupt end to their closeness, she suddenly felt unsure of herself. What was she doing, standing here letting a guy she didn't really know kiss her? Maybe he really *was* the smooth talker Vonda declared him to be, and now that she'd kissed him, maybe he wouldn't ask her out again. After all, this was new to her — so new she wasn't sure what to do next, how to transition from head over heels back to a sane conversation.

But before she could worry anymore, he took her hand and brought it to his lips. With the most tender care, he kissed it, his eyes on hers. "Can I say something without scaring you?"

She could hear her heart pounding, feel it as far down as her knees. "Yes." What could he want to tell her? That he was sorry? That he regretted kissing her when they hadn't known each other that long? She held her breath.

"I have the strangest feeling, Emily." He studied her face, and this time he placed both his hands around her narrow waist.

"What?" She was frozen, waiting.

"Like all my life has been leading up to this one ... single moment."

She wanted to tell him she felt the same thing. But all she could do was breathe and nod her head. For a moment, it seemed he might kiss her again, but instead he tucked her arm in his and walked her back up the hill toward his car. This time the conversation turned to relationships.

"I figured you had a boyfriend." Justin smiled at her, and in the fading light his eyes sparkled. "A girl as beautiful as you. With a heart like yours."

She laughed. "No wonder Vonda called you Mr. Smooth." The air was colder now and she began to shiver.

Justin slipped his arm around her shoulders, and as they walked, they fell into a rhythm that seemed as old as time. "I'm serious. I would've asked you out a week ago, except I figured you had someone."

"Okay." She looked up at him, not sure she wanted to know. "What about you? There must be a line of girls waiting for you somewhere."

"Nah." He laughed and shook his head. "I went to college on a running-start program. Focused on ROTC and graduated at twenty. Never really fit into any group. You know, not a jock, not a druggie, not a musical type, not a whiz-kid. I dated here and there, but I sort of stayed to myself."

When they reached the car again, he hesitated. "I *so* don't want to take you home yet."

"I know." Would he lean against his car and pull her into his arms? The way she sort of hoped he would?

No. He was too much of a gentleman for that. Instead he led her around to the passenger door, opened it, and held it for her. When he slipped into the driver's seat, he smiled at her. "You think Vonda'll be able to tell? Tomorrow when we're at work?"

She giggled. "Probably."

The drive home went too fast, and when they reached her residence hall, he walked her up to the door. "Tonight was amazing."

"Yeah." She wasn't sure what to make of her feelings. A sudden shyness mixed with a longing she'd never known. She wanted so badly to kiss him again, but the timing seemed wrong. She took a step toward the door. "Thanks, Justin."

"See you tomorrow." He hesitated, then turned and jogged down the steps.

When he was gone, she hurried inside, and there in the entryway were three girls from the soccer team. Pam was one of them.

"My goodness, Emily, who was the hunk?"

She looked back at the driveway and the Jeep Cherokee just pulling away. "Justin." She let her eyes find Pam again. "Justin Baker. He's a soldier from Fort Lewis."

"He's hot." Pam whistled.

"He's beyond hot." One of the other girls shaded her eyes and looked out toward the fading taillights. "He's the hottest guy I've seen on campus all summer." She took hold of Emily's shoulder. "Tell me he has a brother, please, Emily."

"He doesn't." She laughed and waved them off. She didn't want to stand there in the entryway making small talk with her teammates. She wanted to get to her room, wash her face, and crawl into bed, where she could relive every moment of the last six hours. While she could still feel his breath on her skin, his kiss on her lips.

While the memory was still so alive she could be absolutely certain she'd spend the rest of the night dreaming about it.

Her last thought before going to sleep made her smile. Vonda was wrong. Love wasn't wasted on the youth. It had found her when she least expected it, and wherever her new relationship with Justin went from here, she had a feeling the journey would be magical.

And that however long the ride, the two of them would enjoy every minute.

$\mathcal{S}$ıx

Shane felt the tension between him and Lauren long before they took their seats on the plane. She was quieter than usual, and once in a while he'd catch her dabbing at her eyes, maybe trying not to cry.

He looked out the window as the plane took off. How had they grown so distant? He still loved her, still wanted to share his life with her. The feelings he had for her, he'd never have for anyone else. After a lifetime of missing her, he knew that, Knew it as certainly as he knew his name and rank.

She hadn't said anything about running, but he had the feeling she was thinking about it. Twice in the past few weeks she'd mentioned emails from her editor, invitations—no, not invitations, but downright pleas—for her to return to the Middle East.

"Is that what you want?" He asked her yesterday, the last time she'd mentioned the emails.

"No." She came to him, looped her arms around his neck, and leaned her head on his chest. "I want you, Shane. I've always only wanted you."

So why did their differences feel more pronounced every time they were together? He wanted to talk about wedding locations and honeymoons, but the conversation always took a different direction.

"Don't you feel bad," she'd said the last time he mentioned a honeymoon, "taking a trip to some luxurious beach when the people in Afghanistan are struggling just to survive?"

"Okay." He took hold of her shoulders and looked into her eyes. "Does it help the people in Afghanistan if we stay home?"

She shook her head and turned away, more upset than was fitting for the moment. "You don't understand me, Shane. I'm not saying we can't go, just that it makes me sad, thinking about the people over there." She hung her head, her voice a million miles away. "I'm sorry. I guess I'm being a real drag."

Through the last part of June and all of July, Lauren spent most of her time on the road gathering information for one story or another. When they talked—in person or on the phone—they discussed the coming trip to see Emily's new school, her new residence, and her new guy, Justin Baker.

Shane had hoped this trip would give them a chance to remember why they were together in the first place. But now here they were, and though Lauren was beside him, she might as well have been back in Afghanistan for how close she felt.

He stared at the city below, watched it get smaller and smaller as the aircraft found its cruising altitude.

He drew a deep breath. *Lord, I can feel You up here. So close it's like I could reach out and touch You. But what about Lauren?* His eyes stung and his throat felt thick. *Father, I've looked for her all my life and now she's here. But her heart seems half a world away. What can I do, Lord? How can I stir inside her the feelings she once had? The feelings she had last winter when she followed me to Fallon?*

Remember, my son, love never fails. Not ever.

The answer resonated in his heart and seemed to come from someplace right behind him. He knew better than to turn around and look. But when God's answers were this clear, they always left him with a sense of awe. The Lord, the Creator of the universe, cared enough to answer his simple prayers. And this time, the answer was especially strong, because it came straight from Scripture. First Corinthians, chapter thirteen.

Love never fails.

He breathed out and relaxed his jaw. Then he turned his head and leaned in close to her. "Hi."

She was reading a magazine. Without hesitating, she slid it back into the seat pocket in front of her and shifted so she was facing him. "Hi."

He framed her face with his hand and worked his fingers into her hair. His eyes met hers, and the confusion he saw there only made his heart hurt more. "Lauren, don't leave me. Please."

"Shane …" She covered his hand with her own. "Why do you say that?"

"Because." He swallowed, searching her eyes, desperate to see the love and certainty he longed to find there. "I can feel you pulling away." His voice was a whisper, one that was barely louder than the roar of the jet engines. "A little more every day."

Tears filled her eyes, and her chin quivered. For a while she didn't speak, then she managed to force tight words free. "I don't want to leave."

"Okay, then." He could feel the tears in his own eyes. "Stay. Please, Lauren. Stay."

The impossibilities lay dark and flat in her eyes, her expression. "We need a bridge. Only …" She gulped, and two tears slid down her cheeks. "Only I'm not sure there's a bridge that big."

"Love is the bridge, Lauren." He ran his fingertips along the side of her face. "I'll never love anyone like I love you."

She nodded. "Okay." Her answer told him only this much: they couldn't talk about forever, couldn't figure things out here, surrounded by the other passengers. She closed the gap between them and touched her lips softly to his. "I love you that much too."

They didn't speak again the rest of the short flight. Their discussion had pulled back the shades and revealed a terror too dark and horrible to imagine, too great even to consider. Later, after they'd had a chance to see Emily, they'd talk about it again. Because whatever was making things worse, whatever was placing this barrier between them, wasn't going to go away on its own.

In the half hour before the plane landed, Lauren rested her head on his shoulder and fell asleep. Shane savored the feel of her body against his, reveled in the sensation of her nearness without her angry opinions, his frustrated comebacks. He stroked her hair, and when it came time to get off the plane, she woke and smiled at him.

"I can't wait to see Emily."

"Me either."

Just like that, they made a silent pact to put all talk about themselves on hold. At least for now. They rented a car and headed straight for the university. The sky was blue with temperatures in the mideighties. Emily had been telling them that the weather was wonderful in Tacoma.

"That or the company you're keeping?" Shane teased her the last time they talked.

"Well—" Emily sounded wonderful, full of life and love and purpose—"let's just say it could be raining every day and neither of us would notice."

On the drive from the airport to PLU, Shane thought about how strange life was. Gary Baker had been one of his closest friends in the Gulf War. They were in different branches of the military, but they were together for planning meetings and strategic multibranch cooperative assignments.

When their stint in the Gulf ended, they remained friends. Over the years, their visits and conversations happened less frequently, but that never mattered. They had the sort of friendship that withstood time.

When Emily chose to take the PLU scholarship, and then when she asked Shane about getting a job at Fort Lewis, he remembered. That was the base where Gary had been stationed before he retired. Now he lived ninety minutes south in a small town called Kelso, the place where he'd grown up and where he and his wife Carol raised their two kids. But still he might know who to talk to at the army base. Shane was on the phone to his old friend that afternoon.

"The timing couldn't be better," Gary had told him. "They're looking for someone part-time. My boy's working at that office a few days a week. I know exactly who you should talk to."

By the end of the week, Emily had a job. But never, not once, had Shane given a second thought to the idea that Gary's son would work with Emily. Not until she called toward the end of June, giddier than he'd ever heard her.

"How do you know, Dad? When it's really love?"

"Well ..." His feelings were mixed at her question. All those years he'd ached because he'd missed out on her life, hadn't known where she was or even *if* she was. Now that she'd found him, it felt strange to hear her so excited about a boy. Strange to have to share any part of his little girl. He cleared his throat and tried to sound paternal. "For one thing, it usually takes longer than three weeks."

"I don't know." Her voice had a dreamy quality to it. "We've gone out almost every night. I think it took us about three hours to figure it out."

By the end of the phone call, just for something to say, Shane asked the boy's name. That's when Emily giggled. "You know him, Dad. I wasn't going to tell you until you met him in person, but you might as well hear it now. His name's Justin Baker."

"What?" Shane about slid out of his seat. Several times Gary and Carol had sent pictures of Justin. He was a handsome kid, but he was a kid, right? Way too young to be talking love with Shane's little girl. "Isn't he still in high school?"

Again Emily laughed. "No. Justin's dad said the same thing. He thought I was like seventeen or something."

"Yeah, because nineteen is so old, right?"

"Almost twenty." She paused. "You and mom were ready to get married a whole lot younger than this."

Married? Shane's heart skipped a beat. The statement must've been for effect. Certainly Emily hadn't met a boy and fallen so hard the two of them were talking marriage. "Marriage, Emily? Are you trying to tell me something?"

This time Emily laughed. "Dad, of course not. I'm just saying ... Justin's twenty-two. He finished college at twenty."

"Well, I wouldn't expect anything less from the son of a man like Gary Baker."

"Good." She made a clapping sound that carried over the phone lines. "His parents are coming up for my tournament, so you and Mom will get a chance to connect with them."

The weeks had flown by since then, and now here they were. He and Lauren, on their way to the first game of the tournament.

They had just enough time to check into their hotel on the way to the field. When they got there, Shane could see a set of bleachers already full of people.

"What if they don't like me?" Lauren was holding his hand, but she lagged a step behind. "And why does it seem like we spend our entire lives around a military base?"

Shane smiled at her. "Practice, Lauren." He tickled the corners of her mouth. "People will like you a lot more if you're smiling."

"I'm sorry." She did, but he could feel her resistance. They drew closer, and Lauren stopped twenty yards short of the bleachers. "I want to look for Emily." She shaded her eyes. "Wait ... there she is! Number seven!"

Suddenly Shane realized what he was watching. Their daughter had spent a lifetime kicking around a soccer ball. Game after game, practice after practice, the people cheering in the stands for her were her grandparents. Never her parents. Until today. Now, for the first time, he and Lauren were together doing what they should've done all of Emily's life.

Watching her play soccer.

Shane linked his arm through Lauren's. "Look at that." They watched their daughter dart around two defenders, dribbling the ball like it was attached to her ankle by a string. Then, at just the right moment, she sent it across the field to a teammate streaking toward the goal.

The defender running just ahead of Emily's teammate didn't have time to adjust her footing, and before even the goalie could react, Emily's teammate shot the ball back to her, and she fired it into the goal. The entire team raised their hands, jumping and running out to meet Emily.

A shiver passed over Shane's arms. "She's amazing."

"She is." Lauren was just about to say something else, when people approaching caught her attention. She looked off to the side and smiled. "Hello."

Shane followed her gaze and there was his friend, Gary Baker. And next to him was a strapping boy four inches taller than Gary. Justin, no doubt. "Hey! I can't believe this!" Shane took a few long strides and wrapped Gary in a big bear hug. "It's been too long, friend. Way too long."

They pulled apart and Gary pointed out at the soccer field. "Your girl's good."

"Thanks." Shane grinned toward Emily, still getting congratulatory hugs from her teammates. Then he turned his attention to the tall soldier standing beside Gary. "And who's this young man? Don't tell me it's your little Justin all grown up?" Shane felt Lauren come up alongside him. He put his arm around her shoulders and stuck his hand out toward the young man. "I'm Officer Shane Galanter. Your dad's buddy."

"Sir." He saluted. "Lieutenant Justin Baker, sir."

"At ease, lieutenant. The question is, when did you get to be taller than your daddy?"

Justin laughed. "He asks me that all the time."

The play on the field resumed, and Lauren stuck out her hand first to Justin, then to Gary. "I'm Lauren, Emily's mother."

"Nice to meet you, ma'am." Justin wore his casual dress: camouflaged pants and a buttoned-down shirt. His manners were impeccable.

Gary smiled at Lauren. "Come meet Carol. I think you'll like her."

They moved to the bleachers, and after ten minutes, Carol and Lauren were talking about the plight of third-world countries and the work humanitarian and Christian groups were doing to alleviate the AIDS epidemic.

Shane leaned in close to his friend. "Did you tell her to talk about that stuff?"

"Who, Carol?" Gary looked at the two women. "No, she's always been interested. Tells me we're going to take a year off and do mission work in Africa someday."

Shane felt the tension in his soul ease. Lauren had found a friend, something neither of them expected. He was about to ask Gary how things had been in Kelso, when the action on the field came to a sudden stop. A girl from the opposing team was on the ground, and instantly a group of coaches surrounded her.

"Paramedic!" one of the coaches shouted. "Someone call a paramedic!"

Shane whipped out his cell phone and dialed 9-1-1. He wasn't sure of the emergency, but in a calm voice he told the operator that a soccer player was down and seriously injured at PLU's soccer field. "I'm not sure of the address."

"That's okay, sir. Your cell phone has a GPS locator."

Shane was relieved. Before he could get off the phone, Justin bolted down the bleachers and out onto the field. "He has medic training," Gary was on his feet, squinting, trying to make out the scene.

Shane finished his call and watched as the young soldier took control. He must've identified himself, because the coaches cleared away. Even from their view in the bleachers, it was clear the player had been cut across her calf. She must've been kicked, the cleats from another player's shoe slicing into her.

Justin didn't hesitate. He took off his shirt and pressed it over the wound. Then he raised the girl's leg and propped her foot up on his shoulder. He was talking to her, still applying pressure on the wounded leg as the paramedics arrived.

Once they'd wrapped her leg with sterile bandages, Justin took his bloodied shirt and returned to his place in the bleachers. Everyone in the stands applauded, and as Shane looked, he saw Lauren. Her mouth was slightly open, her eyes full of awe for the young man.

"That looked serious ..."

"It was. The slice was pretty deep, nicked an artery for sure."

"I wondered." Lauren touched his shoulder. "You might've saved her life."

He shrugged and wadded his shirt in a ball near his feet. "I guess the team trainer was in the locker room helping another player, someone injured earlier." An easy grin played on his lips. "I knew what to do. Anyone would've done the same thing."

Shane gave Gary a look, one that said he too was impressed by Gary's son. When the game was over, when PLU had won, 4–2, one of the coaches from the opposing team came over and thanked Justin. "Thanks for what you did. She was losing a lot of blood." He looked sickened by the thought. "I don't think the rest of us realized how serious it was, that an artery was involved."

Again Justin brushed off the comments. He shook hands with the coach, but his eyes were already searching the field. Shane followed the boy's gaze and spotted Emily jogging across the field toward them. Justin met her partway, and the two hugged for a long time.

Shane wasn't sure where to focus his attention. On the way Justin Baker looked at his daughter, on the beauty of what the two of them obviously shared, or at Lauren. Gary and Carol were making their way down the bleachers, heading for Emily and Justin, but Lauren still sat there, watching from her place on the top row of the stands.

"He's so ... compassionate." She didn't blink, didn't look away from the place where the two young people were talking and laughing. "Did you see that, Shane?" She finally shifted her gaze to him. "Did you see how he responded?"

Whatever was going on in Lauren's head, he wanted to understand it. "Of course he reacted that way." Shane looked from her to Justin, and back again. "He's a trained medic, Lauren."

"But I ..." She bit her lip, and emotion welled in her eyes. "You're kind that way, Shane. But that's because I know you. Soldiers — the soldiers I've written about — are more concerned with taking a life than saving it."

Shane couldn't believe she'd said such a thing. Was that really what she thought? That Shane and his peers were nothing more than well-trained killing machines? "Lauren, that's a terrible thing to say."

Almost as soon as he uttered her name, her expression changed. She put her fingers to her mouth and shook her head. "Listen to me. How could I have thought such a thing? It's like ... it's like I can hear myself for the first time." She looked at Justin again. "Like that young man is the first soldier I've actually seen for myself. Without looking at him through the lens of my training, my experiences."

Shane didn't know what to say. He was still stunned that somewhere in her heart, Lauren had harbored such a warped view of soldiers. But saying so would be overkill, especially when she looked so shocked, almost angry at herself.

Whatever was happening inside her, Shane was sure God had used the actions of a very special young man to open Lauren's eyes a bit. He took his fiancée's hand. "Come on. Let's go congratulate our daughter."

"Yes." They reached the bottom of the bleachers when Lauren turned and looked at him. She hadn't ever looked more serious. "I'm sorry, Shane. For ever thinking that."

"It's okay." He gave her a tender kiss. "Come on. Emily needs us."

They met up with the others in time to see Emily pluck at Justin's white T-shirt. "Good thing you had this on." She stood on her tiptoes and kissed his cheek. "Otherwise the team would've been too distracted to play the rest of the game."

Shane smiled, savoring the feel of Lauren's hand in his. They made small talk, congratulating Emily on her game and her goal, and listening while Emily updated them on the condition of the injured player. "The other coaches heard word near the end of the game. She lost a lot of blood, but she's been stitched up. She'll be fine in a few weeks." Emily held out her hands, her brow raised. "Whoever heard of slicing open an artery in a soccer game? I'm so glad she's okay."

Carol Baker put her arm around her son. "Thanks to Justin's quick thinking."

"Yeah—" Emily grinned at him—"my hero."

"And don't you forget it." Justin laughed and looked around the group. "Emily's next game isn't for a few hours. Let's get lunch."

Shane reveled in the feel of the group, the way his friend and he had so easily reconnected, how Carol and Lauren had found common interests. And now that he saw them together, he couldn't help but be thrilled for Emily. Justin was the sort of young man he could only hope to see his daughter marry one day. The fact that the soldier was his friend's son only made things better.

But none of that compared to what he'd seen in Lauren's eyes as she sat on the top rung of the bleachers. Lauren presented such a strong front, an impenetrable fortress that refused any viewpoint but her own. She was absolutely convinced she knew the truth about issues involving politics or the war, and apparently about soldiers. Today, though, there was a break in that wall.

Shane could only pray that it was a beginning, and that one day very soon, the tender, passionate Lauren he had known and loved would find her way out from behind the wall. At the very least, he had something that day that he hadn't had in months. He had hope.

And for now, that would have to be enough.

$\mathscr{S}$EVEN

$\mathscr{S}$omething was changing in Lauren's heart, and though she didn't want to dwell on it, she was horrified at the realization she'd stumbled onto that morning. That she'd harbored ill thoughts toward all soldiers. Her attitude had been inexcusable.

But what did the experience mean? Would this change of heart go deeper, into the far reaches of her opinions? She wasn't sure.

Not until talk at the pizza place turned to the war.

Back at the soccer field, Carol seemed like such a wonderful, rational person. But now ... she was passionate about the United States' commitment to finish the task in Iraq. "The thing people don't understand is the good our troops are doing." She looked from her husband to Shane, and then to Lauren. "Iraq is a different place today, a better place because of the sacrifice our military is making."

Almost against her will, Lauren felt her defenses rising again. She opened her mouth and then closed it, casting her eyes down at the laminated menu. *What's wrong with you, Lauren? It's one conversation, let it go.* She gritted her teeth and tried to find a diversion. The license plates that hung on the wall. That could distract her, right? She studied them, forcing herself to steer clear of the talk around the table. Fifteen seconds, twenty, and the license plates weren't doing it. Instead she made lists in her mind of the interviews she needed to conduct for her next *Time* piece. But it was no use. The conversation drew her like gravity until she couldn't hold back a minute longer. Carol was still waxing on about the benefits brought to the people of Iraq because of the war.

Lauren sat up straighter and found a tight smile. "But the insurgents will only take over again as soon as the U.S. pulls out. So what's the point?" She bit her tongue, but it was too late. Her words had escaped before she could run them by the filter in her mind, the one that was supposed to help her act with more social graces.

Shane shot her a look across the table. She softened her tone and managed a smile. "I mean, how much longer will it take?"

"There's two ways to tell that we're winning this war." Justin took a sip of his root beer and set his cup down. "First, U.S. citizens have been safe on our own soil. And second, we're building an infrastructure of freedom through trade and government that has never been known in the Middle East."

Lauren nodded and turned her attention to her ice water. Why couldn't she be more like them? And how could the young man across from her be so compassionate one minute, and so committed to what basically amounted to killing the next? It was one of those times when she felt like a fish flopping around on dry ground, crazy in need of a place where she might fit in.

She said little throughout the rest of lunch, but in the car on the way back to the soccer field, she looked at Shane and frowned. "I'm sorry. Again."

"Whatever." He smiled at her, but his eyes held frustration. "I thought maybe today, after your reaction to Justin's rescue …" His voice trailed off. "I don't know. I guess I thought you might see everything else differently too."

"I sort of wondered about that." If she could take back her comments at lunch, she would. Or she'd say it more carefully. But that didn't change how she felt. "I'll try harder the rest of the trip, okay?"

Shane sighed. He worked the muscles in his jaw. "That's just it. I don't want you to have to try, Lauren." He looked at her. "Don't you see?"

She did, and there was nothing more she could say. Instead she reached out and took his hand. Because as long as he was there beside her, as long as his fingers were woven between hers, she had proof that they were still together.

Even if good-bye was feeling closer every day.

~

Something was wrong with her parents.

Emily said good-night to Justin earlier than usual and stood at the window of her room, tears in her eyes. *God ... they're not getting along. I can feel it. Show me what to do.*

She pressed her forehead against the cool glass and remembered the conversation at the pizza parlor. Her parents' politics were still coming between them. Which was crazy because they were supposed to have all that stuff worked out. A small circle of fog built up on the window, and she rubbed it with her fist.

Her mother needed to be more careful with what she said, that's for sure. But her dad too. The couple of glances he gave Mom must've hurt her feelings. Emily turned away from the window and plopped down on her bed. Pam was out, probably studying with a few of their teammates down the hall. The solitude felt good; she needed to think.

If her parents didn't start trying to understand each other a little more, then something tragic could happen. She let herself fall back on the bed and stared at the ceiling. All this time ... all this time she'd been thinking everything was okay, that they'd agreed to disagree on the war, and that they'd found a peaceful way to handle their differences.

But if what she'd seen today was any indication, things between them were far from worked out. In fact, as they all left the pizza parlor, she could feel the tension between her parents. Emily let out a slow, painful breath. *God, they can't fall apart now, not*

when they're supposed to be planning a wedding. Please, God ...
whatever it takes, please help them work through their differences.

The war was a complicated issue. Emily might work at an
army base and understand her father's opinions, but she understood her mother's too. Her mother had seen the harsh reality
of war firsthand. Of *course* she hated war. Anyone who'd been
through what she had would hate it.

Emily sat up and hunched over her knees. Her body ached
from the soccer games that day, and there were more to come
tomorrow. She needed to get to sleep so she'd be ready to play.
But after she washed her face and climbed into bed, it was still
another half hour before she fell asleep. When she did, it was with
images of her parents filling her heart and mind.

And the certain belief that somehow God would close the
gap between them.

For the next three days, Lauren alternated between cheering
for Emily—whose team made it to the final game—and studying Shane and his friends. Gary and Carol were some of the nicest
people she'd met. Much nicer than anyone she'd connected with
in Fallon.

Even so, their views and hers were worlds apart.

The night before the tournament championship, Emily
pulled Lauren aside at the soccer field and searched her eyes. "Are
you okay? You and Dad?"

A few seconds passed while Lauren caught her breath. "The
two of us?" She made a silly face. "Of course, honey."

Doubt remained in Emily's eyes. "I've been watching you.
It's not like it was at Grandma and Papa's house. Something ... I
don't know, something's different."

Lauren thought for a moment and then decided. She needed
to be at least partially honest with her daughter. Otherwise, if

things didn't work out, the girl would be blindsided. Lauren took hold of her hands and looked to the worried places in Emily's soul. "We have a lot of differences, your father and I. Things we're still trying to work out."

Fear threw itself into the mix of emotions playing out in Emily's expression. "But you love him, right?"

"Of course." She soothed her thumbs over the tops of her daughter's hands. Her tone changed. "But you need more than love, Em. Sometimes you need common ground." She hesitated, and the familiar sting of tears poked at the corners of her eyes. "Your dad and I are still working on that."

"So … how can I pray for you?"

Of course this was Emily's answer. She'd spent a lifetime praying that she'd find them, and that if she did, they'd find love again together.

"Seeing Justin, getting to know him, that's helped a little." She gave her daughter a sad smile. "Just pray that God'll give us a bridge, a way to understand each other better."

Emily studied her. "You understand, right, Mom? That none of us want this war."

"That's what I keep hearing." She refused to get into a debate with her daughter minutes after a soccer game.

"Well, it's true. We don't want war." She pressed her hand against her heart. "We want a safe country, and we want the people of Iraq to be free. If it takes a war to make that happen, then we'll fight to win." She paused, seeming so sure of herself. "Can't you see how that makes sense?"

Lauren wanted to dig a hole and hide from all of them. Shane and the Bakers, even Emily. How could she be so different from the rest of them? How could they not see that fighting was never the answer? A safer America? That could be accomplished through peace talks and treaties. Wasn't that what parents always taught their kids — talk things out, don't resort to violence?

So why couldn't the people she cared most about in the whole world see the situation in that light? Or why couldn't she see it in theirs?

Emily was waiting, so Lauren pulled her close and hugged her, stroking her back. "You know what makes sense?"

"What?" There was such angst in Emily's voice. She inched away, clearly still wanting answers.

"Why PLU gave you a soccer scholarship." Lauren grasped at the upbeat tone, the one that felt more familiar, easier when it came to Emily. "Honey, you're wonderful! It makes me so sad to think how many games I missed."

Gradually, Emily's expression changed until it was clear she'd made a conscious decision to let go of the previous topic. A smile replaced her concerned look and her eyes began to dance. "It doesn't matter how many you missed. It matters that you're here now."

"And tomorrow's the championship!"

"Exactly." Emily leaned in and held her mother for a long while. "It'll all work out, right, Mom?"

Her daughter's simple words were like swords pricking the surface of her heart, allowing a pain that knew no bounds to slip free. "I hope so, sweetheart. I truly hope so."

The topic didn't come up again that night or the next day as they wished Emily luck before the championship. Again Lauren sat with Shane and the Bakers at the top of the bleachers. This time they didn't talk about war or politics or the Middle East. They simply cheered Emily on.

Just after halftime, Lauren's cell phone rang. She checked the caller ID and felt her breath catch in her throat. Bob Maine, her editor. She stepped down from the bleachers and took the call several feet away. "Hello?"

"Lauren, tell me you're at the airport." The man's gruff voice belied a heart as big as the magazine's towering offices in New York City. "You haven't answered my emails."

"Because I've been busy working, Bob. Remember that? This is the first week I haven't turned in a story."

"But they're stories anyone could write."

"Thanks." She kept her tone from getting too serious. This wasn't the time to make a decision about returning to the Middle East.

"Lauren ..." He gave a frustrated groan. "Okay, not *anyone*. You're doing a great job reporting stateside. But we don't have anyone like you over there, baby. We need you. Even just for six months."

Six months. The thought bounced around her mind like an errant pinball. She could do that, couldn't she? Make a six-month commitment, go overseas, report on the war, and maybe while she was there, try to look at things the way Shane and his peers saw them.

She turned and saw her group in the bleachers. Shane caught her eye, his smile as genuine as the summer sky. "Bob." She pinched the bridge of her nose and shook her head. "I can't make that decision now. I need ... I need time."

"How much time?"

"A month, at least."

He sighed. "I'd like you there first of September. I'm serious, Lauren. Do what you have to do, but make it happen. That's where you belong, and you know it."

The conversation ended, and Lauren returned to her place next to Shane.

"Who was that?"

She kept her answer matter-of-fact. "Bob Maine."

Shane rested his elbows on his knees. "Still bugging you about getting back to the Middle East?"

"He won't let up." She looked away and turned her attention to the soccer field. For the rest of the game, while Emily's team won the championship and then on into the evening during the celebration at a nearby restaurant, she didn't dare look too long into Shane's eyes. Or Emily's.

She'd told Bob the truth, she would think about it. Soon. But right now she couldn't do anything of the sort. Shane knew her too well. And if she let herself think about leaving, and then looked too long into his eyes, she'd break down there in front of everyone. Because Bob Maine's offer gave her more than just the chance to see things the way Shane did.

It gave her an escape. Back to the familiar danger of reporting war firsthand. And that thought stirred a longing deep inside Lauren. If she gave in, then sometime in the next few weeks she'd have to do the impossible. Look into the eyes of the only man she'd ever loved and tell him good-bye. Yes, just for six months. But if she fell into her routine the way she expected she would, the good-bye might last a whole lot longer.

Maybe even forever.

～

Emily couldn't shake the terrible feeling.

Yes, the tournament had gone perfectly. She'd played some of her best soccer ever, even scoring the winning goal for the tournament championship. She'd been giddy after the game. Then, when she saw her family and Justin's together, it gave her a kind of premonition. As though, just maybe, the two families would be together again this way—not for soccer games, but for life.

The terrible feeling had nothing to do with her game or her guy. She was in love, and everything about Justin Baker was more wonderful than she'd ever imagined. Rather her fear came every time she looked at her mother. The feelings she'd had that night in her room and the conversation with her mother the next day only served to worsen her fears. Something *was* off between her parents—and she was worried. Maybe their troubles were why they'd avoided a summer wedding.

Ever since they found their way back to Fallon together, Emily believed without a doubt that her parents had worked out their differences, that the wedding plans were in full force, and that the toughest conversations between them were probably about where they'd honeymoon. Something like that.

But now, all her certainty about her parents had changed.

Her mother was quieter than usual and less affectionate around her father. She seemed distant, and no matter what Emily's dad did to include her in the conversation, her mom acted out of sorts. As if she couldn't quite connect with anyone.

Not even Emily.

As her parents left after the last game was over, she hugged them both, and when she was in her mother's arms, she whispered near her ear. "Be happy, okay?"

Her mom looked into her eyes, longer than usual. "I will, Emily." She paused. "The important thing is for you to be happy, okay?"

Now that her parents were gone, now that Emily and Justin were heading back to her residence hall in his car, she was struck by a thought. Her mother must've meant something by her comment. Like maybe the important thing was for Emily to be happy because she, herself, wasn't. Was that it? And what about the other part?

I will, Emily …

Did that mean she was about to find her happiness somewhere other than with Dad? Some other way than being Dad's wife? By the time they reached the PLU parking lot and the place where Justin always dropped her off, Emily was so tense she was sick to her stomach.

"Hey—" he took her hand—"what's on your mind?"

"My mom." She looked out the window at the shadowy branches in the trees that lined the lot. "I get the feeling she and my dad aren't happy."

"Hmmm." He released her hand and gently moved his to the base of her neck. He massaged her tight muscles, slow and easy. "I sort of saw that."

"But Justin—" she looked at him—"you don't understand. My parents love each other so much."

"That's what you've said. You were going to share some of your mom's journal pages about how much she loved him, remember?" His voice had a calming effect on her heart. He kept working at the knots in her neck. "I still want to see them."

"Okay." The thought of her mother's journal entries restored some sense of calm to her world. Her mother might be confused, even conflicted about how her viewpoints didn't line up with the rest of her family's. But Emily's parents loved each other. There was never any question about that.

Justin leaned in and kissed her. "One day, when we're a whole lot older, we'll be dancing at their ten-year anniversary dinner and we'll remember this night. Because I'm going to pray every day that God works a miracle for your parents." He kissed her again. "The way He's worked a miracle for us."

Emily's fears dissolved like the tension in her muscles. "When we're a whole lot older, huh?"

"Yep." He pulled back and searched her eyes. "The timing's a little unclear right now, but just for the record—" he grinned and the sparkle in his eyes shone even in the dark—"I'm never letting you go, Miss Emily. Not ever." He held up his pinky finger. "Pinky swear."

She giggled. He could always make her laugh. That was one of the things she loved most about him. Before Justin, she'd been a little too serious. Now she laughed so much more easily. Even times like now, when she was worried about her parents. She clasped his little finger with hers. "Pinky swear."

"I mean it." He laughed as he let his head fall back against the seat. "It's not exactly a diamond ring." His eyes held hers. "But that'll come in time."

Sure, she'd just met him and they'd only been together a matter of weeks. And yes, when they talked like this, it was more silliness and flirting than anything. But somehow deep inside, Emily had no doubts. Even knowing he would return to Iraq in a month or so, she was certain Justin was right. That one day she'd wear his ring and they would dance together at her parents' tenth wedding anniversary. God had brought her parents back together for a reason, and one day soon they'd have the answers to the questions that never quite went away.

"You know what I love about you, Emily?" Justin smoothed his hand over her dark hair and brushed his thumb along her bangs.

"What?" She wished it weren't so late. They could hang out in the commons room, watch television, and snuggle together the way she loved. But the coach had called a meeting for the morning, and she needed to be at her best. Even if coach cancelled practice, which most of the players assumed he would do after such a sound tournament win.

Justin slipped his hand around to the back of her head and kissed her once more. "I love that it's enough for you that we live happily right now. And the whole ever-after stuff can come later."

Emily grinned. This time she shifted so she was closer to him, and the kiss came from her. "There's plenty of time for ever after." She was breathless. She needed to get inside. Otherwise the feelings he stirred in her would keep her awake all night. "And right now, nothing makes me happier than you."

He drew her close, and she let him. But finally she pulled away. "Good-night, Justin."

"Good-night."

She was halfway up the outside steps when he rolled down the car window and yelled as loud as he could, "I'm crazy about you, Emily Anderson."

At first those words had been hard for her. Love, the way she thought of love, was something her parents defined, not something she'd ever really considered for herself. But now there was no stopping her feelings, no lying to herself. Justin Baker was the most amazing guy she'd ever met. She cupped her hands around her mouth. "I'm crazy about you too!"

He stretched over to the passenger seat so she could see him better. Then he held his little finger out the window. "Pinky swear?"

She laughed but held hers out toward him in return. "Pinky swear!"

By the time she got inside and climbed into bed, her thoughts had nothing to do with her parents or her fears about their relationship. All she could think about was Justin and the way he made her laugh and love. And how, with him in her life, every day felt better than the last.

Happily, indeed.

She didn't need a ring or a promise or a date to convince her that Justin was right for her. Neither one of them was going to walk away, not after what they'd found. They could survive however long it took.

Even if they had to wait years for the ever after.

EIGHT

Word came on a cloudy Saturday morning, the third week of August, as Justin was heading out to meet Emily. PLU's soccer practice had been early that day, and Justin had planned a surprise for the two of them—a hike in the foothills of the Cascade Mountains east of the city.

His commanding officer saw him heading out and pulled him aside. "Lieutenant Baker, I need to speak with you." He ushered Justin into his office and handed him a slip of paper. "You leave for Iraq Monday, September 24. You've been assigned to a six-month tour, shorter than before." The man's tone was matter-of-fact. After all, this sort of news went out every day around the base. "I just received notice." He paused. "I wanted you to have as much time as possible to prepare."

"Sir, thank you, sir." He felt the familiar thrill, the rush that in just a month or so, he'd be back on the front lines doing what he loved—wearing the army uniform and taking a stand for justice. Helping people who had no help and safeguarding American soil. He stood a little straighter. "I'll be ready, sir."

The man nodded. "Dismissed, soldier."

Justin saluted as he left the office, but not until he reached his Jeep did the news actually sink in. Facts swirled in his head and made him dizzy. The most obvious was this: He and Emily would say good-bye in just one month. Four weeks to continue the crazy, wonderful, magical whirlwind that had been their lives ever since their first date. He wanted to take her to the Space Needle and Blake Island and Issaquah. He planned to walk with her along the trails of the Washington Park Arboretum and kiss her halfway down Azalea Way, the path that wound through the grounds.

All of that in just a month.

But there were other bits of information filling his mind as well. He had to be ready physically and mentally, emotionally and spiritually. There was no other way to take on a task like this. Iraq was a tough place, and he wouldn't do the United States Army justice if he wasn't prepared.

Then there was the fact that this tour was going to be shorter than the first. Six months instead of a year. Before meeting Emily, he would've wondered about that, even complained. If he wanted to be a leader one day, then he needed to spend his share of time on the front lines. That was only right.

But six months would count just fine. That, plus the year he'd already done. He'd have plenty of experience by the time he finished this next tour. Besides, he'd signed up for a year, and if that's what they wanted, they would've assigned him to a full twelve months. The shorter tour could only mean one thing. God was smiling down on him, knowing that every day without Emily would feel like a month, and that half a year was probably all either one of them could take.

Justin did the math.

Six months in Iraq meant staying through the holidays and into the spring, but by the end of March he should be on his way home. With no more tours ahead of him, he could do the thing he'd wanted to do since the first time he'd taken Emily on a date.

He could ask her to marry him. It didn't matter how fast things had moved. He was more than crazy for her; he loved her. He had no doubts. He would ask her to marry him and then maybe a year later, the summer before her senior year, they could plan on a wedding. That would give him time to get additional training and take a paid position. They could get a nice apartment and start their future together, living and loving, waking up in each other's arms.

But the proposal would have to wait. Because though he knew how to survive with the danger, nothing was really certain until he came home. Even six months was a long time—long enough that Emily's feelings for him could change, or he could get assigned to permanent duty overseas.

Still, the odds of either one of those things happening were slim. The possibilities came to life like so many summer wildflowers, dotting and coloring the hillside of his future in ways that took his breath. The news—knowing his departure date—would be sad for her at first. But they could stand anything for six months. He climbed into his Jeep and drove to PLU. Never mind the clouds. The future was so bright, he had to squint to look at it.

He only hoped that after hearing his news, Emily would feel the same way.

Hiking the nearby hills was the best idea Justin had come up with that week. He was never at a loss for ideas. They'd been dating steadily for more than two months, and he'd treated her to the sort of memory-making summer that seemed like something from a dream. Every day was more magical than the one before.

Justin was amazing.

Emily had known it from the beginning, when his cheeks turned red beneath Vonda's relentless teasing. She'd known it when he took her to the small church just off the base, when she watched him hanging on every word of a message on sacrifice, and when he'd lifted his chin and closed his eyes during the praise music. And she knew it when he made a point of asking her to go every Sunday morning after that.

He'd opened up his heart and shown her the picture of a man who was as gentle as he was strong. She knew more about his background now. He and his sister were very close—though, according to Justin, they were known to have drawn-out arguments. And his entire family saw him as a hero. Not just because of his time in Iraq either.

That wasn't all she found out. A few days after the soccer tournament, the two of them were editing news briefs in the public information office when Vonda set down her telephone receiver.

"Justin Baker, how many things are you involved with, anyway?" Her voice boomed across the office.

Emily looked up from her computer.

He made a silly face and shrugged. "Take a message, Vonda. I'll call them back at my break."

"The senior center, the teen center, the city-subsidized daycare center, the local grade school ..." She shook her head and returned to the phone call. After she'd taken a message, she hung up the phone and did an exaggerated sigh. "Boy, you make Mother Teresa look lazy. How'll you find time for that pretty girl of yours if you stay so busy?"

"It's nothing." He winked at her and then looked at Emily. His expression told her that there were things about his life she didn't yet know. Things he wanted to share with her.

"It's something, all right. And anyway, you don't need involvement to keep yourself on your toes. That's what you've got me for!"

Justin laughed and Emily did the same thing. But a strange and wonderful feeling spread from her heart outward. Justin volunteered his time? And how come he hadn't talked about that before? She'd known guys in her past who bragged about the least little bit of charity or community work. Anything to look good.

Justin had done the opposite.

"Why?" she asked him later. They had taken their lunch outside to a picnic table. "Why didn't you tell me?"

"Come on, Emily." His easy laugh filled the air between them. "How would that sound? We're just getting to know each other, and I bore you with a list of things I'm involved in?" He grinned. "Besides, the Bible says don't let your left hand know what your right hand is doing." His shrug seemed to dismiss whatever praise was due him. "It's not like I'm saving the world. Just spending time with people."

She was awed, intrigued. Over the course of lunch she found out that he spent a few hours every week or so at the Veteran's center. If he didn't admit to fighting with his sister every now and then, Emily would've been tempted to search his back for wings.

"I love Veterans." She studied him, still trying to figure him out.

"People forget about those old folks." His tone was nonchalant, as if every guy his age took time to visit with Veterans. He swallowed a bite of his sandwich and looked at her. "They served our country with everything they had. The World War II Vets and the Vietnam guys." His eyes grew deeper, more serious. "The stories they tell would make you cry, Emily. How they watched friends fall and die in battle, and how they wept over having to kill the enemy."

He was quiet for a moment, and the silence felt comfortable. Then he looked at the blue sky beyond the trees and his voice grew more intense. "The sacrifice they paid, they paid for all of us. So we can go to church and choose our careers and," he smiled, "even so we can sit here and eat lunch together." He looked at her. "Freedom is as basic to us as breathing." He shrugged. "It's easy to take for granted. I don't know." The sunlight caught his eyes. "I guess the least I can do is spend a little time getting to know them, letting them know that their sacrifice wasn't in vain. That people haven't forgotten."

Emily could barely eat. She hadn't thought guys like this existed. When her surprise let up a little, she pushed harder, asked more questions, and learned that he spent an hour every Saturday after lunch at the city's teen center. Justin had played soccer and basketball in high school. Even though he hadn't run with the popular jock crowd, he still knew sports and was athletic enough to jump in and play with the kids who came to the center.

"Most of them don't have dads." He narrowed his eyes and looked up for a minute, toward the branches of one of the big evergreens that lined the picnic area. "I can't imagine growing up without a dad." His eyes grew watery. "When I was in grade school, a buddy of mine had a father in prison. A real bad guy, into drugs and gang stuff." Justin's voice grew softer, and his expression changed as he drifted back.

"One day when my friend was twelve, he climbed on his bicycle and headed out to the prison. He wanted to talk to his dad, whatever it took. His mother wouldn't take him, didn't want the guy having an influence over her son. So my buddy rode off to find him on his own. Only he never made it. Got his bicycle tires stuck in a rut along some rural road and flipped his bike right in front of an oncoming bus."

Emily gasped and put her fingers to her mouth. "That's terrible." When she looked up, she saw tears in Justin's eyes.

"He never knew what hit him." He sniffed and his voice grew more determined. "I couldn't get over that. The boy just wanted his daddy. Wanted him so badly he would've done anything to get to him." He exhaled. "A lot of the kids who enlist in the armed services were raised in single-family homes, did you know that? Either their dad was gone all the time or in prison, or divorce took him away and off to another family."

"I didn't know."

"It's true. Lots of the kids who come here have a brilliant future ahead of them. But a good number are looking for a way out, any way but the way they were raised." He set his sandwich down on his plate and pulled a few sesame seeds from the bun. "Those kids are so hungry for an older guy in their life, it's unbelievable.

I think about my dad, what a great guy he's been for me." He angled his head. "So what if I show up and play hoops with them once in a while. No big deal. But maybe when they hit the pillow that night, they miss their dad just a little bit less because someone took time to hang out with them."

"Do they ever give you a hard time about the war?"

Justin considered her question. "You know, for now these kids think the world of soldiers." He smiled, slightly embarrassed. "I guess by going out and meeting with the kids, I'm helping that generation have the right understanding of the military. The world will tell them soon enough that we're the bad guys, that we're warmongers. I want them to know the truth—that we're willing to give our lives so that they'll have a safe place to go to school, a safe neighborhood where they can live and play and grow up."

When Emily returned to her room that evening, she was dumbfounded. Justin truly cared for the people he helped. The Veterans and the lost teens and the innocent youth. It all came back to his understanding of what constituted a leader: "Being a leader means making sacrifices, Emily, and what've I really sacrificed? The things I do are fun. I'm a people person. What can I say?"

She wanted to pick up the phone and call her father, brag to him about how wonderful her new boyfriend really was. But that day as she reached for the phone, she changed her mind before she punched in the first number. Justin hadn't shared the information with her to impress her, but to help her understand him. And he'd only done so after she found out about it through Vonda. That made it all the more special. She made a decision that day that she would keep the details about Justin quiet and close to her heart.

The recent memories faded, and she looked at her watch. Justin would be there any minute. She grabbed her backpack and headed for the foyer of her residence hall, where she always waited for him. Yes, if she and God were the only two who knew how special he was, then so be it.

She reached her spot and anchored herself against the wall. Again, images of the past few weeks came rushing back. She'd gone with him to the teen center a few times, once to visit with the schoolkids, and twice to play basketball. She had Saturday afternoons off, and basketball was a great cardio workout. But more than that, her times to go to the center with Justin gave her a chance to see him in action.

He was a natural leader, no doubt.

Both times she'd joined in the pick-up games, and he would make sure she was on his team.

"Come on, Baker," one of the teens said the first time she went. He thumped his chest. "She's too pretty for you, man. Put her on the sidelines where she can cheer nice and proper."

"Not all pretty girls are cheerleaders." Justin chuckled. He was completely at ease around the tougher kids. "Here's how it is. She's on my team, and even though she's pretty, we'll still beat you."

The guys laughed and shoved each other, talking smack. But once the game got underway, Emily worked beautifully with Justin. His passes were right to her, giving her one easy layup after another. The final score had them on top by four points. Justin took his camera with him everywhere, and as they finished, he took it from his backpack and handed it to one of the teens. "Get our picture, okay?"

The guy shook his head. "Girls."

"I know, I know." He took her hand but kept his distance as he raised a brow at her. "Don't stand too close. I need a shower."

She laughed and took her place beside him.

"Ready?"

They smiled and the boy took the picture. Another memory made. But it wasn't so much the game that Emily remembered from that afternoon. It was the way Justin hung around with the guys afterward. He brought a twelve-pack of Coke and gave everyone a can, and for more than an hour, he sat on a set of steps listening while the guys talked about school and sports and girls. Whatever was on their minds.

Her thoughts shifted, and Emily looked at her watch. He was ten minutes late. She checked her cell phone, but no text messages, no missed calls. Strange. Justin was late once in a while, but usually he'd call. She leaned forward and scanned the parking lot. Then she let herself fall back against the wall again. He would have a good reason, whatever it was.

She smiled and remembered the ride home from the teen center that first time they'd gone together. She had studied him. "Don't you have any faults, Justin Baker?"

"Me?" He pointed to himself and gave her a mock look of surprise. "How can you even ask?"

She giggled. "Come on, I'm serious. I've never known anyone like you."

"Truth? The list is too long to go into."

"Like what? You don't wash your car once a week?"

"That too." He loosened his grip on the wheel and looked at the road ahead of him. "Let's see. Okay, I have this dog, Buster. He was my best friend until I enlisted, and now I almost never make it home to take him on walks. That's a big one." He held up two fingers. "Second has to be my room. It's been a mess since I was old enough to walk. No matter what my mom tried, I couldn't keep it clean." He gave her a wry look. "I guess that's sort of a warning. If you wanna break up with me, I'll understand."

"Confession." She winced. "My room's probably worse than yours."

"Yikes. We'll have to hire a housekeeper for sure." His laughter faded. "But that's only the beginning of the list."

She felt her heart opening to him. "What's at the top?"

He stared at the road for a handful of seconds. "Fear." He gave her a side glance, and for the first time she could see cracks in her soldier's armor.

"Fear of what?"

"I don't know." Clouds had gathered and it gave the moment a quiet depth. "Of being in battle and doing the wrong thing, of letting my squad down." He looked at her again. "Of dying before I ever have the chance to live."

She sat back and absorbed this revelation. After a while she put her hand on his knee. "I didn't know."

He grinned, trying to lighten the mood again. "I don't think about it much, because, well ... you know. I'm never gonna die, right?"

"Oh, you mean that big *S* on your chest, Superman?" She giggled.

"How'd you know?" He chuckled. "No, seriously. Most of the time I can convince myself I'm not afraid of that stuff. The risk is my choice, you know?"

"Yes."

"But if I'm honest—" he drew a long breath—"if I'm really honest, I sometimes struggle with it. Way down where no one can see."

"Except me." She moved her hand to his.

"Except you. Because you and I share that X-ray vision."

They laughed, and that night after dinner they drove south to his parents' house. Buster was an English springer spaniel, black and white with gray around his whiskers. "Buster—" Justin hooked the leash onto the dog's collar—"I'd like you to meet a special girl." He went through with formal introductions, but Buster couldn't have cared less.

He only had eyes for Justin.

Clearly the dog hadn't forgotten the days of his youth, when Justin was young and had all sorts of time on his hands. The dog stayed close by his master's side throughout the walk, glancing up every few minutes with a look of admiration that said it didn't matter if Justin came to walk him only once a year. The dog's love for his boy was undying.

When they were finished, Justin crouched down and nuzzled his face against the dog's. "Atta boy, Buster. It's a good thing Dad takes you for walks when I'm not around, huh?"

The dog licked Justin's cheek and then whined as they walked away and headed into the house.

"See?" he told her later. "That dog deserves better. Definitely a big-time fault."

There were others, but not many that Emily could see. Once in a while he'd be late picking her up because he'd tried to squeeze too many events into a single day. But overall, it had been perfect. The weeks had flown by like a wonderful movie heading all too fast toward the ending.

And today would be one more amazing experience. Hiking the foothills east of the city. She exhaled and moved to the door. Where *was* he? He'd never been this late before. At eleven forty, when he was a full fifteen minutes late and she was about to call his cell phone, his Cherokee pulled into the lot and zipped around to the driveway just outside. She smiled and skipped down the stairs. As she climbed in, she grinned at him. "I was beginning to think the clouds had scared you off. But I checked the forecast. No rain for days." She squinted out the windshield. "I guess this is more of a marine layer, and according to the paper, it should burn off in an hour or so, as long as ..."

Suddenly she felt it.

He wasn't smiling, wasn't saying anything in response. She'd been rambling about the weather without even stopping to ask how he was or whether there was a reason he was late. She stopped midsentence and looked at him. "Justin?"

"My commander pulled me aside on my way out." He didn't look afraid or upset. Just very serious. He put his hand on her shoulder. "I ship out September 24."

The news knocked the wind from her. She pressed her fists to her stomach and hunched over a little. *Come on, Emily, breathe.*

You knew this was coming. And she had known. But for the past six weeks she'd lied to herself, convinced herself that maybe Justin was wrong, maybe the army wouldn't need him back in Iraq for another tour. Maybe the summer they were sharing really would go on forever, endless and perfect.

But now ... now there was a date, a time when she would have to say good-bye and trust God that somehow Justin would return to her, that He hadn't brought a boy like Justin Baker into her life only to take him away forever. She swallowed hard and lifted her eyes to him. "For sure?"

"For sure." He massaged her shoulder. "But there's good news, Em. It won't be for a year like I thought. Only six months."

"On the front lines?"

He smiled. "That's where they need medics most."

She was still barely catching her breath. Six months on the front lines in a war where there were casualties every day. She had no idea how she'd survive a single week, let alone six months. "Have you ... have you told your dad?"

"Not yet." He bit his lip. "I wanted you to know first." He brushed her hair back from her face. "Now listen, no sad eyes, okay? Six months is nothing, Emily. I'll come back and we can do what I've wanted to do since the first time we went out."

She felt the dark cloud lift just a little. "What's that?"

"Well—" he came closer and kissed her, longer than usual and with a passion that left them both breathless—"I guess you'll have to wait and see."

She kissed him again and gave him a pretend pout. "What if I don't want to wait."

He rubbed his nose against hers. "Ever after's worth waiting for. Don't you think?"

Ever after. Emily put her arms around his neck and held him close. He was right. He'd come back in six months and they could talk about forever, about how God had made them for each other, and how once he was back they would have an entire future to plan.

They continued on with their hike that day, lost in a world all their own, laughing about how Justin's dad had found an old sweatshirt of Justin's and given it to Buster, and how the dog wouldn't sleep without it now. "Talk about a guilt trip." Justin stayed right behind her as they hiked, and halfway up the trail, when she slid on some loose rocks, he caught her in his arms.

"Well, that settles it." She steadied herself and grinned at him. "You definitely have a talent for saving lives."

Justin glanced at the hillside. The drop-off was maybe ten feet. "You would've skinned your knee, but I don't think that fall would've killed you. Just to be honest."

They laughed and she started out again. "Just stay behind me, okay? You never know when I might fall."

"You got it."

The day was full, and Justin took pictures left and right, even finding a passerby to snap one of the two of them near the top of the trail.

When they finished their hike, they drove to the teen center for basketball. Later, after the games, Justin told them about his leave date.

"Man!" One of the teens, Bo, the one who seemed to be the group's leader, had a sweaty T-shirt in his hands. He wadded it up and tossed it on the ground. "That stinks."

"Yeah, how come Uncle Sam gets you two times around?" Another teen crossed his arms, doing his best to look tough. But there was no hiding the tears that had sprung to his eyes. His chin quivered. "Stupid war, anyway."

Justin took a slow breath and looked at each of the kids. "It's not a stupid war, guys. Really." He picked up a pebble, turned it around in his hands, and tossed it out onto the basketball court. "The stuff I've seen over there would amaze you. The war's helping more than you'll ever hear about."

"Still—" Bo cocked his head back—"you already been there once."

"I wanted to go back." Justin rested his elbows on his knees and looked from Bo to the others. "When you believe in something, you put your whole heart into it." He looked at Emily. "Whether that's a girl, or fighting for your country."

Emily studied the guys. A lump formed in her throat. She tried to swallow, but she couldn't. The teens looked like the most lost group ever, devastated and not sure how to react to the fact that Justin would be leaving them.

One of the teens, a smaller kid who hadn't said much, looked up and nodded. "I'm proud of you, man. When I'm eighteen, I'm enlisting too. My mama says it'll set my whole life straight, being in the service."

"Yeah." Another boy, one who'd hung his head at Justin's announcement, looked up at his friends. "Me too. I'm enlisting soon as I graduate high school."

"But man!" Bo shook his head. "What about all that danger?"

"Okay, well, that's why I'm telling you." Justin's voice was kind, but stern. "Not so you can hang your head and be mad at the military." His expression softened. "So you can pray. Pray for me every day, and pray for the other guys out there. We're doing a good thing. Pray that we'll make progress and that God'll use us while we're there."

"Pray you'll come back in one piece, you mean." Bo smiled, but as he did, a single tear rolled down his cheek. He cussed under his breath. "I mean it, man. Come back safe."

"Hey, now." Justin gave him a friendly punch in the arm. "I'm not leaving for a month. You have lots of time to take me in hoops between now and then."

"Yeah." Bo returned the punch. "Just come back."

Emily wiped at her own tears, and on the way to her residence hall later, she and Justin were quieter than usual. Finally she reached for his hand. "Did you ever think that maybe you don't need a second tour? Maybe … maybe you're doing enough over here to get all the leadership skills you could ever use."

"The way I see it, the good leaders all go twice, Emily." His voice held something she hadn't heard before. Not the fear he'd confessed, exactly. But a sense of duty, obligation. Every other time he'd talked about his second tour, it was with a tone that suggested he almost looked forward to it. But this time was different.

"So you've thought about it at least?" Her voice was soft.

"A second tour is expected of any committed soldier. Most of us don't have a choice, and just because I'm a lieutenant, because I have more training, more education, doesn't mean it's not expected of me." His eyes held a longing. "It's the right thing, Emily. But that doesn't mean I wouldn't rather be here with you."

Those words made her feel more loved than anything he'd told her so far. Yes, he was going back to Iraq and yes, it was the right decision for him. But he'd given her a glimpse through a chink in his heroic armor.

In a perfect world, he would never leave her side. But that was just it.

The world wasn't perfect.

When they arrived at the parking lot, he turned off the engine and reached into the backseat. "I brought my Bible." He opened it. "I want to show you something." He turned to Genesis. "Listen to this. It's from chapter 29." He began to read.

The story was about Jacob and Rachel, how Jacob had loved Rachel from the beginning, and how working seven years for her seemed like only a few days because of his love for her. When Justin reached that part, he stopped. He looked at her, his eyes full of questions. "Do you know what I'm trying to tell you, Em?"

She felt hesitant and unsure. Her eyes fell to the open Bible, but she shook her head. "Not really."

He pressed his hand to the page. "That's how I feel about you." He took her hand and looked long at her. "At the end of summer I'll have to go away, but time can't separate us, Emily. Not six months or six years. Because that's how much I love you."

Her heart melted. "Justin—"

"I mean it." He leaned close and kissed her. "Go on in. But remember that, okay."

"You're amazing."

He smiled. "Go."

As she headed up the steps that evening, she remembered how she'd slipped during their hike, and how he'd been right there to catch her. It was how the teens felt, how the Veterans probably felt too. Justin was their fallback guy. The one they could count on when no one else was around.

She could only do what he'd asked the teens to do. Pray for him, for his effectiveness in the Middle East and for his safe return. So that whenever life gave her a reason to trip up, he would always be there, ready to catch her.

Justin Baker, her fallback guy. Her hero.

NINE

The weeks of summer disappeared, and finally Lauren had to face the facts.

There had been no improvement between her and Shane, nothing to convince her she should stay. He'd been busy at work, training a new group of pilots and preparing for a series of raids that would take place from naval aircraft carriers located in the waters off the Middle East.

They were covert operations, plans to bomb headquarters where new terrorist cells were gathering and making plans for attack. All Shane could tell her was that the U.S. government had discovered more terrorist activity, that they knew the whereabouts of the terrorists and which compounds they were using, and that they intended to eliminate them without civilian casualty before they could formulate a strike against the United States.

He was taken up with the plans while she'd given herself over to stories that seemed empty and meaningless. A feature on the college dropout rate, the difficulty college grads had getting jobs that paid enough, the success of a reading program in inner-city D.C., and the humanitarian work being done in New Orleans more than a year after Hurricane Katrina.

Okay, so those stories were important to a segment of people. But the war affected every citizen in the U.S. and the Middle East. When she wrote from Afghanistan, she could help sway public opinion, help people know how wrong and ineffective the war was, and what hardships it created for the Afghani and Iraqi citizens. She could tell the truth about civilian casualties and show that the U.S. had been overzealous in declaring war in the first place.

Maybe her stories would be strong enough to help voters know that it was time to bring in a president who would put an end to the horrors being committed in Afghanistan and Iraq. Those countries would figure out their own way to freedom. If they wanted it badly enough, they'd find a way. But American boys needed to be back home. No matter what Shane thought.

The longer she pictured Justin Baker bent down using his own shirt to stave off the soccer player's bleeding, a girl he'd never met, the more she'd changed her thinking. It wasn't the soldiers' fault they were in Iraq. They'd been taught that what they were doing was right.

If Justin was what U.S. soldiers really were like, then all the more reason to pull out of the war. America couldn't stand to lose a generation of young people like that. Kids who might grow up to be police officers or firefighters or judges, doctors, or lawyers. The very ones who would bring about change in a society that desperately needed it. No, the cost was too great if it meant losing a single kid like the one Emily was in love with.

She'd tried to talk about it with Shane one night, but the conversation hadn't gone well. They shared dinner at his house, and afterward they took a walk to the nearby park.

"Remember when we were freshmen?" Shane held her hand. He stopped and looked at the swings. "We'd walk home together every day past the grade school."

"And if classes were out, we'd stop and swing together." She smiled. The memory was as clear as if it had happened last week. "We'd see who could get the highest."

"You won almost every time." He grinned at her, released her hand, and took a few running steps toward the swings. "Bet I can beat you now."

They both laughed, and the feeling was wonderful — so much better than the tension that seemed to always settle between them. She jumped on the nearest swing. "Race you to the moon."

"And back again."

The same words they'd said every time they'd done this as kids. And as they stretched their legs to the sky, Lauren could almost believe it was possible, that they could look past their differences if only they could spend more time doing this, playing and laughing together.

Shane won easily that evening. When they slowed their swings, out of breath from laughing and the exertion, Shane held up his finger. "Winner. Definitely the winner."

"Okay." She set her swing into gentle motion and waited until her breathing was normal again. "Hey ... guess what?"

"What?"

She narrowed her eyes, still holding onto the swing chain. "I've changed my mind about soldiers."

He looked nervous, as if he was having too much fun to talk about war. "After you got to know Justin, right?"

"More than that." She looked into the deep blue sky. "I used to think they were the bad guys, sort of. The people who were in favor of war — " she gave him a quick look — "which could never be a good thing."

Shane moved his swing ever so slightly. He let out a heavy sigh and stared at the ground. "Lauren ..."

"No, really. I have a point here." She kept her tone light, so she wouldn't shut him off from listening. "I know differently now. The soldiers, the kids like Justin, they're the good guys, aren't they?"

"Yes." Shane looked at her, but his expression was wary, as if he knew better than to agree to anything she might say about the war or the military. "They're definitely the good guys."

She twisted her swing from side to side, her eyes never leaving his. "So that's all the more reason why war's wrong. Because we can't afford to lose the Justin Bakers of this country." She tried to smile, but it didn't come easily. "Does that make sense?"

He stood slowly and held his hand out to her. "We better get back. I have an early day tomorrow."

Lauren had noticed a trend.

When they shared an evening together, if she didn't talk about the war or his job or the Middle East, then they'd find their way to the cozy sofa in his living room. They'd whisper about the past and share kisses — sometimes far later than they meant to. Shane had made it clear that he wouldn't sleep with her, and she agreed that it was best not to. She'd gotten pregnant once. It could happen again. Besides, no matter how liberal her views, she believed sex outside marriage was wrong. The Bible said so, and she truly wanted to do things God's way.

But if the taboo topics came up, their kissing would be quick and marked with strain and distrust, as if both of them knew it was only a matter of time before she'd leave again, and that would be that.

Now it was the first of September and she'd made up her mind.

She couldn't leave Shane, not on her own. Couldn't tell him she didn't love him and care for him when she still did, when her feelings for him had never been deeper. But she couldn't stay either. Shane deserved a wife who would praise him every day for his commitment to national security, who would celebrate covert air strikes as one more sign that America was in safe hands.

Men needed compliments. Her mother had taught her that when she was a teenager. But how could she build Shane up when she disagreed with what he was doing? And since she didn't have the strength to break things off, she'd made a different sort of decision.

To tell Bob Maine yes. Yes, she would go back to Afghanistan, and yes, she would work alongside Scanlon. She would report on the war the way she'd always done, and she would look harder this time — in case she was wrong. She would commit to a full year, and when it was over — if Shane was still interested — they could talk, see if they'd come any closer to finding the common ground she'd prayed about. See if they'd figured out a bridge long enough to span the distance between them.

They were meeting at the park again that night. Lauren didn't want dinner — she wasn't hungry, and after she told him her news, he wouldn't be either. She arrived ten minutes before Shane and took a spot at their usual picnic table. She had just long enough to study the endless expanse of mesquite bushes that covered the dusty, dry hills surrounding Fallon, just enough time to watch a pair of fighter jets zooming out of sight in the distance. Why had she ever thought it could work?

Lord ... I don't understand how we got into this mess. Why did You let us find each other? And how come I ever thought I could survive here in Fallon?

She listened, and after a minute she began to see a Scripture verse forming in her mind. *My ways are not your ways.*

The verse was one she and Shane had talked about before. God's ways were different than man's, right? Wasn't that what it meant? But why would the Lord place that verse in her mind now? She sat still, observing the world around her. Not too far away, an older couple held hands as they walked along the paved perimeter of the park. Closer still, a family with two young boys was having fun on the play structure.

My ways are not your ways ...

Did God want her to see that maybe her way of thinking wasn't right? Was that it? If so, she was willing. *Lord, if I'm wrong, show me. I only want what's best for this country, for the soldiers*

*and the people of the Middle East. If my ways aren't Your ways, then
please, Lord … show me Your ways.*

She realized then that her prayer was one of the most common ones uttered throughout the Bible. Not a prayer for her will to be done, or for her way of thinking to be right. But a cry for wisdom.

What did the Bible say? Wisdom was more precious than gold or silver, better than honey, and worth any amount of searching, right? Wisdom was seeing things as closely as possible to the way God saw them, understanding them the way He understood them.

And it was admitting that maybe she was wrong—or maybe she and Shane both were—and being open to whatever God wanted to teach her. That was wisdom. *Fine, Lord … I'm here, I'm open. I never wanted to hurt Shane this way, never wanted to hurt myself. So please, God … give me wisdom.*

As she finished the prayer, she spotted Shane pulling into the parking lot. He got out of his car and walked over, his steps slower than usual. *He knows,* she told herself. *He has to see what's coming.*

He took the seat opposite her and folded his hands on the table. "You know something?" His expression was open and vulnerable, and it reminded her of the night when he drove to her house, the day before his family moved him to California. He had come as a last-ditch effort, desperate for a way to avoid saying good-bye.

"What?" She felt like a schoolgirl again, lost in his eyes. This was her Shane, the man she'd looked for all her young adult life.

"My heart still beats faster every time I see you." He reached across the table and she did the same. Their fingertips touched, and the sensation was warm and intimate. "I'm here because you want to talk." A sad smile played on his lips. "And knowing you, that can't be good. But even so," he looked deep into her eyes, "I see you and I want to shout to the heavens. You're here. You really are here after all those years apart."

"Shane…" She couldn't be doing this, could she? Meeting with Shane to tell him good-bye? She swallowed hard and searched his eyes. She was right; he knew what was coming. But even so, he wasn't angry or distant. Instead he held his whole heart out for her. "I'll never regret coming here, following you here to Fallon."

"Hmmm." His eyes never lost contact with hers. "Why don't I like that opening?"

"Because—" She hung her head and made a sound that was more cry than laugh. When she lifted her chin, she could already feel tears in her eyes. "I admire you, Shane. I don't tell you enough." She brushed her fingertips against his again. "You've committed your life to doing what you think is right, to living the way you believe is best." She let her voice drop a notch. "Most people could go their entire lives and not be able to say that."

"You admire me, Lauren?" His words were a caress. The longer they sat there, the harder this was going to be. "Is that what you came to tell me?"

"No." Her answer was quick and bathed in compassion. "But it's true. And I don't think I've told you enough. I might not—" she waved her hand around, frustrated at herself—"I might not agree with you, but I admire you for taking a stand. Really, I do."

"Okay." He looked like he didn't want to ask the next question. But he had no choice. "So why are we here?"

She brought her hand back to his. "Because—" she held her breath—"I'm leaving in the morning." There was no way around the obvious, not anymore. She had to tell him, because if she didn't say the truth soon, she'd run around the table and fall into his arms and make promises to him that she could never keep.

"Leaving? For an assignment?"

"Yes … no." She breathed out and let the explanation come. "My editor wants me back in Afghanistan, Shane." Her emotions caught her off guard. This was the only sane choice, the only answer. The only way even to find out if God's wisdom went against her own, or if compromise was something she was supposed to work on. She pressed her finger to her upper lip and fought for control. "I've told you before. He's been asking me all summer."

Whether he had expected this or not, Shane's face grew a shade paler. "You're going back to the Middle East?" He tightened the hold he had on her hands. "Tomorrow morning?"

"Yes." She felt terrible, and she wondered at her sanity. If she hadn't run off to California looking for him, if she hadn't turned her back on her family twenty years ago, then everything would be different. Back then she would've driven to the moon to find Shane, to reconnect with him. Now, here they were, together again, and she was choosing to walk away.

"So that's it, huh?" He sat a little straighter, and for the first time since he arrived, there was anger in his eyes, in his tone. "That's all the warning you're giving me?"

"Shane, if I'd told you any sooner, I wouldn't go. I'd change my mind, because that's what being with you does to me. It makes me think impossible thoughts, like we could work things out, when nothing that's happened between us since I moved here makes that look even close to plausible."

He released her hand, stood, and turned his back to her. When they were teens, Shane had been willing to live with friends or with a teacher so he could stay in Illinois and marry her the way he wanted to. He would've worked three jobs so that after graduation they could live on their own and raise their child.

But the choice hadn't been his. That summer, when Lauren was weeks away from delivering, Shane's parents moved their family across the country. Oh, they promised he and Lauren would stay in touch, but that was a lie, same as the lie her parents had told her — that they'd connect with the Galanters as soon as they settled in California.

Now it was like the same thing was happening all over again. Shane had been willing to make things work, willing to listen to Lauren's arguments, willing to go to counseling or take longer trips away from Fallon.

But like before, the choice wasn't his.

He crossed his arms, his shoulders stiff and unmoving. If his heart was breaking, he wasn't showing it. She sat there, helpless. "This is all my fault, Shane." A couple of young moms walked by. Lauren waited until they had passed before finishing her thought. "I don't expect you to understand."

"Understand?" He spun around and put one foot on the bench where he'd been sitting a few moments ago. He leaned closer. "Lauren, you give me no time even to breathe, let alone understand."

"That's because I just made up my mind last night." She wanted to go to him, fall into his arms, and stay there. But it wasn't the time. "I've thought about it all summer, Shane. Wondered if I was crazy to want to leave, or crazier still to think I could stay."

"I *love* you, Lauren." He clenched his jaw and shook off the emotions that seemed to battle in his eyes. "What do our views on the *war*—" he spat the word like it was poison—"what do they matter? Certainly there must be more we can talk about than that." He waved his hand over his head. "Like the years we lost … and our role in Emily's life and the stories you're writing and what plans we have for the future. We can talk about our faith, and how important it is to find a church where we'll both fit in." He did a single laugh, one that held no humor whatsoever. "See, Lauren? Have you thought about those things?"

While he was talking, another pair of fighter jets soared into the sky overhead. The sound shook the park, and the little boys with their parents looked up, staring and smiling. Lauren waited until the sound died off. Her shoulders slumped and she shook her head. "I live in Fighter Town, U.S.A., Shane. Sometimes I can't think at all for the constant sound of the jets overhead."

"So that's it?" He tossed his hands and put his foot back down on the ground. "We meet here and say good-bye, we go our separate ways like we never found each other again?"

"No." She was on her feet now. She moved around the table and stood before him. "I'm not leaving you, Shane. I'm taking a job in the Middle East. One year, that's what I've promised. And something else." She waited until he met her eyes. "I've asked God to show me if my beliefs are wrong or too strong. If I should compromise somehow. I've asked Him for wisdom." Tears clouded her eyes. "I don't know what else to do."

For a long while, the anger lingered in his expression. But then the fight seemed to leave him. He held out his hands and took her into his arms. "A whole year? What if He shows you before that?"

"Then I'll come home." She met his eyes and touched her fingers to the side of his face. Then she brought her lips to his. Their kiss was borne of desperation and longing and sorrow. When it was over, there were tears on both their cheeks. "I'll come home, and I'll pray with every fiber of my heart that you'll still be here waiting."

"And in the meantime?"

"In the meantime ... you'll have a lot less stress at dinner parties."

He smiled, but it faded before it reached his eyes. "Promise me something?"

She wanted to tell him yes, anything he asked. But they both knew that wasn't true. Instead she angled her head and prayed he'd see her heart. "I can try."

"Promise me you'll go back with open eyes." His tone was tender, filled with meaning.

"Okay." It was an easy promise to make. She'd already prayed for wisdom, and though she expected to feel even more strongly against the war a year from now, she could promise him to keep her eyes open. At least that. "If I'm wrong, I'll say so."

His eyes grew wet and he blinked twice. "Me too."

She traced his brow and his cheekbone. "I only know that nothing will change if I stay here."

He nodded. "You'll have email?"

"I will." She didn't want to commit to writing. Life in Afghanistan or Iraq, depending on where they stationed her, would plunge her into a different way of living. Besides, it would only hurt worse to keep Shane on the line as a pen pal. "I don't know how often I'll write."

Her words were one more blow, and she watched them hit their mark somewhere inside him. "Don't take risks, Lauren. There's nothing valiant about going places where the military warns you to stay out."

"I know. I'll have my jacket and helmet, my gear. I'll be careful." It was what she had to say, what all reporters told their families and loved ones. But they both knew the truth was something else. If the story meant going to areas of conflict, then she'd go—same as her colleagues. They all lived and worked with the understanding that they were observers, the ones who captured the news, never the ones who made it.

But after being shot at that day at the Afghanistan orphanage, Lauren knew better. Constant danger was a very real part of the job. Many journalists had died covering the war. She could only promise to be as careful as possible, nothing more.

"Hey—" Shane put his hands on either side of her face—"did I ever tell you what I thought that first day, when I came down the airport escalator and walked into the baggage area, and there you were? Standing next to Emily?"

She smiled, even as another layer of tears clouded her vision. "I don't think so."

"I thought I was dreaming." He drew her close. "Because all my life I looked for you, Lauren. The month before Emily called, I was supposed to get married."

"I know."

"But I never told you why I broke up with her."

Lauren waited, savoring the feel of his arms around her, knowing this would be the last time they held each other for a long time. Maybe forever. "She wanted you to be a politician, right?"

"Yes, but that wasn't why we broke up." He looked past her, as if he were seeing those days again. "I kept a picture of you in my top drawer, the way you looked when you were seventeen. And at night, in my dreams, I would imagine how you must look now, nearly twenty years later." He paused. "I'd be walking downtown or at the mall or at the gym, and I'd see a blonde woman with your profile, and I'd chase her down."

"What?" Lauren couldn't keep from giggling. "Are you serious?"

"Yes." He smiled, but again his expression held more sorrow than laughter. "I'd get just close enough to call out your name, and the woman would turn around and I'd know. It wasn't you." He narrowed his eyes. "The last time I did that was the night Ellen and I announced our engagement."

"Shane, that's terrible." She tried not to sound jealous. She hadn't heard the details of the story before, but her heart hurt even imagining him that close to another woman. "What happened?"

"I was heading up in the elevator and the door opened a few floors shy of where the party was about to start. Through the doors I saw a blonde woman who looked like you. At least, I thought she did." He brushed his thumb against her cheek. "I slipped out and chased after her, ran down the hall and into the indoor pool area. I must've looked like some sort of crazy man, running in there dressed in a three-piece suit."

"What did she say?" She was flattered and sad all at the same time. He cared so much for her. How could she leave him? "Did she know you were following her?"

"I stopped just inside the pool deck area. She had two teenage boys with her, and an older guy with gray hair came up and kissed her. That was the first time I saw a clear view of her face, and I knew two things. First, that it wasn't you."

"And second?"

"I couldn't get married. Not when my heart had never let go of the dream, the hope of finding you."

The story filled her heart. She pressed her head against his chest, and for a long while she listened to his heartbeat. "I didn't know."

"So when I saw you that day in the airport, at first you were just one more blonde woman who looked like my Lauren. I was about to rush up to you and ask if you were her, when I spotted Emily. Emily who looks so much like you and so much like me. And that's when I knew. Every prayer I'd ever uttered on your behalf had been answered."

She closed her eyes. Every prayer but one. Because his prayers had been like hers, like Emily's. That if they ever found each other again, they would find the same love they'd shared before. That they would never say good-bye again.

Only here they were.

She was about to tell him they should get going, she had to pack before she caught her flight in the morning. But he beat her to it. "I guess we better get it over with."

Already something in his voice had changed, something that told her he was steeling himself to the pain that lay ahead for both of them. The beginning of letting her go. She stared into his eyes and tried to memorize the look there, tried because there would be dark days ahead when the only way she might hear God's voice, understand His wisdom, was by remembering this moment.

They kissed, and when they came up for air, they were both quietly crying. "I love you, Lauren. Take that with you, okay?"

"I love you too, even if—" she sobbed twice—"even if I'm the most stupid woman on the planet for letting you go."

His lips touched hers one last time, and when he pulled back, he wore the look of a broken man. He mouthed the word, "Goodbye," and for a long time held her gaze. Then he turned and made his way back to his car.

She watched him go, and with every bit of distance that came between them, she felt herself grow weaker, until finally she dropped to her knees and sat back on her heels. *Don't go, Shane... tell me I'm wrong! Make me stay!* She wanted to shout at him that it wasn't too late. He could still talk some sense into her. But the words wouldn't come. Almost as if her mind knew better than her heart what needed to happen next.

He looked at her one final time before he drove away, and even from her place on the ground, she could see he was crying. Not just teary-eyed or choked up, but weeping. And she knew then that this was the hardest thing either of them had ever done.

It was one thing to say good-bye back when they were teenagers, when the decisions were being made for them. But they were adults now who had found their way back together. And this good-bye was of their own choosing. Or of her own choosing. And in that moment, as a torrent of tears filled her heart and overflowed onto her face, she wondered if maybe Shane was right after all. Maybe everything about the last season of her life had been nothing more than a wonderful, terrible dream, from which it was inevitable that one day they would both awake. And they'd be right back where they started.

Alone in the world and wondering what would've happened if they'd never had to say good-bye in the first place.

TEN

Justin had their final day together all planned out.

Neither of them had any commitments, nothing to do but spend the time together. He was going to miss celebrating Christmas with Emily, so he took some money he'd been saving and stopped by a jeweler at Tiffany's in downtown Seattle's Pacific Place, a store they'd visited a few times on their dates there. What he found was perfect for Emily, and maybe — just maybe — wearing it would help the time go by faster.

Fall was in the air, but the days were still long and sunny. Emily had asked where they were going, but he kept it a surprise. "Trust me, it'll be perfect."

"I know." Emily had told him that the night before. "I just wish it wasn't happening so soon."

He made some joke to lighten the mood, and they both laughed. Because laughing felt so much better than crying. But now the day was here, and he was minutes away from leaving to pick her up. Everything was all set and loaded in his Jeep. The last thing he grabbed before he left his barracks was his camera. All summer he'd been good about taking pictures. It was part of what was going to make this day special.

He had just enough time to do one more thing. He sat down at his desk and pulled out a piece of lined paper. His words would come easily. With her, they always did.

Dear Emily . . .

He stopped there and remembered how this rollercoaster had all started. At the office of public information.

Nothing had changed about Vonda. Back at the beginning of August, she looked at them one day, clucked her tongue against the roof of her mouth, and shook her head. "Now listen here." She aimed her eyes at Emily. "Don't go acting like you're not in love. The whole office knows about it."

"But this is work." Emily grinned at her. "There can't be fraternizing at work, right?"

She brushed her hand like she was swatting at a pesky fly. "Fraternizing? You two wouldn't know how to fraternize if it meant a pay raise." She pounded her fist on the counter. "I say life's too short. If two people are in love, then don't hide it. In fact—" she stormed over and jerked her thumb in Justin's direction—"get up, young man."

Justin did as she said, chuckling under his breath. She made a big show of sliding his chair to an open computer next to Emily's. "This is your new work space." She took Justin's hand and led him to his chair. "Go on, take it." She rolled her eyes at Emily. "I have to tell you two everything." She waited until Justin was sitting down. "Good. This way you two lovebirds don't have to keep puttin' on a show, and you can hold hands when you want to."

She gave a firm nod of her head.

From that point on, Justin sat next to Emily. It was better that way, because Vonda was right. Being with her at work and pretending she wasn't sitting on the other side of the room was by then almost impossible. Love had caught him off guard and now it consumed him, especially at work when they'd tried so hard to keep their feelings hidden, to separate their jobs from life outside the office.

Justin looked out the window, the memories still playing in his mind. He'd had his last day at the office on Friday, and Emily and Vonda threw him a surprise farewell party. Afterward, when it was time for him to go, Vonda gave him a kiss on the cheek. Then she waved her hand at him. "Go on, get out of here." She drew back and froze, her eyes never leaving his. Suddenly her expression changed. Her chin began to quiver and her eyes welled up. Then she brought her hand to her mouth, and two trails of tears overflowed onto her cheeks. "Now look at me! All blubbery and everything." She wiped at her eyes, took hold of his shoulders, and looked straight at him. "Justin Baker ... you come back now, you hear? That's an order."

His throat thick, he saluted her. "Yes, ma'am."

She gave Emily a hug. "I'm the one who told you about him, so you make sure you do your praying, got it? We all gotta do our praying."

Before he left, she pressed a tissue first to one eye, then the other. "You're a good boy, Justin. I've seen my fair share of kids go off to war and never come back. But that ain't you, understand? This old world needs the likes of you, and I mean it. So don't do anything to get yourself killed."

He wasn't sure how to react. Vonda was always the strong one, the most blunt woman he knew. But now she was showing a side he hadn't seen. He hugged her, and when he and Emily were out in the hall, he realized Vonda wasn't the only one crying. Emily was too.

"Hey." He pulled her into a hug. "What's all this?"

"I don't know." She pressed her head against his chest. "I just want it to be March."

"It will be, sweetie. Soon enough."

But no matter how strong he acted around Vonda or Emily or the teens at the center or even his parents, deep inside he was waging a different kind of war. The one against fear. Before when he'd gone to Iraq, he had nothing to lose. He only wanted to do his part, fight for the United States, and make the war effort that much stronger. But when he left back then, he left with his whole heart and soul and mind.

Not so this time.

He looked at the paper before him and tried again.

Dear Emily,

I can't believe the worlds you've opened up to me this past summer. Things I never would've dreamed have come true and …

The words flowed as if she were standing before him and he was getting one last chance to tell her everything he felt. When he finished writing, he folded the page and tucked it in an envelope. There. Now he was ready to go. He hadn't overlooked a single thing.

So he was a little afraid. That was something he'd have to live with. Because Emily was worth longing for, and that's exactly what he would do. Every day while he was in the desert, no matter how important the work, he would long for her.

And one day very soon, he would come back home, and if he had his way, never — as long as he lived — leave her side again.

ELEVEN

Emily had steeled herself for this day, prepared for it by praying and journaling and taking long walks across campus just so she could think. With her mother back in the Middle East, her entire world felt like it was spinning out of control. And now this—her last day with Justin. When she woke that morning, she had tears on her cheeks even before she stepped out of bed.

Her parents had failed. Sure, they told her they might have another shot at a relationship someday. Sometime. But the dream of seeing them married was over. Even still, today was harder. Justin was leaving. There could be nothing sadder than that.

He picked her up a little after noon, and from the moment she joined him inside his Jeep, she felt something different between them, a sorrow that neither of them had allowed until this day.

"I have a few surprises for you." He grinned at her as he drove off the campus and entered the freeway. He wore his dress uniform, and he'd never looked more handsome.

"Me too. For you." She turned her eyes to the road because it hurt too much to look at him, to imagine him with grime on his face and mud on his boots, working the front line and kicking in doors. Her heart felt heavy inside her, and it remained that way until they pulled into a parking spot near Seattle's waterfront. She laughed, because if she didn't, the tears were bound to come. "The same place?" She slipped her bag onto her arm. "You're taking me to the same place we went for our first date?"

"Sort of." He swung a backpack over his shoulder and held her hand.

Even the air felt the same as it had the first time they were there. They walked past tourists and burly fishermen lugging buckets and poles over their shoulders. A chorus of seagulls filled the air, and every once in a while, Justin's eyes met hers as they strolled along. She savored the sights and smells, breathing them in. She would remember this day forever. When they reached the water, instead of going to the restaurant where they'd shared their first meal, he took her out onto Pier 55, to the place where a three-level white cruise ship was loading.

"Justin, are you serious?" She stopped and stared at the ship. "You're taking me on a cruise?"

"Yeah, well." He rubbed his knuckles on his shoulder. "The Bahamas seemed a little far for an afternoon ride, so, you know—" he grinned—"I settled for this."

She'd heard from a few of the kids on campus that the lunch and dinner cruises that made their way around Elliott Bay and Puget Sound were worth every penny. The perfect place for a romantic date. But she and Justin had been forced to catch their moments between their other commitments. Though some of the cruises lasted only an hour, most were longer, and besides that, they were expensive.

Before they boarded, Justin snagged an older couple strolling past on the pier. "Please ... could you take our picture?"

Both of them lit up. The man held out his hand. "Absolutely, young man." He gave Justin a handshake before taking the camera from him. "And thank you for the fine job you and your guys are doing for our country."

Emily's heart swelled with pride. He *was* doing a fine job, even going to Iraq showed what sort of man Justin was, what sort of man he was going to become in later years.

"Thank you, sir." Justin took Emily's hand and moved her back a few steps so they were standing with the cruise ship behind them. "Okay, whenever you're ready."

Before the man snapped the picture, his gray-haired wife leaned in and smiled. "Oh, dear, aren't they the most adorable couple? Just like you and me at that age."

"The way we looked an hour ago." The man grinned and then looked at them. "Okay, one … two … three." He snapped the picture and handed the camera back to Justin. "Someday, when you're old and gray like us, you'll look back on that picture and understand about the passing of time. Don't blink, young people!" He jabbed his finger in the salty air and smiled. "Enjoy every minute."

"Thank you. We will, sir." Justin waved to them and then turned to her. "Good advice."

Emily could only nod. Could the man possibly have known how accurate he was or how timely his message? They boarded the ship and spent the first hour eating a lunch of grilled chicken. After that, they went up on deck and found a secluded bench on one side, a spot where the view was breathtaking. The ocean air felt wonderful, and with the design of the ship, the wind wasn't too strong.

"I can't wait another minute." He set his backpack down and went to unzip it.

"Wait." She put her hand on his. "Let me go first. Please."

He grinned at her, and the sun on the water made his eyes look greener than ever before. He sat up straight again. "Okay. You go."

Her heart beat hard. Gifts weren't always her thing, but she'd thought long and hard about this one. She pulled the wrapped item from her bag and handed it to him. "Here."

He looked puzzled. "Hey … I didn't know you were doing this." He slid his fingers beneath the paper, and in a matter of seconds he could see what it was. "A scrapbook? Are you serious, Em?"

She'd been working on it every night, long after she would normally be in bed. Even her coach had noticed that she wasn't as peppy as usual on the practice field. A few weeks before, she'd asked him for a copy of all their photos, the ones he'd been so careful to take ever since the summer began.

He burned the entire file onto a CD, and she'd made two sets of prints. One for herself, and one for him. Now every hour of effort felt more than worth the time. "Your mother told me you like scrapbooks."

"You talked to my mother?" He ran his fingers over the red linen cover and the photo at the center, one someone had taken of the two of them after her championship soccer game.

"Yeah. That day we went there to walk Buster." She giggled. "I'm good at secrets."

"I guess." He looked at her. "Actually, I've never made a scrapbook. I just take the pictures. I sent my mom a ton from my last tour in Iraq, and she put them into a book. Gave it to me that Christmas." His smile faded. "It was the best gift she's ever given me."

"That's what she said."

"I can't believe this ..." He opened the book and looked through it, taking time to read the captions she'd written beneath each picture, to admire the time she'd put into decorating each page and creating a theme around each layout. There were pictures of their strolls along Puget Sound, and the one Bo had taken after their basketball game that first time at the teen center. Photos from walking Buster, and of them working side by side at the public information office.

Beneath those, she'd written: *Smooth Talker, indeed.*

Another photo showed where Vonda had slipped in behind them, and Emily had written, *Vonda knew before either one of us. And Vonda's never wrong.*

There were pictures of them with their parents taken the weekend of her soccer tournament, and one of him with the teens at the center, and another of him playing cards at a table full of Veterans.

Justin, she'd written. *You'll always be my hero. But you'll always be theirs too.*

Slowly, page by page, he worked his way through the book. On the last page, was a picture of the two of them at the end of their hike that day in the foothills of the Cascade Mountains, east of Tacoma. *One thing I ask of you, Justin Baker,* she'd written beneath it. *That whenever I fall, you'll always be there to catch me.*

When he finished, he looked at her, his eyes glistening. "I'll keep it with me wherever I go."

"Okay." She'd created it on lightweight paper, careful to keep the size small enough that it would fit in his backpack. "Every time you look at it, just know that I'm thinking of you, praying for you." She pointed to the last page and an envelope she'd taped there. "Inside is a letter. You can't read it until you're in Iraq."

"How ..." He swallowed hard, and a tear slipped onto his cheek. "How am I ever going to walk away from you at the end of the day?"

"I don't know." She pressed her palms to her eyes and tried to stop her own tears from forming. "If you figure it out, tell me, okay?"

They both laughed, and the sound lightened the moment. It was a beautiful day, and but for a six-month stint in Iraq, they had no reason to be sad. Justin wrapped the paper around his scrapbook and tucked it into his backpack. Then his eyes met hers. "My turn."

She hadn't given any thought to what he might be doing for her. She'd spent all her energy creating the scrapbook, putting it together and believing that somehow — another world away — it would bring him the strength and determination he needed to keep going, to keep being careful, and to come home again, safe and whole.

Now she wondered what he'd planned for her. She took hold of the bench on either side of her and watched while he lifted a small wrapped rectangular box from his backpack. "Start with this."

"Justin ..." She couldn't still her racing heart and wondered if maybe she would faint from the mix of joy and impending sorrow. She opened the paper carefully and then lifted the velvet lid of the box beneath it. There, nestled on a piece of satin, was a white gold bracelet with a single heart charm at the center. Her breath caught and she had to work to make herself heard. "It's ... it's beautiful."

"Read it." He pointed to the heart.

She took the bracelet from the box and held it close. On one side of the heart, in delicate engraving, it read, *Justin and Emily.* On the other side, it said only, *Genesis 29.*

The memory came back in a rush. The Bible verse he'd read to her the day he got news of his deployment date. He'd written it at the end of several notes since then, *Genesis 29.* She looked at the engraved words now and tried to see them through her tears.

"I meant what I said the first time I read that to you." He leaned his head against hers, his voice so soft she could barely hear it over the sound of the cruise ship. "I might be going away for six months, Em, but I'll work my tail off every hour, knowing that nightfall will bring me one day closer to coming home to you."

She couldn't speak. She was trembling, overwhelmed by feelings she'd never known before. She handed him the bracelet and held out her wrist so he could place it on her. When it was secure, she looked at it, admiring how it glistened against her tanned skin. "I'll never take it off."

"Good." He sat up straighter and dug back into his backpack. This time the box was longer, but it was wrapped the same way. He handed it to her. "This one means even more."

She removed the paper and opened it, and inside lay the most delicate white gold necklace, one that matched the bracelet, and at the center, another tiny heart.

He took it gently from her and fastened it around her neck. "It's belonged to you for a long time now." He hooked it and then adjusted it so the heart was in the middle. "But this way you know for sure." His eyes found hers. "My heart belongs to you, Emily. It'll belong to you forever."

Joy and sorrow and longing and disbelief all mixed together and swirled inside her. Justin Baker's heart belonged to her and her alone. She touched the tiny piece of jewelry and then brought her fingers to his face. "It's perfect."

"Like you." He kissed her, and when he pulled away, his eyes danced. "Just one more thing."

"Justin, you're spoiling me." His thoughtfulness was more than she'd ever imagined.

"I figure this is our Christmas." He reached into the backpack once more and pulled out a bulky, round package. "Here. This one's a little more practical."

She laughed and felt the heart on her bracelet jingle as she opened this last gift. Inside was a Starbucks travel mug, one big enough for even a large drink. The outside was a collage of their pictures, the same ones she'd used for his scrapbook. He'd sized them onto a single piece of paper, some large, some small, and he'd printed it off and slipped it inside the plastic casing.

"I know how you like your coffee." He gave her a quick kiss. "This way you can know that wherever you are when you're drinking one, I'll be over there in Iraq drinking something a whole lot more like mud than coffee. And wishing I was here with you instead."

She studied the pictures, basking in the array of memories they represented. "I love it."

"And I love you." He worked his hand around her waist and slid closer to her, kissing her the way she longed to be kissed. Only a few seconds had passed when he pulled back and snapped his fingers. "I almost forgot." He reached into his backpack one more time and pulled out an envelope. "I wrote this for you. But you can't read it until I'm gone."

She took the envelope and pressed it close to her heart. "This might mean more than all the other gifts put together." She slipped it into her bag, next to the travel mug.

And then, suddenly, they had nothing left ahead of them but good-bye. He took her hands and searched her face. "How's your dad?"

"Sad."

"I'll bet." He looked out at the water. "And your mom?"

"Busy back at her job. They're moving the whole *Time* magazine team to a building in Iraq." She frowned. "Maybe you'll see her there."

It was a topic they'd already spent hours talking about. Her mother had called from the airport the day she was leaving for the Middle East. "Honey, I had to tell you before I left. I'm going back to Afghanistan, back to my job writing about the war."

Emily couldn't have been more shocked if her mother had said she was moving to the North Pole. "But ... you and Dad ... you're getting married in December."

"No, Emily. We're not. Not this year, anyway." Her mother had sighed, and Emily wasn't sure, but it sounded like she was crying. "I need to see the war again for myself, be there and experience it. Write about it." She made a little coughing sound. "Maybe I'll find out that I've been wrong about our involvement over there. Or maybe ..." She hesitated, her voice tight. "Maybe I'll find out I've been wrong about thinking I could ever make things work with your dad."

Emily had begged her to change her mind. "Mom, no. Go home and think it through. Remember your journal? All the things you felt for Dad, remember that? You can't give up now. So what if you don't agree with him?"

But it was too late. Her mother had made up her mind. The phone call was only her way of being courteous enough to tell Emily herself, rather than waiting for her father to tell her the news.

She'd called her dad the moment she hung up from her mother. By then she was crying, unable to grasp what had happened and at a loss to do anything about it. "Dad ... tell me it isn't true."

He waited until she had control of herself, and then he told her that yes, it was true. "Your mother has a lot of searching to do, Emily. Maybe we both do. Pray for us. This isn't what either of us really wants."

Later she'd shared every detail with Justin, how frustrated she'd been and how helpless she'd felt. She peered out across the water. The subtle vibration of the cruise ship engine vibrated against her back. "Before, I always knew there was something I could do. Like it was up to me to find my parents and reunite them." She looked at him. "But now ... now this is their decision. Her decision. It doesn't matter what I want, they have to work things out for themselves."

Justin took her in his arms and stroked her back. "It's something they need to figure out. Especially your mom." He released her but kept his hand around her shoulders. "God has a plan for them, just like He has a plan for us. If that means the two of them should be together, then they'll figure it out." He kissed her. "I'll pray for that, okay?"

A trio of seagulls swooped low along the side of the ship and then lifted out over the Sound. Emily watched them fly away, and she remembered something. She'd never shown Justin the pages from her mother's journal, the way her parents had been so in love with each other. A week ago, she'd made copies of the writings and tucked them in her purse, intent on showing him. But she'd forgotten about them until now.

"Hey—" she picked her purse up and dug around in one of the side pockets—"I almost forgot."

"What?" His voice held a desperate knowing. They had only hours left, after all.

"My mother's journal. I was going to show you, remember?" She pulled out the folded pages. "I only have to look at this to know they belong together."

He leaned his shoulder into the side of the ship. "Read it."

She smiled. This was something else she liked about being with Justin. The easy way they had together. She scanned down the page and found her favorite spot. "This was what she wrote their junior year of high school. Spring of 1985." She hesitated, then with a steady voice, she began. "'Shane and I talked about love. Real love. We both think it's weird that our parents don't understand how we feel about each other.'" She smiled at Justin.

"Parents never change."

"Nope." She found her spot and kept reading. "'They act like we're a couple of kids who have no clue what love is. But here's what I've learned when I'm with Shane.'" She bit the inside of her lip, staving off the surge of emotions in her heart. "'Real love waits in the snow on your front porch so you can walk to school together in the fifth grade. It brings you a chocolate bar when you fall and finish last in the seventh grade Olympics.

"'Real love whispers something in the middle of algebra about your pink fingernail polish so that you don't forget how to smile when you're doing math, and it saves a seat for you in the lunchroom every Friday through high school. Even when the other baseball players think you're stupid.'" Emily laughed and caught Justin's eyes.

"Your mom was quite the writer, even back then."

"Yes." She ignored the tear rolling down her right cheek. "'Real love has time to listen to your hopes and dreams when your parents are too busy with the PTA or the auxiliary club or the business they run at the local bank.

"'Real love stays up late on a Saturday making chocolate chip cookies together, flicking flour at you and getting eggshells in the batter and making sure you'll remember that night the rest of your life. And real love thinks you're pretty even when your hair is pulled back in a ponytail and you don't stand perfectly straight.'" Emily's voice cracked and she had to stop for a moment. When she regained her composure, she finished. "'Real love is what I have with Shane. I just wanted to say so.'"

"Hmmm." Justin put his arm around her again. "That's beautiful."

"Exactly." She dabbed at her tears, folded the note, and put it back in her purse. "Sometimes I wonder how long it's been since my mom read her own words."

"You could send that to her." He stroked her shoulder. "Make a copy and mail it to her."

"True." She hadn't thought of that. When she found her mother last winter, she gave her an entire box of her short stories and journals. But she doubted her mother had read through them, the way Emily had—line for line—when she wasn't sure she'd ever even find her mother. She looked up at Justin. "I might do that. Maybe it would help."

"Right." He stood and moved to the railing. Then he held out his hand to her.

She took it and found her place beside him. "The water's so dark."

"It's like that off Kelso too." He lifted his chin, and the ocean breeze washed over his face. "Growing up, my dad used to take me fishing along the waterfront and he'd always tell me the same thing. 'Don't go out past your ankles, son. The water's deep along the Northwest coast.'"

"I love how you and your parents are, how close you are." They rested their elbows on the railing, and she noticed her new bracelet. She'd told him the truth. She wouldn't take it off, not as long as he was away and she was praying for his return.

"I'll miss them. And my sister." He turned his head and looked at her. "But not like I'll miss you."

She didn't want to talk about that yet. "Tell me about Kelso. What was it like growing up there?"

"Very different than Wheaton." He grinned and turned his attention back to the water. "At least that's my guess."

"Wheaton was nice, but it'll always be a suburb of Chicago. The big city feeling's never very far away."

"I used to long for a place like that." He chuckled. "But by the time I was in high school, I began to appreciate what I had in my own little town. The fact that my teachers had students who were the *kids* of students they'd had twenty years before." He was quiet for a moment. "There were parades and community picnics, and after spending a lifetime there, you couldn't go to the grocery store without running into ten people you knew."

"Really?" Emily liked the idea. "They probably gave you a big send-off when you enlisted."

"They did. My family held my going-away party at the American Legion hall, and half the town showed up." He looked like he was picturing the event. "Kelso's a blue-collar town, really. Lots of folks in shipping and construction. And they fly the flag higher than any people I know."

"I love that. How America's working class is so patriotic. They're the heartbeat of this country, for sure. The soul and strength." The wind was making her cold. She moved closer to him, so their sides were touching. "You could see it at the last election, the way the heartland, the country's backbone, was so supportive of family values and military strength."

"Yep. My hometown'll be supporting me this time, same as last. Tying yellow ribbons around trees and flying flags. That sort of thing."

The captain came over the loudspeaker then and announced that they'd be returning to the pier in five minutes. Emily looked at Justin as the message ended. It was one more reminder that their time together was borrowed.

"Someday, I want to take you on a real cruise." He turned so he was facing her. They were still alone on the deck, trying hard to be lost in the moment as if they had forever and not just five minutes. "We'll go somewhere warm where the water is shallow and clear and pale blue green."

"Sounds wonderful." She faced him and slid her feet between his. "But this was wonderful too." She gave him a shy smile. "Thank you. For everything."

He slid his arms around her waist and held her tighter than before. "I wish I had another week. Even another day."

Her hands came up along the back of his neck. "Not me. I want the six months to be over. The sooner the better."

Fifty yards away, a small speedboat whizzed by, and a group of guys on board howled in their direction. "Hey!" one of them shouted. "Go for it, man!"

Justin grinned and nuzzled his nose against hers. "Yep." He let out a soft moan. "I wish that too sometimes."

She felt her face grow hot. She understood what he meant, what the guys on the speedboat meant. The feelings she had for him took her places she knew better than to hang around. "Someday."

"I know." He kissed her, moved his lips over hers in a way she would remember long after he left in the morning. When he drew back, there was no denying the passion in his eyes. "Someday."

They felt a gentle thud as the ship reached the dock, and again the captain came on, thanking the passengers for joining them on the cruise and asking everyone to drive safely as they left. Justin laughed and took a step back. "I think that's our cue."

Her body ached to be near him, to stay near him. But God had provided a way to protect them from making bad choices before, and today was no different. They joined hands and left the ship. It was still only four o'clock, and for the next two hours they walked through Pike Place Market, checking out the shops and smiling at the strange people they saw along the way, the man juggling raw fish, and the girl in flowing gauze playing her harp blindfolded.

"You wouldn't see that in Wheaton!" She laughed and linked her arm through his. The hours flew, and before they left, he took her to the same restaurant where they ate on their first night out together. He even requested the same window table.

After dinner, he took her back to PLU and parked. Both of them knew the hour that lay ahead would be neither quick nor easy. They walked to their favorite spot, the bench just down the path from her residence hall. It was sheltered by a hedge of bushes on one side and a grassy field and evergreens on the other. Every time they sat there, they felt completely alone.

They looked at his scrapbook again, and she admired once more the travel mug he'd given her. The sun set before nine o'clock, and for the next half hour they sat there sharing kisses and sweet memories of every happy time they'd spent together that summer.

Finally, it was time for him to go. His flight was set for six in the morning, which meant he needed to leave the barracks by four. His commanding officers wanted the group that was deploying in bed by ten-thirty. His family would pick him up and take him to the airport, saving their good-byes for his final hours in Tacoma. But tonight belonged to her.

He walked her to the steps, and then — in a spot where no one in the building could see them — he eased her into his arms. "What a summer, huh?"

Her heart raced. She felt like they were on the Titanic, sliding off the deck with no way to stop, no way to keep from falling into the icy waters below. "Justin." She held onto him, needing the feel of his arms around her. And suddenly she could see him, crouched down behind a broken wall, gunfire zipping through the air overhead. "Please!" Her voice was a desperate cry. "Don't go. Don't leave me."

"Baby ..." He ran his hands down her back, along her arms, then he eased back and searched her face. "I'll come back. I promise. Everything's going to be okay."

"Don't." She shook her head, terrified of the feelings that stood like crumbling mountains all around her. "You can't promise that."

"But I believe it." He touched her face, and the feel of his hands was like velvet. "I've done this before, remember?"

She clung to him, and every heartbeat felt like the clock ticking, counting down the time they had left together. Tears filled her eyes and spilled onto her cheeks. "Take ... take me with you. Wherever you go ... I wanna be there too."

"I wish I could." He kissed her tears, kissed them as they fell from her eyes. "You have my heart." He held her necklace, the tiny heart that hung there. "Don't forget that."

Sobs came over her then. She hadn't wanted to do this, hadn't wanted to break down until she was safe in her room. But if she never let go, if she held him this way and never said good-bye, then he would miss his plane and maybe he'd change his mind. Maybe Iraq didn't need him, after all. Not when the Veterans and the schoolkids and the teens at the center all needed him. Not when Buster needed him.

Not when she needed him.

"Hey." He kissed another tear. "Every now and then, when you have a day off, maybe you could drive down to Kelso and take old Buster for a walk. Tell him I'm thinking of him."

She hung her head against his chest and grabbed three quick breaths. "O-o-okay."

"And stop by the teen center. Give 'em updates for me, alright?"

She couldn't bring herself to respond. She held onto him; he felt so whole and good and right. Justin Baker, the greatest guy she'd ever known. *Bring him home, God ... please. Don't let anything happen to him.*

"Emily?" He eased back a bit and lifted her chin. "Will you do that, will you go there for me?"

She nodded. There was a question she wanted to ask, and now seemed like the time. "Are you afraid?"

He waited, searching her eyes. "Yes."

She sniffed. "You hide it well."

"Thanks." He breathed in slowly. "Soldiers aren't supposed to be afraid."

"Justin ..." Never mind that she looked like a mess, that her tears were coming in buckets. She wanted to stand in the middle of Fort Lewis and make an announcement. *You can have any soldier you want, but not this one. Because this is the one I love! He's too good to work the front lines, too good to lose.* But the time for announcements, for changing his mind, had passed.

He was going, and she was only making it harder by losing control.

She steeled herself against the pain and stood straighter than before. "Have you figured it out yet?"

"What?" He had tears in his eyes too, but he was keeping his composure.

"How we're supposed to say good-bye?" She allowed a handful of quick sobs, and then she held her breath. *Enough. Get a grip, Emily. Come on.* She pursed her lips and blew out. "Okay, wow." She tried to smile, because otherwise she would fall to the ground and weep for a month. "Sorry."

His expression sobered. "No." He kissed her, the sort of kiss like he'd given her before, the kind that left them both dizzy. When it ended, he moved his thumb tenderly over her lips, his voice a whisper. "No, I haven't figured it out."

"Me either." She looked at him as long as she could, and then she flung her arms around his neck. "Be careful, Justin. Please. And when it's all over, come back to me."

He kissed her once more, and this time he held onto her the way she'd held onto him a moment earlier. Like he was terrified to walk away. But finally, he did. He took her hand and held it until his feet moved him far enough away that they had no choice but to let go. "I'll write."

She nodded, angry with herself for her tears. Not because they gave away how she was feeling, but because they blurred her eyes. And she wanted to remember every second of this good-bye, every detail of his face and his eyes, his strong shoulders and the crispness of his dress uniform.

"Good-bye, Emily." He was ten feet from her. He blew her a kiss, his eyes never leaving hers. "I love you."

"I love you." She mouthed the words, and it took every ounce of her resolve not to run after him, not to insist that he find a way to take her with him. So she could be sure he wouldn't place himself in danger, because she would never let him. Not for a minute. She held onto the stairway railing to keep herself in place. "Write."

"I will." With one long, last look, he turned away and jogged to his Jeep. He slid into the driver's seat and drove away. She watched him go, and already she could feel the distance between them. *Hold me up, God ... don't let me fall apart.* When his taillights disappeared, she clutched the stairway railing and bent over it. *God ... no. How can he be leaving?*

Daughter, I am with you. Even now, I am with you.

The words spoke peace to her soul, life-giving, life-saving peace. And they reminded her that with Christ, she wouldn't fall, because He would give her the strength to stand. She would stand as the days passed, stand every time she heard news of an American casualty, and she would stand even as her heart broke for missing him.

She would visit his parents and Buster and the teens at the center, because that's what Justin wanted her to do. Besides, for the next six months she didn't dare fall. Not when Justin Baker would be too far away to catch her. She would stand, and she would do it all in God's strength.

All for the love of a boy who had stolen her heart in one unbelievable summer. A guy whose heart she would wear on a chain close to her own. A soldier who was everything good and pure and strong and right about the U.S. military, and who had already given her a summer of happily.

Now all she had to do was wait six months for him to come home, so that one day that spring he could promise her the rest. A lifetime of ever after.

$\mathcal{T}$WELVE

The compound in Iraq was more primitive than the one in Afghanistan, but it suited Lauren's mood. She and Scanlon had connected again; they'd gone out and shared dinner and talked about everything that had gone on since their last time together.

"So —" Scanlon looked at her over the rim of his glass of red wine — "did you come to any conclusions?"

"About Shane?" This was the discussion they'd had before she left for the States, before she made her decision to move to Fallon. Scanlon understood the situation, and he'd let her go easily, the way a friend would let another friend move on to a better place. But still he was curious, and she didn't blame him. She was drinking green tea. She picked up her small cup and took a sip. "Yes."

"And?"

"I love him." This was the tough thing about Scanlon. They'd kissed once, a lifetime ago, and she knew his feelings for her. If he had things his way, they'd fall in love and get married, a sensible relationship built on all the things they shared in common — their work, their views, their passion for seeing the war come to an end. But her heart could never quite agree. She shrugged one shoulder. "I love him more than ever."

"Then why are you here?"

"I love him …" She looked down at what was left of her tea. "But I'm not sure I can live with him." She shook her head and found Scanlon's eyes again. "We're so different."

He didn't look glad, and his tone held nothing in the way of celebration. He only reached out and squeezed her hand. "I'm sorry, Lauren."

"Me too." She pictured Shane, the way he'd looked the last time she saw him. "So sorry, sometimes I think I might get on the next plane and toss every view I've ever held."

"Only you can't do that." Scanlon's voice was simply matter-of-fact. "Because the views you hold run to the very core of your being, Lauren. You know that."

Yes, she did. She considered Scanlon's words throughout those first weeks while she grew reacquainted with the people of Afghanistan. But then word came from the main office in New York City. Bob Maine wanted them in Iraq. The action was there now, and no story about war in the Middle East would ring completely true unless it was being written there, from the middle of the battle.

She and Scanlon celebrated the decision. The closer the better, that's the way Lauren saw it. She'd given up Shane for this, after all. And she'd prayed for wisdom. There could be no place like Iraq for God to show her the answers she was looking for.

The move took place at the end of September, just after Justin Baker and his division arrived in one of the war's hot spots outside Baghdad. Lauren had spoken with Emily about their goodbye, but her daughter had been brief, almost short. "I keep trying to find something in my life that's going right."

"Emily!" The comment stung Lauren and gave her a chance to see just how hurt her daughter was by her return to the Middle East. "Your whole life is right. You're intelligent and beautiful. You have your whole future ahead of you."

"I know." She sighed. "It's just ... a few months ago the whole world seemed perfect, and now ..."

Again Emily's words hurt. She remembered herself kneeling on the ground, too heartbroken to stand. "Leaving your father was the hardest thing I've ever done." Her words were clear, certain. "It's complicated, but I had to come back here, Emily. So that I'd know if there's any way your dad and I can ever have a future together."

Emily's tone eased some. "I'm sorry. It's just ... sometimes I feel like the timing is pretty lousy. First you leave. Then I barely have time to breathe and Justin's gone. I keep thinking you could've worked it out if you wanted to."

Of everything Emily had said in that conversation, that last part was the most painful. She'd wondered if sometimes her viewpoints gave those she loved the impression that she was the enemy. They hadn't talked again since then, though they'd exchanged a few emails. Phone service was spotty in the new compound, and once they got situated, two weeks ago, the story assignments came at them in bunches. Everything from the coverage of roadside bombings, to the progress of rebuilding the infrastructure in Baghdad.

In Iraq, she was visible enough that she no longer wore the khaki shorts and tops she could get away with in the journalists' compound in Afghanistan. Now she wore long skirts and blouses over her protective gear, and a handkerchief around her blonde hair—her way of showing respect for the cultural mandates that still existed in Iraq. So far her stories all had the feel of those she'd done from Afghanistan. Futile fighting, frequent failures, and the stories of fallen men who died for reasons that seemed as dusty as the desert.

Still, she would drop into her bed each night with the same prayer: *Show me, Lord. If there's something I'm missing, show me. Give me Your wisdom.*

Now it was mid-October, early Wednesday morning, and she and Scanlon were heading out to the heart of the city, to the place where protests were taking place over the upcoming election. Lauren was tempted to have her story all but written. The protestors were obviously citizens who didn't want a puppet government, the leaders assigned by U.S. influence. They wanted their own people.

She could already imagine the quotes she'd get.

"Could be dangerous today." Scanlon was working with one of his cameras. They'd been given an SUV to use while in Iraq, and this time she was driving.

"Definitely." The people loved reporters, at least that was her experience. Other than the time at the Afghanistan orphanage when she and Scanlon became targets, for the most part locals relished the chance to have their voices heard. Still, Scanlon was right. Anytime there were protests, there were bound to be crazy people, insurgents or radicals intent on making a statement, suicide bombers who would proudly drive into a crowd of protestors.

She steered the SUV around a pothole and wondered if Justin was working nearby. Were he and his company stationed in the area? If so, he might be working the same protest. According to the military party line, soldiers made their presence felt whenever an agitated crowd gathered, especially when the protest centered around an election.

The reporters she associated with felt differently. With the U.S. military flexing its muscle around Iraq's election time, the only voice that would be heard was one the United States approved of. Lauren made a right turn onto the main highway through Baghdad. The U.S. involvement, that's probably what the protest was dealing with. Either way, she was about to find out.

A few miles down the road, she spotted a crowd. *Stay away from crowds*, Bob Maine told them. *Park at a distance and walk in. You'll have a better sense of danger that way.*

Good counsel. She pulled the SUV over and parked it along the roadway. Then she turned to Scanlon. "Ready?"

He stuck his camera into his bag, latched it, and took a deep breath. "Ready."

The temperatures had started to drop around Iraq, and that day was cooler than any that week. Even still, the surroundings never changed. Everything — sky, ground, buildings — all the color of desert dirt. She swished her skirt out from the car door and swung her bag over her shoulder. "Let's go."

As they came closer to the crowd, Lauren stopped. She'd been a journalist long enough to know better than to rush into a situation, even when she was stateside. Sometimes more could be learned by observing than by any interview she might get.

Scanlon took his camera from his bag and began shooting. The scene was one of chaos—vendors selling wares from dilapidated card tables, protestors waving signs and shouting, and U.S. soldiers dotting both sides of the road, armed and ready. Like their leaders said, in case violence broke out.

She took a notepad from her bag and grabbed two pencils. She slid one beneath the scarf that hid her hair, and with the other she wrote down her observations. *Protestors angry ... soldiers stiff, stonelike.*

"Let's get closer." Scanlon led the way, and they moved to within thirty yards of the action.

That's when she spotted something.

In a vacant lot, amidst the rubble of what must at one time have been a building, a group of U.S. soldiers was holding what looked like a picnic. Children played all around them, and two of the uniformed Americans stood near the back of a U.S. Army vehicle, handing out bags. A strange feeling stirred in Lauren's heart.

All during her time in Afghanistan, she'd heard about the good U.S. soldiers were doing in the Middle East, but she'd never seen proof. Until now.

Scanlon lowered his camera. "Are you seeing what I'm seeing?" He took slow steps into the street and looked both ways. "Come on."

She followed him, and that's when she saw something else. One of the young soldiers—one of those playing with the Iraqi children—had a familiar build, a familiar way about him. Could it be Justin Baker? She and Scanlon found a spot on the sidewalk, right on the edge of the action taking place in the vacant lot.

"Okay, catch!" The soldier and three others were tossing a football with fifteen or twenty street kids. The children were laughing and jumping and waving their hands, each of them wanting the ball. When one of the kids snagged it from the air, the soldier grinned. "Good job!" And then he said something else, something that sounded similar, only it was in Arabic.

Lauren could hardly believe her eyes. The lot was filled with at least thirty soldiers, and all of them were helping the kids in one way or another. The bags being handed to the children contained a sandwich, a water bottle, and some sort of toy. Lauren could see that now, because as the kids walked away, they tore into their bags, chattering in happy exclamations about what was inside.

Scanlon held up his camera and then lowered it again. He looked the other direction, toward the angry mob of protestors. "Looks like we have a choice."

"Looks like two stories." As soon as she heard herself say the words, she was struck by the notion. Two stories. Two sides of the same assignment. There were the gruff soldiers, the ones making their presence known to the protestors. But there were these men too. Americans, giving to the Iraqi children out of their own time and resources. No, not out of their own resources. Out of the resources of the U.S. military.

She shaded her eyes and squinted. Maybe it was Justin. Could she possibly have run into him this quickly, this easily? She could've gone an entire year and not seen him. The soldier took out a camera and snapped a picture of three little boys, each of them holding onto a part of the same football. That's when he turned and spotted her, and she knew.

It was Justin, Emily's guy. Hadn't he told them over pizza that day that the U.S. was doing good in Iraq? Hadn't he said that no one stateside would believe the changes taking place or the good-will being spread to the people?

Of course, she hadn't believed him. Not a word of it. Because she'd based all her information on what she'd seen herself, on what she read in her own magazine, and on what she heard from the other news sources. CNN and the *New York Times* and *Newsweek*. They all said the same thing: no one wanted the war, people were tired of the losses, nothing good was coming of it.

So where were the stories on this sort of event, this chance for the soldiers to interact with the Iraqi kids? She caught Justin's attention and nodded her hello. He looked surprised, but then he smiled and waved. Lauren nudged Scanlon. "Start shooting. I want this feature in the next issue."

"But ..." He looked at the protestors. "That's not what we came for."

She studied him. Of course he was hesitant. They'd been told what to cover, and this certainly wasn't it. But this was part of the story. She was starting to understand that. "Scanlon." She kept her tone level. "We were sent here to cover the war." She looked at Justin once more. He was catching the ball and flinging it back to the group of young boys. "This piece hasn't gotten a whole lot of coverage."

They spent an hour, Scanlon taking pictures and Lauren talking to the kids and taking notes. The soldiers she spoke to seemed wary, and small wonder. What had she told herself on the way here? That the story was really already written, right? A chill passed down her arms and legs. What if she hadn't been sent to get the news, but only to verify it? The story had been chosen long before she and Scanlon arrived on the scene. *Cover the protest*, Bob told them. *Find out why they're angry at the U.S.* She was still in the middle of the soldiers and kids, but she peered down the street to the protestors. She would find out. She turned her attention back to her notepad. But first she would get this story.

Finally she worked her way to Justin. She wasn't sure what to make of the feelings inside her ... betrayal and anger and remorse and uncertainty. This was just one story. No matter how unexpected, it wasn't enough to change her views. But it certainly had her attention. For the first time, she even felt a little awkward, uncertain about her role as a reporter. She lifted her eyes to those of the young soldier's.

"Ma'am." He nodded at her. "I wondered if I'd see you out here."

"Me too." It was easy to see why Emily was so crazy about this boy. "I've never ..." She glanced around at the merriment taking place. "I haven't been to Iraq. I ... I didn't think things like this really happened."

He grinned. "I tried to tell you."

"I know." She held his gaze. "I'm sorry, Justin. I've asked God to show me where I'm wrong, to help me find balance." She looked at the dusty ground, and then back at him. "I guess this is one of those times."

"Yes, ma'am." He winged the ball back to the kids. "You talk to Emily much?"

"No. We're writing."

"Us too." He wiped the grime from his forehead. "I miss her like crazy."

"She feels the same way."

He nodded and grabbed the ball from the air again. Once more he grinned and shouted words of praise at the children in their language.

"How did you learn that?"

"Our job is twofold, ma'am." Justin looked slightly confused, as if she should already know the information he was sharing. "We need to hunt down the insurgents, the terrorists, and we need to help Iraq become a free country. We couldn't really do that without knowing some of their language."

English was fairly common in the Middle East, but Justin was right. If they were going to reach out to the children and help introduce democracy to a nation that hadn't known it before, they'd need to know the language. At least enough to play a little football with the kids.

Lauren didn't want to take up more of his time. "I'll tell Emily we saw each other."

"Okay." He jogged back a few steps and threw the ball again. "Tell her I love her." His eyes shone. "Tell her I'm counting the days."

"I will." Lauren's throat hurt. If she could whisk this young man to safety, to a plane that would take him home to Emily, she would.

She and Scanlon had all the information and photos they needed. It was time to move down the street toward the protestors. As they drew closer, Lauren stopped to survey the crowd. Some of them were hopping and waving fists, grouped in a tight circle and chanting something she didn't understand. Something anti-American, no doubt.

As she watched, a man ambled up and studied her. "You from U.S.?"

She felt suddenly vulnerable. Yes, she had her protective Kevlar, but that didn't matter. Cameramen and reporters could be blown to pieces same as soldiers—even with their safety gear. Lauren took a step closer to Scanlon. Scenes like this protest were rare in Afghanistan, though flare-ups continued. She held up her press badge, the one she wore around her neck. "Reporter."

The man nodded and pointed at the protestors. "You hear what they say?"

"No ..."

Scanlon moved in close beside her. He had his camera, but he also had a can of mace. Just in case.

Lauren squinted at the mob. "What are they saying?"

"They say no more violence against voters, against leaders." The man's weathered eyes grew watery. His English was difficult to understand. "Every time good man try take office, insurgents kill him, kill supporters. Kill voters."

"What?" Lauren hesitated, but slowly, like the first few pebbles in an avalanche, the meaning of his words hit her. As they did, she felt her world turn upside down. She lowered her brow and looked at the man. "You mean ... they want the U.S. out of Iraq?"

The man's mouth went slack and his eyes widened. He held up his hand and bowed his head, shaking it as hard as he could. "No ... never! Not yet, no." He said the same thing until finally Lauren interrupted him.

"Sir, please. I need to understand."

"My people—" the man lifted his eyes to hers—"so grateful to Americans. So grateful. We have hope now, a chance to work and grow and live with our families." Anger twisted his expression. "But some want old ways, old terror ways." He shifted his attention to the protestors. "Now we say, enough. Time to stop the violence." He pointed at a few of the soldiers. "Americans try to stop violence." He bowed twice. "We glad for Americans."

"Okay." Lauren looked at Scanlon, then back at the man. "Can we take your picture?"

"Yes." He pointed at her notepad. "You write down what Yusef say. We glad for Americans!"

Lauren wasn't sure which way was up. She began scribbling, capturing the things Yusef wanted to tell her. Then she looked at the protestors again, but this time through new eyes. These weren't the insurgents, the terrorists opposed to the United States. If they were, then where were the flag burners? The men who would gleefully burn an image of the U.S. president?

They weren't around, because these people wanted the same thing the U.S. wanted for Iraq. Democracy and peace, a safe place to live and work and raise their families. Suddenly a connection became clear. Lauren looked at the empty lot, where the children and the soldiers played together. She aimed her question at Yusef. "Whose children?"

"Those men." He pointed at the protestors. "Most people want free election and personal rights." Tears filled his eyes again. He nodded at the children. "They are our future. They want live in world without terror."

"Yes." Lauren could almost feel her beliefs being ripped to shreds, the foundation she'd stood on crumbling as fast as the words falling from the old man's mouth.

He jabbed her notepad, more intense than ever. "You tell them Yusef says so."

She looked at him a moment longer. Did he know? Was he aware of the news that came across the televisions and daily papers in America? Did his compatriots know that the reality playing out here in the streets was not the story being told to the citizens of the United States?

Suddenly, the weight of her responsibility hit hard. All along she'd seen herself as a Pied Piper, a solitary voice with the ability to make people fall in line with her way of thinking. Never once until now had she felt guilty about how she'd used that power, about how maybe she hadn't told the full story.

She felt sick to her stomach. What if she'd been wrong? What if, even half the time, she'd missed the story in her zeal to uphold her beliefs? She accused the U.S. military of using unnecessary strength, but what had she done? What about her colleagues? To come into a situation like the war in Iraq with a predetermined mind-set was to do the entire world a disservice, wasn't it?

Yusef ambled off to join the other protestors, and Lauren realized she was shaking. "Did I just hear what I thought I heard?"

Scanlon filled his cheeks with air and let it out slowly. He removed his baseball cap and raked his fingers through his short hair. "If I didn't know better, I'd think the whole thing was staged, something set up by the army."

Her question and his answer sent another wave of alarm through her conscience. Were they that conditioned, that even witnessing the truth, they doubted what they were seeing? All because it didn't line up with their viewpoint? "I feel sick." She rummaged through her bag and pulled out a bottle of water. Without stopping for a breath, she downed it.

At that instant, before she could put the empty bottle back into her dusty canvas bag, an explosion of gunfire rang out from what looked like a deserted brick building across the street from the protestors.

Screams filled the air, and Scanlon grabbed her, slammed her to the ground. "Lauren, don't move!" He whispered a string of obscenities. "We gotta out get of here!"

From her place on the ground, she saw three protestors fall, squirming, twisting in pain, their blood spilling into the street. Lauren sat up, too horrified to look away. One of the men was Yusef. Kind, passionate Yusef. Who wanted so badly for the children in the empty lot to get a chance to grow up in a free society. Now everything he believed in was draining away on the streets of Baghdad, where the truth screamed as loud as the wailing protestors. The life Yusef spoke of would never be. Not for him.

Yusef was dead.

ℱHIRTEEN

Lauren tore her gaze from Yusef's fallen body. Scanlon hovered over her, both of them low to the ground. Her breathing came fast and hard, and she stared at the dirty road inches from her face. *Focus, Lauren. Come on, focus.* She wanted to run to Yusef, see if there was something she could do to help. But that would be too dangerous. Besides, he was gone. She had seen enough death to know. Sweat broke out on her forehead, and her heart pounded so loud it was deafening. *Watch, Lauren. Observe. And tell the story. The true story ...*

She eased herself free from Scanlon's protection and lifted her eyes to the horrible scene. "I want to *do* something," she hissed.

"We can't." His voice was breathless, thick with fear. "Stay low until it's safe. Then we run for it."

He was right. Here, low to the ground, they weren't a target. The streets were full of people cowering low. She looked at Yusef again, what she could see of his body. Other protestors surrounded the victims, wailing and waving their fists at the place where the shots had rung out. At the same time, a dozen U.S. soldiers—the ones who had been standing stiff-faced along the edge of the protest—sprinted toward the building, weapons drawn. They broke down the door and raced inside.

Lauren looked at the empty lot in time to see Justin and his fellow soldiers round up the children, hiding them behind the army vehicles. Several of the little boys, who moments earlier had been tossing a football, were weeping and screaming, clinging to the Americans.

More gunfire exploded from inside the building, and Lauren had just one thought: *Please, God ... let those be American guns.* Because that would mean the assailants were dead, the way Yusef and his friends were dead.

The protestors only wanted what most people wanted—freedom and hope and a chance for a future. Yusef had believed with every syllable that the election could be held in peace, and that the Americans would help make it happen. But now ... she watched, aching for them as the protestors fell to their knees beside the fallen, rocking back and forth, wailing over their loss.

Next to her, Scanlon aimed his camera at the empty building, at the grieving protestors—and finally at the American soldiers protecting the children—shooting a few dozen quick pictures.

Then, in the time it took for Scanlon to grab her arm and pull her to her feet, a whole new array of thoughts hit her. If there had been more support for the war, more aggression on the part of the U.S. troops, maybe the men who fired those shots would've been hunted down long ago. Maybe they'd be in jails or eliminated. But so many Americans had helped spread a mind-set that made any support of the war taboo.

Americans like her.

She took one last look at the place where Yusef's body lay. As Scanlon led her from the scene, she couldn't keep herself from looking. "I'm sorry, Yusef." She whispered the words at first. Then she shouted them, so loud that across the street she was sure Justin Baker could hear her. "Yusef ... I'm sorry!"

"Come on!" Scanlon sounded terrified. "We have to get out of here."

She turned and ran along behind him, leaving the battle to play out as it would. And now what? She was supposed to go back to her compound and open her laptop and pound out a story undermining the U.S. military and its role in the war in Iraq? After she'd seen U.S. soldiers handing out food and water to kids? After she'd watched with her own eyes as they played football, and even as they rounded up the kids and protected them with their lives? As they ran into a building full of insurgents in an attempt to protect the Iraqi protestors?

She was supposed to look the other way about the things Yusef had told her? Write a story that made the protestors into something they weren't? Anti-Americans anxious for the U.S. to leave them alone?

Scanlon took the driver's seat as they headed back. Lauren was glad. It allowed her time to cover her face and let the tears come. Was this how Justin Baker and his company spent their time? Lending as much safety and hope as they could to the people who wanted what Yusef wanted?

How could she ever look in the mirror again, ever write another story the way her editor expected her to write it? Her stomach rumbled and her heart lay in a heap, just like the gunneddown protestors.

Oh God ... God ... have I been wrong all this time?

Daughter ... I am with you.

The answer sounded so loud, she wondered if the Lord was in the backseat, guarding her, helping her, answering her constant cry for wisdom. She let her tears come.

"Lauren ... it was one day, one scene." Scanlon seemed to know what she was thinking. "You can't throw out everything you believe because of that."

"Maybe I can." She dragged her hand across her cheek and glared at him. It wasn't his fault, the turmoil twisting within her, but it felt good to take it out on someone. "Maybe we've all been wrong."

"War's more complicated than that. Than one side completely right, one side completely wrong." He kept his eyes on the road, his voice calm. "You're a journalist, you should know that."

"Yes, I should." She made a sound that didn't come close to releasing her frustration. "So how come I've been so one-sided? How come so many of us have been?" She covered her face again. War *was* complicated. Valid debate might exist over the way a war was carried out or whether one target was more dangerous than another in the battle. But the core of *why* it was happening and its purpose?

She'd never allowed the possibility that the stories she'd heard from soldiers and commanders might be true, that the U.S. really *was* doing a good thing for the people of Iraq, or that by dismantling terror cells, they really *were* protecting the interests of the United States.

It had sounded like so much military rhetoric, and sometimes at the end of the day, she would join Scanlon and other U.S. reporters and practically mock the news being handed them by the military's public information officers.

"Do you realize what happened out there?" Lauren lifted her head and looked at her friend. "We discovered a lie, Scanlon. One that too many of us have believed for way too long. That nothing good could come from war, that nothing could ever justify it." She pointed over her shoulder at the scene they were leaving behind. "But that ... what we just saw. That at least makes this war understandable, doesn't it?"

What was wrong with the insurgents, that they'd fill a building, hiding like cowards, and shoot into a crowd of people whose sole intention was to help build a better Iraq? The factions that tore apart the country were so different it was frightening. Were these the people she had wanted the president to reason with?

She leaned back against the passenger seat and tried to get a grip on her emotions. It was one day, one incident. Her beliefs hadn't been formed in a day, and neither could she release them that quickly. Scanlon was right. Maybe she was overreacting. Witnessing a killing could do that to a person.

The road was bumpy beneath them, and Lauren still couldn't catch her breath. *God ... what did I just see? That was just one flash of a moment in this terrible war, right? What am I supposed to feel?*

Daughter, I have given you wisdom. You would do well to listen.

Lauren shut her eyes. The response was so clear, Scanlon might as well have said it. But it wasn't Scanlon speaking. The voice—the still, small voice—was God's. And what was He telling her? He'd given her wisdom? When? In the events that day?

No ...

Her eyes widened. Not the events, but the heart of the matter—the passion behind the events of war. Maybe that's what He had shown her today. Suddenly she remembered something. Months ago Shane had tried to tell her everything Yusef had said. Shane had reminded Lauren of September 11, of the terrorists who in cold-blooded exactness would take control of jetliners and fly them into buildings.

"Reason with someone like that, Lauren?" He gave her a sad look. "No one wants war, but how are we supposed to protect the U.S. from that sort of killer without going after them?"

Today's images flashed in Lauren's mind like a horror film. She closed her eyes but they wouldn't go away. Justin and his buddies playing with the Iraqi children, the protestors shouting and ranting, Yusef jabbing her notebook. *You write down what Yusef say. We glad for Americans!*

She gritted her teeth and opened her eyes. God's answer was clear. There *was* wisdom to be learned from today, and the best thing she could do was look for it, listen to it.

If she'd been wrong in her views, her staunch beliefs, then she needed to say so. Even if it meant losing her job. She leaned back against the headrest and stared at the desolate roadway ahead. She had begged God for wisdom, and in a single morning He had nearly drowned her in it.

Yes, war was complicated.

But what she'd seen that day was as simple as breathing. And every word of her story would reflect the truth about it.

She willed herself to relax. If she was going to write the stories in her heart, she needed to be calm, at her absolute best as a journalist. Otherwise her editors would think she'd gone soft, that her time in Fallon hanging around military types had tainted her thinking.

Shane's face came to mind.

Nothing could've been further from reality. She had left Shane — knowing she could be leaving for good — all so she could defend her way of thinking, her absolute belief in the inherent evil of the war and its perpetrators.

God, I want to see Your wisdom from today. Give me the words as I write. Please. Is this just one day, one instance? Are there really people swarming the streets of Baghdad, wishing Americans would stay and help? She pictured Justin, the look on his face as he played catch with the kids.

Last year she'd written a story about how violent soldiers were teaching a generation of Iraqi kids to be fighters. She had based her story on the same sort of rhetoric she accused the army's public information office of spilling. Her research was covert, interviews with people in a clandestine setting. The contact usually showed her something small-scale. In the case of the story about soldiers teaching violence, the contact had introduced her to three young boys, all of whom had rifles.

"We fight Americans," the chosen young spokesman for the group said. "We fight them until they leave."

Lauren wanted to kick herself. Looking back on it, she had to admit it was just as likely the kids had been young terrorists. Because only the terrorists would want U.S. soldiers removed from a scene like the one she'd just witnessed. Still, she'd written an entire piece on the notion, leaving millions of Americans who read the story with a sense that the army was somehow bringing harm to the people of Iraq.

God ... I feel faint, sick inside. Please ... if I've been wrong, if I've written stories that furthered the cause of people like those in that building, then please ... use me to change that thinking, to balance it. Please, God.

She wasn't ready to call Shane and tell him she was wrong about much of what she'd believed ... but she was close. When she returned to the journalists' compound, she said very little to Scanlon. There was no time to waste. She hurried to her room, opened her laptop, and started a new document. Then, as though her next breath depended on it, she began to write a story.

A story different from any she'd written in all her life.

FOURTEEN

Justin saw it.

As clearly as he saw the protestors fall in the hail of bullets, he saw the change in Emily's mother. It was in her eyes. The widely read, famous journalist Lauren Gibbs hadn't been to Iraq before. In Afghanistan, according to Emily, the few times she'd witnessed anything like the soldiers and the kids, the events had seemed staged to her. But today was different. It had been spontaneous — there was no way she couldn't see that truth. And in the time it took for their eyes to meet, he knew what was happening.

Justin sucked in air, trying to catch his breath, very aware of the danger around him. He hovered over a group of kids, most of them crying or whimpering. "It's okay." He soothed his hand along the shoulders of two of them. "It's okay." He looked over his shoulder, but Lauren Gibbs was gone. Even in the midst of the chaos, he couldn't help but smile. God was answering their prayers. His and Emily's and Emily's father's. Probably even the prayers of Lauren Gibbs, herself. Emily said her mother had asked God for wisdom. At the same time, she didn't believe her mother was open to God's answers. Not really, anyway.

But Emily, at least she's praying, Justin wrote in a recent email to her. *Wherever people are praying, there's always hope. Don't forget that.*

Another round of gunfire rang out across the street, and the children pressed in more closely to him and the other soldiers. Justin was torn by what to do next. The kids needed protecting, certainly. As long as he and the guys from his company stayed, they could keep the kids from running into the streets and getting killed.

But from the gunfire echoing all around them, there was a battle raging in the building. What if the guys needed help? One more soldier could make the difference in taking the insurgents out. He looked at the terrified faces of the kids, felt the way they clung to him, tugging on his shirt, begging him with their eyes not to leave. Not to ever leave.

He had no choice, of course. He would stay with the kids. But still his eyes found the building and he uttered a constant prayer for the safety of the soldiers.

"Help." One of the boys looked up at him, pleading with him in Arabic. The child couldn't have been more than five years old. He held out his arms to Justin. "Please."

The sound of bullets, the screams, the wailing coming from the men that were the kids' fathers—all of it was more than this little boy could take.

Justin picked the child up and swung him on his hip. He pressed the boy's head to his shoulder and motioned to the other soldiers. They needed to get the kids behind the convoy of military vehicles. "Make a wall!"

His buddy Joe Greenwald nodded at the others down the line. "You heard him, make a wall!"

Good ol' Joe. The two had served side by side during their first tour and now they were rarely apart. Joe shared his faith and his passion. They bunked next to each other, and now that they were back in the theater of action again, they were as close as brothers. Already he'd shown Joe his scrapbook from Emily, and Joe had whistled long and low.

"Lucky guy, Baker."

"I know." He ran his finger over the picture of the two of them on the front cover. "Lucky and blessed, all at once."

Joe was stationed at Fort Lewis too. He looked a little harder at her face. "Isn't she the girl we saw in the hall that day?"

That first day, when Emily started working at the base, Joe had been the one walking with him in the hall. She smiled at both of them, and when she was gone, Justin had elbowed his buddy. "Bet she's the new girl in my office."

"Bet you're not that lucky."

A few weeks later, Joe shipped out for Iraq, anxious to get back to the action. They hadn't met up again until Justin arrived at the end of September. That day when Justin showed him Emily's scrapbook, he pointed at the picture. "It's her, isn't it?" He gave Justin a playful shove. "You *dog*. You were right. She wound up working with you, didn't she?"

Justin let his eyes linger on her photo. "Yeah, she certainly did."

Joe didn't have a girl. He was a big guy with an even bigger heart, but he was too shy for most girls. "Know why I like hanging out with you?" he'd ask Justin every now and then.

"Why?"

"Cause—" Joe smiled—"you have a reason to get back home. That makes you the safest soldier out here."

Now Justin watched Joe come alongside him, helping him get the guys in line. Joe positioned himself at the other side of the group of kids and directed the soldiers near him until the entire company had done what Justin ordered. In a few seconds, they placed themselves between the building and the horde of frightened children.

The little boy in his arms snuggled close against his shoulder. Was his father one of those who lay dead? Justin hoped not. He held the child for almost an hour, until the U.S. soldiers spilled out of the building carrying four covered bodies on four make-shift stretchers. A small American flag lay across the first one.

Justin looked away. Another one down. He prayed it wasn't one of the men from his company. He clung to the child in his arms and waited while a few of the soldiers crossed the street and reported on the situation. The snipers had been insurgents, of course. Members of a new terrorist cell. Like cancer, the cells took root wherever they could, and these few had been operating in the abandoned building, probably no more than a few days.

The good news: all three terrorists were taken down. But not before an American lost his life. The soldiers gave them the name of the casualty, and Justin felt the slightest sense of relief. He was from the East Coast, a soldier from another company. But even so, he was a life lost, someone's son and someone's friend. Someone's high school love. He was here for the same reason they were all here, because it was the most right thing he could think to do with his life.

Joe circled the guys around the kids and nodded at Justin. "Pray for us, will you?"

Justin bowed his head, and around him, several of the Iraqi children did the same thing. His throat was tight, but he found his voice anyway. "Father, we are sad and broken by what's happened here today, by the loss of life for freedom's sake." Justin opened his eyes enough to see a little boy watching him. His eyes were wide and he was still shaking. Justin gave him a look that said it was okay, he was in good hands. "Lord, give us strength. Help us look to You, who went to the cross for freedom's sake. You know all about sacrifice, God. Thank You for our fallen comrade ..." He hesitated, steeling himself against his emotions. "Thank You for his sacrifice."

He coughed and his voice grew stronger. "Be with his family, and let them know that their soldier ... didn't die in vain."

"In Christ's name," Joe said, his voice strong. "Amen."

The kids lifted their heads and looked around, not sure what to do next.

A gust of wind and sand blew across the empty lot. Justin shielded his face and held the boy in his arms a little tighter. The child and his friends would never fall to the bullets of the terrorists who had taken up residence across the street. Not if he had anything to do with it. He set the little boy back on the ground and pictured Lauren, the change in her eyes. If he'd seen right, she would never be the same after what she witnessed today on the streets of Baghdad.

None of them would be.

That night they turned in to their barracks earlier than usual. They weren't in tents anymore, but old buildings. This was one the U.S. military had taken over just outside the city. Justin pulled out the scrapbook. He stretched out on his cot and positioned his light overhead so he could see better.

"Her again?" Joe was already lying on his bed, his hands beneath his head. He grinned at Justin. "I mean, not that I blame you."

"Yeah." Justin opened the cover and stared at the first page. "You spend enough time out there, and life back home starts to feel like a dream, like it never even happened."

"It happened, alright." Joe gestured toward the scrapbook. "Pictures don't lie, Baker."

Justin sighed. "I know." He kept the book open and reached for the printout of Emily's latest letter. He kept a stack of them inside the makeshift nightstand that stood between his bed and Joe's. "Neither do emails."

"At least you got someone writing to you." Joe smiled. He didn't feel sorry for himself, Justin could tell. Being around the guys, around the other soldiers in the company, had changed Joe actually. Made him funnier, more social.

"There's a girl waiting for you too." Justin felt his mood lifting. He tossed his friend an easy grin.

"I know, I know. I just haven't met her yet."

"Exactly."

They were quiet for a while, and Justin fiddled with the paper in his hand. He wanted to read it again, but not until he looked at their pictures, not until he let himself hang around the sunny halls of yesterday. He turned the page and studied himself, the way he looked sitting on the steps of the teen center, talking smack with the guys.

Had Emily found time to visit them? If she had, she hadn't said so. But from the sound of it, Buster was in good shape. She spoiled him every time she had an afternoon off. Justin felt the note in his hand, and again he resisted the urge to read it. Notes from Emily had to be savored, like everything else about her.

"Oh, Baker, come on." Joe turned onto his side and propped his head in his hand. "Go ahead and read it. You're killing me with the suspense."

"What?" Justin gave him a teasing look. "I thought my emails from Emily bored you."

Joe rolled his eyes. "Not much else going on for entertainment." He motioned with his hand. "Get on with it, already."

Justin laughed and moved the scrapbook aside. He liked nights like this, when he and Joe bantered back and forth. It helped wipe out memories from the day—especially days like that one, when the violence had come so close it was unnerving. He and Emily wrote to each other about once a week, since it took almost that long for the letters to come through. Like the other soldiers, he had only limited access to the computer, and so they'd earmarked Mondays as the day to check for letters from each other.

As he'd done with several of her previous emails, Justin opened this one and began reading it out loud. "'Hey, Justin, it's me …'"

"As if it could be anyone else." Joe rolled over onto his back again and grinned at the ceiling. "Go on."

"I was trying." Justin kicked his buddy's cot. He could feel his smile growing, and it felt great. A reminder that he was still alive, no matter how much death happened around him.

"Okay, okay."

Justin looked back at the paper. "'I visited Buster again today. Your family is sort of feeling like the one I always wanted to have. Hope you don't mind, but you know—you being so generous and all—I didn't think you would.'" Justin chuckled and shook his head. He loved when her letters had this humorous tone. It was better than the times when he could practically hear her crying between the lines of her emails.

"Don't skip parts."

"I'm not." He found his place. "'Anyway, Buster's missing you bad. I thought you should know. He's still sleeping with your sweatshirt, but now—I guess he sort of associates me with you. Because, I'm serious, he looks at me for half a second and then he looks right past me. As if he expects you to walk around the corner. Only it doesn't stop there. I hook him up to his leash and we start walking, and about every few steps he stops and cranes his neck around my ankles and stares—just stares at the empty place behind me.'"

Justin laughed out loud. "I wish I could see that."

"Me too." Joe smiled. He kept his eyes on the ceiling as if he was picturing everything Emily had described.

Outside the wind had picked up. It howled through the cracks in the doorjamb. Justin held up the paper and started in again. "'Anyway, I admit it. I think your dog's a little loony. But he's growing on me. Lately I've been bringing him chicken scraps from the cafeteria. I'm pretty sure by the time you get back, he'll be looking around your ankles trying to find me! Ha! Just kidding. The dog would sit at the window waiting all day for you if he didn't get hungry once in a while.'"

She painted a funny picture, but it touched him at the same time. Buster mattered to him, and she knew it. She was spending time with the dog for him, because the time he'd missed with the dog grated on him. And she was taking it upon herself to right that wrong the only way she knew how. By being Buster's friend.

"Is that it?" Joe looked disappointed.

"There's a little more." He took a quick breath. "'Anyway, you said you wanted scores, so here goes. We won both games last week, 5–1 and 3–2. I know, someone on defense must be slipping if we allowed two goals. But you'll smile at this. I scored two of the three goals and had another assist. The coach says giving me a scholarship was the best decision he ever made. I figure you'd have to agree. Imagine if I'd gone to San Diego State, like I thought about doing? Well, Justin ...'" He skimmed the next few lines. "'Missing you like crazy. Love you, Emily.'"

"Hey!" Joe sat up. "You skipped a part."

"That's the deal." Justin chuckled and leaned back against one elbow. "I have the right to censor."

"Shoot. I miss all the good parts." He made an exasperated sound. "You still walking around with her picture in your boot?"

"Yep. Every day."

"Man, I can't relate." He shook his head. "I'm hittin' the hay. You can read over the lovey-dovey parts in peace."

Justin smiled. "'Night, Joe."

"'Night." His buddy flipped off his light switch and rolled onto his other side.

"Don't forget your prayers."

"Ah, man!" He craned a look over his shoulder. "You interrupted me. I was already past the *Dear God* part."

A bit of laughter shook Justin. How great it was having Joe's friendship. These Baghdad nights would be too lonely without his buddy. Some nights they didn't talk about Emily at all, but pulled out their Bibles and went over the book of James or Colossians or Hebrews. Anything that might give them peace and hope to fight another day.

He opened the letter again and found the part he'd skipped.

Justin, I can't believe you've been gone nearly three weeks. It feels like three years. Whoever said absence makes the heart grow fonder was right. Only I'm not sure how much fonder my heart can get without bursting through my chest. If you come back and find a hole where my heart used to be, you'll know why.

It made him smile, Emily that crazy over him. *Let her know, God, let her understand that I feel the same way.*

He sighed, careful to keep quiet so Joe could get some sleep. He found his place and kept reading.

I'm drinking coffee out of the mug you gave me. That means I'm thinking of the mud you're getting over in the desert and yes, I know. You wish you were here with me, drinking a latte instead ... just for the record, I wish the same thing. Thinking of you, Justin. Missing you like crazy. I love you, Emily.

Justin folded the letter and placed it in the drawer with the others. Then he reached for the scrapbook. Slowly, he worked his way through the photographs. By the time he finished, Joe was out to the world, snoring louder than usual. He put the book away. It was late. Tomorrow he'd need to be as sharp as he'd been today. Careful to keep his head low when the bullets started to fly.

He turned off the light and lay in bed, his eyes open. A lot had happened today, a lot that filled his head with images he'd have for a lifetime. But the one that stayed with him as he fell asleep wasn't the protestors lying in a pool of blood or even the Iraqi children—before and after the attacks. It wasn't the little boy who'd clung to him for so long. It was a different image.

The one of Lauren Gibbs, her eyes truly opened for what Justin guessed might've been the first time in her entire life. And as he fell asleep, he wondered what she must've been thinking as she drove away. And he wondered something else.

What she would write for *Time* magazine as a result.

FIFTEEN

B ob Maine reached the end of the story on his computer
screen and leaned back in his chair. He cussed under his
breath. "Gibbs ... what'd you go and do?"

He'd known it was coming. Half a year in the shadows of Top
Gun could change a person. Still ... Lauren's first stories hadn't
seemed different. Same cutting-edge reporting, same skepticism.
He stared at the screen. But this? He shook his head. Children
clamoring after U.S. soldiers, protestors trying to thank the United States? It sounded like something the military public information office would cough up on its own behalf.

Whatever was going on, he had to get to the bottom of it.
He'd placed an urgent call to the compound and left a message
for her. He knew her schedule; he was expecting her call any minute. If this was what she was going to produce from Iraq, she'd be
better off stateside.

"Hurry up and call, Gibbs." He tapped his finger on the desk
and scrolled to the top of the story. He'd already read it twice. He
was partway through the first paragraph for the third time when
the phone rang. He grabbed it. "Bob Maine."

"Bob?" The connection wasn't great, but the static couldn't
hide her defensive tone. "This is Lauren. You read my report?"

"Gibbs!" Across the room, a line of reporters looked his way.
He lowered his voice. "Are you *kidding* me? This PR babble you
sent me is your coverage of the protest?"

"I was there, Bob. I saw every bit of it." Her tone was passionate. "No, it isn't what I usually find when I go out to cover a story.
But I'm a reporter, and a very good one. You said so yourself." She

161

took a breath. "You sent me over to Iraq to get the news, right? Isn't that right?"

Bob wasn't sure what to say. He hadn't expected this. A sheepish promise to edit her story, yes. But a fierce defense of it? "What are you trying to say, Gibbs? That the report you gave me is fair and accurate?"

"Yes." She didn't hesitate. "More fair than anything I've ever written."

"Meaning what?"

"That's exactly what I'm going to tell you." And for the next thirty minutes, his star war correspondent not only explained the events she'd covered in the report, she explained her personal biases and how they'd affected her reporting. She sounded sharp and intelligent—and troubled.

When she finished, Bob was still frustrated. But she'd made her point. "You should've been a lawyer. They get paid more."

"But this—" her tone held vindication—"this means more."

"Fair and accurate?" He was still skeptical, but now his doubts seemed unfounded.

"Fair and accurate."

At the end of the day, when Bob sent the story on to copyediting, he could only hope one thing. That the readers of *Time* magazine would agree.

⌒

Shane had heard very little from Lauren.

Not that he expected to hear much. She'd left with her mind pretty well made up, her viewpoints firmly in place. Which was why he couldn't wait to get his hands on a copy of *Time* magazine, the issue that was circulating through the offices at Top Gun. Something's happened to Lauren Gibbs, he kept hearing.

Pilots had stopped him in the halls twice that morning. "Sir, your fiancée ... what happened to her?"

At first Shane had been terrified. Had she been kidnapped or killed? But the pilot must've seen from his expression what he was thinking. "She's not hurt or anything. She's just ... I don't know, changed. Read the articles in the latest *Time*. You'll see what I mean."

Shane's heart pounded and he turned around, headed back to the lobby where the latest issues of a dozen magazines would be sitting on a table. He was halfway there when another pilot stopped him. "Did you read Lauren's recent stuff?" The guy grinned. "What'd you do, brainwash her?"

Something about the guy's tone bugged him. "Haven't read it." He kept walking. He wasn't trying to brainwash Lauren. She was entitled to her views. He only wanted her to find balance, to see where he was coming from. He found a copy on the table. The cover showed a scientist holding a test tube, but one of the smaller headlines read, "Democracy Suffers a Blow in Iraq."

Okay, so how was that headline different from anything Lauren had written in the past? The headlines were nearly all negative, intent on showing the ineptitude of the war effort. He took the magazine, stepped outside, and found a bench a few feet away. If something had changed in Lauren, he would know it. As surely as he knew her voice, he would know by her words if God had helped her see the war in a new light.

He flipped to a layout near the middle of the magazine. The pictures were graphic, as they often were in *Time*. One small photo showed three bodies, broken and bleeding, with what looked like protestors gathered around, obviously grieving the loss of the men.

But it was the center photo that caught Shane's attention. Lauren never would've chosen to have her photographer get that shot. Not the old Lauren, anyway. Then he realized not only what was happening in the photo, but who it was. The photo showed a grinning U.S. soldier tossing a football to a cluster of

Iraqi children. But not just any U.S. soldier. This was Justin Baker. His friend's son.

Shane stared at the photo, studying it.

Beneath the picture, the caption read:

> Lieutenant Justin Baker and a company of soldiers from Fort Lewis spend an afternoon playing with Iraqi children and handing out food and water. The children's fathers were protesting insurgent violence a hundred yards down the street when gunfire broke out, killing three of the protestors.

What? The emotions assaulting Shane were too deep, too many to identify all at once. First there was pride. Good for Justin —stationed in the middle of Baghdad near some of the worst violence, and still finding a way to bring joy to the kids. Shane closed his eyes for a moment, and he could hear the boy talking about the war at the pizza parlor that night.

We're doing good over there, really. The kids need to know that we're their friends. We want democracy and freedom for them, so that they'll know a different life than the one their parents were forced to live.

Shane blinked his eyes open and stared at Justin's face. That night, Lauren had looked away, played with the straw in her drink and acted like she hadn't heard him.

But here he was, he and his buddies, and no amount of political discussion could change the simple fact. Good was being done. Period. The picture proved it. Shane let his eyes wander over the rest of the photo. In the background a convoy of military vehicles seemed to hold bags, and a group of soldiers could be seen passing them out to the children. A small box near the picture provided statistics about how many humanitarian bags had been given to children in the past year, and a list of some of the things the children had been given. Water, food, candy, paper, pens, and toys.

Shane looked to the top of the layout and there it was: *Story by Lauren Gibbs.* And the photos — he scanned the bottom of the first page. Yes, *Photos by Jeff Scanlon,* Lauren's closest friend from *Time.*

Confusion came at him then. Photographers took hundreds of photos in a given afternoon, so why use this one when it told a story the media typically chose to ignore? Wouldn't Lauren have had a say in which photos were used? Especially on a spread like this one?

The answer was obvious. Of course she'd had a say. She and Scanlon and their editor.

Hope and disbelief fought for position in his heart. He'd looked at the photos. Now he needed to read what she'd written. There were two stories. The first bore a headline that said, "U.S. Soldiers Come to the Aid of Protestors, One Soldier Dead."

A slow breath leaked from between his lips. Another death, another loss. He read from the top of the story.

> A U.S. soldier was killed Wednesday in Baghdad while defending a group of peaceful protestors. Violence erupted when insurgent terrorists rained down bullets from a vacant building at the Iraqi protestors, killing three Iraqi citizens. U.S. soldiers stormed the building where the terrorists were hiding, fatally wounding all three insurgents. The single U.S. casualty was a nineteen-year-old soldier, the first to enter the building in pursuit of the terrorists.
>
> Minutes before the attack, one of the protestors, a man named Yusef, explained that his people were pro-testing violence by terrorists.
>
> "We protest violence against voters, against leaders," Yusef explained. "Every time good man try take office, insurgents kill him, kill supporters. Kill voters." Yusef said he was passionate about the need for a protest, especially

in the days before the upcoming elections. "My people so grateful to Americans. So grateful. We have hope now, a chance to work and grow and live with our families. We glad for Americans."

Glad for Americans? Had Lauren really heard those words? And then chosen to use them? He kept reading.

Tragically, Yusef was one of the protestors killed in the violence.

"The Iraqi people, for the most part, are in favor of the war, because eventually it will buy them the freedom they want," said one military commander at the scene. "When this war is over, we will have severely restricted terrorists' ability to work and operate from this part of the world, and we will have secured a democracy for the Iraqi citizens."

Debate rages over whether the cost for such a victory is too high, in taxpayer dollars and in human life. "We believe in freedom and a safe place to live — both in the United States and in the Middle East. It's not something we take lightly," the commander said. "Yes, the cost is high. But it's a cost we must be willing to pay if we're going to see change."

The article went on, but Shane couldn't see the words, couldn't absorb another sentence without stopping to think through what he'd just read. Countless times, he and Lauren had debated the power of the press. "You go to cover a story and you see what you want to see," he'd told her. "A million things happen at a newsworthy event. You take the hundred pieces you want to use and place them in the order you want. And you tell me that's fair reporting. There's no such thing, Lauren."

"The facts rise to the top, Shane. I get assigned to a story, and I talk to the people in charge, and I report the facts."

"*All* the facts?"

"Of course." She resented his insinuation that somehow the news ran through a filter in her mind.

But here, in the article in his hands, Lauren had presented the facts in a way that could've been totally different. If she'd written the story a year ago, she would've pointed out that U.S. soldiers carelessly engaged in a gun battle with Iraqis while children played nearby—something that would've given the picture that American soldiers were heartless killing machines.

This ... this story was nothing of the sort.

As he kept reading, the picture was very clear. Not only because of the way Lauren had written it, but because it was one he'd heard described to him tens of times before. He kept apprised of military briefings and updates on the war, and the scene that had played out in Baghdad the day before was a sadly common one.

The citizens of Iraq, with their first taste of freedom, were anxious to have a new way of life, passionate about capitalizing on the democracy that had been shown to them so that their families and their children's families would never know the terror of an evil dictator. Having taken reams of bad print, the U.S. soldiers rarely went on the offensive during a peaceful protest, rarely searched buildings or alleyways looking for terrorists.

Instead they stood guard, giving the citizens their chance to protest, to make a plea to their fellow Iraqis to take a stand for freedom. Then, when something went awry as it often did, the soldiers stepped in and came to the defense of the Iraqi people. Too often, such a rescue involved the loss of American life.

Always, when he spoke about the war with other military leaders, the consensus was the same. The president needed more support, morally, politically, and financially. The U.S. had the ability to hunt down terror cells, dismantling them and putting insurgents in prison, or destroying them along with their plans for destruction.

But the military had been forced to work with one hand tied behind its back—largely because the media had convinced the masses that funding and manpower for the war in Iraq was no longer necessary. Worse, that it was a waste of American life and money to fight the war even one more day.

Shane looked back at the page. A sidebar story ran with it, explaining the work Justin and other soldiers in his company were doing, how they felt the need to befriend the children of Iraq.

Lauren... are you trying to tell me something? Has God worked on you this quickly? A shiver passed down his back and along his legs. *What's happening in your heart that you'd show this side of the war?* He could hardly wait to talk to her, but he wouldn't make the first call. If she'd turned in a story like this, then she was in a great amount of inner turmoil. The facts—a balanced view of the facts—had come smack against her longtime beliefs.

Yes, he'd definitely be better off waiting until she'd had time to think things through. One day soon, Lauren would call him. In the meantime, he would keep praying for her. He read a little further into the sidebar.

> "If these kids' parents wanted us out of their country,
> they'd never be allowed to spend a morning playing with
> us, receiving handouts from us," Baker, 22, said. "Spend-
> ing time with the kids here helps them see life is going to
> change. Democracy will win in the end."

Shane smiled. *Good for you, Justin. Good for you.*

He pulled out his cell phone and looked at the time. Emily would be on her way to her first class, but he couldn't wait. He dialed her number. As it began to ring, he scanned the article once more.

"Hello?"

"Honey, it's Dad." The joy inside him came out as a quiet laugh. "Have you seen the new *Time* magazine?"

"No." She sounded breathless. "My roommate and I jogged this morning, and now I have five minutes to get to class." Her voice held concern. "Does Mom have something in it?"

"She does." He wasn't sure where to begin. "But nothing like we've seen before. First of all, the main picture is of Justin. Right there in the middle of *Time* magazine."

"Really?" He could tell by her voice that she'd stopped cold, no longer concerned about her class schedule. "Are you serious?"

"Yes. Your mother must've seen him in Baghdad the other day." His tone changed. "A soldier died, Emily. It was a hard day at war, but your mom ... I don't know what's happening to her, but the story is so much more balanced than anything I've seen her write."

"I'll get a copy in the library." She hesitated. "Dad, are you sure? You really see something different this time?"

"You've been praying, right?"

"Right."

"Mom tells me even she's been talking to God." Shane smiled. "Read her stories. The pictures alone are something most Americans have rarely seen." He remembered that she was in a hurry. "I'll call you later. I want to hear what you think about it."

"Okay."

"Hey, and also ... I want to fly out to see you one of these weekends so I can catch a game."

"We're still undefeated."

"That's my girl." He ran his fingers over the still open magazine. "Talk to you later, sweetie. I love you."

"Love you too."

They said a quick good-bye and Shane slipped his cell phone back in his pocket. Once more he read the article, and this time he could almost hear Lauren talking to him through the lines of the story. Yes, war was tragic, yes, it was complicated. No one wanted war, least of all the members and families of the military.

But some things were worth defending. Freedom and democracy and a way of life that Americans had become accustomed to, a way of life the people of Iraq were only now getting to taste. He could hear her saying all that, and something else.

Not yet, maybe, not so soon, but if these were the types of stories she might find in the middle of Iraq, then one day not so far off, the two of them might figure out that they weren't that different after all.

The article might be the bridge they'd spent most of the past year looking for. Because only a change of heart would've allowed Lauren to present the story the way she'd done here. And in the quiet of that morning, he had to wonder. Maybe events like these, stories like this, would become a regular part of her war reporting. If they did, then her time in the Middle East just might give them the thing they'd never been able to find.

Common ground.

$\mathcal{S}$IXTEEN

$\mathbb{E}$mily couldn't get to the library fast enough.

She believed her dad, that something in her mother's article was proof that God was opening her eyes, changing her heart. But even more, she wanted to see the photo of Justin. She carried her books in her backpack and jogged down the paved path to the old brick library, the place where she'd spent countless hours studying.

She'd chosen a minor in sociology, something she'd fallen into because of Justin. The impact he had on the Veterans and schoolkids—and especially on the teens—was impressive. She'd always pictured herself as a writer, even a reporter. Only she would present the facts without bias, at least as much as possible.

But now she wasn't sure she could be a responsible journalist without also being involved in the community around her—volunteering the way Justin did. Her writing courses had always been easy, and she wasn't far enough in her studies to work for the campus newspaper yet. So her fall schedule had three sociology classes. But social studies required hours of homework and reading. After the soccer field and the little campus chapel, the library was where she spent much of her time.

She came to the stairs and took them two at a time. The image she had of Justin, the one she carried in her heart, was the one of him in his dress uniform, standing beside her along the railing of the cruise boat. He was tanned and at ease, his eyes shining with love. Twice so far, he'd sent her digital photos of himself in Iraq. He and a buddy named Joe, standing in front of their barracks, or him and a group of Iraqi children, where it was impossible to tell who was enjoying the moment more—Justin or the kids. She hurried through the double doors and over to the counter where the library kept its periodicals. She found it almost immediately, several copies of the newest edition of *Time*. *Okay, God ... show me what my dad saw. Let me know if she's starting to see things differently. Please ...*

She grabbed the top copy and plopped down in the closest chair. It took her seconds to find the layout. And suddenly there he was. She brought the magazine closer and studied him. Somehow seeing him in *Time* magazine made his situation terrifyingly real.

It was one thing to look at a digital photo attached to an email. But here ... there was no denying the obvious. Justin was a world away, smack in the middle of one of the most dangerous parts of Iraq. She inhaled sharply, refusing to give in to the tears building in her throat. Her feelings were a mix of sorrow and longing and the very deepest pride.

Because there was Justin, doing what he did best. Helping people, leading by example. War was raging a hundred yards down the street, but Justin was watching over the children of the protestors. If he and his company hadn't been there, then what? Then the little boys and girls in the picture would've been gathered around their protesting fathers.

And when bullets rang out, the children would've likely been among those killed. She studied the faces of the children. No doubt some of them had lost dads that day, but they hadn't lost hope. Because the American soldiers in their midst gave them and their parents and their city a reason to believe that no matter how great the losses along the way, freedom would win. Democracy would rule.

But even as her heart swelled with pride, a sick feeling spread through her. *Justin ... what are you doing so close to snipers, on the same streets as terrorists?* As she looked at his smiling face, at the strength in his arm as he cocked the ball back, ready to release it, the magazine in her hands began to tremble.

Not even one month had passed, and every day, every hour, placed him in danger. She tried to exhale, but only a tiny bit of air eased through her lips. Panic surged inside her. What if he didn't have the right safety gear, the right weapons? What if on that same street, that very day, terrorists in another building took aim — in his direction?

Her lungs wouldn't work, and she felt a layer of perspiration building on her forehead. Her legs shook — and suddenly she realized what was happening. She was having a panic attack, something she hadn't felt since the days before she found her parents. Sometimes she got so caught up in worry — that she'd never find her parents, that they might already be dead, or that they wouldn't want to meet her even if she found them — that her body simply tried to shut down.

That's what was happening now.

The what-ifs loomed larger than life, towering over her, suffocating her. Her eyes darted around the room, searching for someone who might help her, but the only one she could see was the librarian — far in the other corner of the library.

God! I can't breathe! She set the magazine on the table and bent over, resting her arms and her forehead on the hard surface. What if Justin never came home? How would she ever survive the loss? How would —

Daughter, I am with you ... my peace I give You.

Like a punctured tire, the air slowly released from her too-tight lungs. *Lord ... is that you?*

Be still and know that I am God.

Every cell in her body felt the command, heard the words. Her muscles responded, relaxing, and finally her lungs filled with air. The Lord was with her. He was here watching over her as she looked at the magazine, here listening to her thoughts as panic began to take hold of her.

He wasn't going to let her fall apart, and He wasn't going to abandon Justin or her mother. She exhaled again. *Thank You, God.* She straightened slowly and leaned back against the hard, cold chair. She could do nothing to change the facts. Justin was in Iraq because he believed in being there. He was doing what he felt born to do—defending the cause of freedom, no matter the cost.

She mustn't do this again, let her thoughts and fears run away with her. Okay, Justin's picture was in *Time* magazine. That didn't make his being there more real. He was there. For another five months he'd be there, and she would have to find a way to deal with her feelings, her fears.

The way was obvious. *God ... I forgot You were with me, but You are. You're right here.* She closed her eyes and felt herself beginning to cool down, felt the panic leaving her body. *You spoke to me even before I called out.* She took another breath, a cleansing, slow drink of oxygen.

Then she turned her eyes to the story, her mother's story. Fifteen minutes later, when she'd read every word, she knew two things for sure. Her father was right—something was changing in her mother; otherwise she never would've presented the day's events in this light.

And second, God wasn't only with her, helping her through the panic. He was with her mother and with Justin and with every child smiling in the picture. For a long moment, she considered the loss of the U.S. soldier, the nineteen-year-old who had been first into the building, shot down by insurgents. Somewhere on the East Coast, the boy's family was getting the news, being dealt the worst blow of their lives.

The cost was high, and too often the cost had a face, a name, a history. But the young soldier had gone into battle knowing the risks, aware of the costs. Same as Justin. She could only hope that in the days to come, as the boy's family and friends gathered to pay him tribute, they would thank God this generation included young men and women willing to sacrifice everything—the way military people had been willing to do since the country's inception.

All so that Americans could go on living a life they'd come to expect, one they so easily took for granted.

She no longer felt sick, and the panic that had threatened to dominate her minutes ago subsided entirely. The Bible had much to say about peace. But almost always the picture Scripture presented wasn't one of God calming the storm. Rather He calmed the person caught in the storm. John 16:33 told the truth about life on earth: "'In this world you will have trouble. But take heart! I have overcome the world.'"

It was that last part that made all the difference. And after she checked out the magazine, as she headed off for class, Emily could feel God's peace the way it was described in Philippians, chapter four. A peace that passed all understanding.

Her classes lasted until after lunch that day, and soccer practice kept her on the field in the pouring rain until three. When it was over, she did something she'd been doing at least once a week. She went to the teen center. This time she took her copy of *Time* magazine, tucked safely in her backpack. It was too rainy to play basketball, but inside the center was a ping-pong table, and the guys were just as competitive about that as they were about hoops.

The teens seemed to look forward to her visits, and though at first they intimidated her with their tough exterior and baggy pants, now she saw them the way Justin saw them—as boys without dads, kids lost in a world that often moved too fast to notice them.

"Hey, pretty mama! You came back!" It was Bo, the teen who'd been most affected by Justin's absence.

Emily grinned at the group. "Today's the day, Bo. You and me at the ping-pong table. You're going down."

He made a sound that told everyone in the room she was as wrong as she could possibly be. "I'm ready, girl. Say the word."

"Okay." She came closer. "But first I have to show you something." She set her backpack down and pulled the magazine from inside.

"You brought us something to read." Dexter, another of the guys who'd been close to Justin, made a teasing sort of frown. "Come on! I thought this was a teen center, not a library."

The others laughed, but Emily held up her hand. "Justin made the magazine."

It took a few seconds for the information to sink in. Bo was the first to her side. "My main man, Baker?" He peered over her shoulder. "Show me."

The guys gathered around, and she turned the pages to the spread in the middle. "See?"

Bo took the magazine from her and scrutinized the photo. As he did, as his buddies pressed in behind him getting a closer look, something in Bo's face changed. His eyes softened, and the tough-guy exterior fell away. He smiled and a quiet chuckle came from his throat. "That's my homeboy ... out there saving the world."

Dexter took hold of the left page, and for a moment Emily thought about warning them. She still needed to buy her own copy. This one had to be returned to the library intact. But Dexter didn't damage the pages. Like the others, he was transfixed by what he saw.

"See, man?" One of them shook his head. He tapped the article with his finger. "That's what I'm talking about. That's why I'm enlisting." Marcus — the shortest in the group — jabbed his finger in the air for emphasis. "That's what Justin's always telling us, how the war's getting things done over there."

"Over here too." Another teen bobbed his head, pride written in the lines on his forehead. "When's the last time you saw a plane crash into a building, huh? That's what I want to know."

Bo was silent, his attention still fixed to the picture of Justin. Emily had stepped back. They needed their space, needed to have their moment, proud of their friend, awed by the sight of his face in *Time*. Absently, she touched the small heart that hung around her neck. Justin's heart. She turned her attention to Bo again, and that's when she saw it. Two teardrops fell from his face and splashed onto the page. He wiped at them, clearly embarrassed. Then he sniffed hard and lifted his eyes to Emily. "Can you give him a message?"

"Of course." Her throat was thick, her heart heavy for Bo.

"Tell him ..." Bo's eyes fell to the picture again. He touched Justin's face with his fingertips. "Tell him that he's doing a good thing, okay?" He looked at her again. "But tell him to hurry himself on back here, because we —" His voice was strained with tears. He made an angry face that hid his sorrow. He pinched the shoulder of his T-shirt between his thumb and forefinger and plucked it, the way kids sometimes did. He sniffed again. "Because we need him more than they do."

"Yeah." Dexter nodded and slung his arm around Bo's shoulders. "Tell him that for me too."

Later, when the magazine was put away and a dozen ping-pong games had been played, Emily was headed back to her car when Bo stopped her. "Could you do me a favor?" He looked over his shoulder, as if he didn't want the rest of his group to hear him. "Could you bring me a copy of that magazine? Maybe we can, you know, put it up on the wall here. So we don't forget to keep watching the door for him."

Emily reached out and squeezed the teen's hand. "Of course."

Back at her residence hall, Emily hurried to the bank of computers on the second floor. This was what she'd been waiting for all day, the chance to hear Justin's voice through the lines of his email. She signed on, feeling the jangle of her bracelet against her wrist. While the computer worked, she glanced at the engraved heart. *Emily and Justin. Genesis 29.* Suddenly her mailbox appeared. Sure enough, there was his email address and a subject line that said only, "Missing you."

Her heart skipped around, the way it always did when she was about to read his letters. God's peace kept her going, but Justin's letters gave her something to look forward to, one way of counting down the days until he returned.

Her eyes raced to the first line, ready to drink in his words like a person dying of thirst. She pictured him, the way he'd felt that last day, hugging her, whispering good-byes. With his voice alive inside her once again, she started to read.

Dear Emily,

The violence is heating up. We can feel it. It's always this way before elections, and it underlines the reasons we're here. These people want democracy, and we won't win this war until they have it, until they're capable of hunting down and capturing terrorists on their own, so that nothing could threaten their freedom ever again.

Okay, enough of that.

I have to tell you, you're spoiling Buster. Scraps from the cafeteria? By the time I get back home, he won't remember me.

She smiled. They both knew that was hardly true. Buster's loyalty ran straight through him. She kept reading.

The days are getting cooler here, which is a good thing. But nothing seems to make the time pass fast enough. I guess you probably know I saw your mom. Maybe when you get this, you'll already have the next magazine. I'm anxious to see what she writes. That day was pretty intense. I think it touched her, Emily. Really. I guess time will tell.

Oh, Joe says to tell you he's jealous. I get all the email and he gets none. But don't feel too bad for him. I read him

your letters and that makes him feel a little better. Enter-
tained, he says. And don't worry. I reserve the right to cen-
sor as I'm reading. Some things need to be just between the
two of us.

Hey, help me out on something, okay? Don't let Bust-
er kiss you. He can't if I can't, that's the way I see it. And
how about the guys at the teen center? Have you been back
to play ping-pong with them? Oh, and ask Bo about his
grades. He's a junior this year, and he promised me nothing
less than a C. Especially in science and math. Tell him I'm
talking to God about him — every day. The other guys too.

You won't believe this. Joe says I'm a slob. Even when I
only have a duffle bag full of stuff to take care of, I still can't
keep things clean. Oh well. There's not much around here
that's really all that clean, anyway. And something else. I
haven't made much time for my morning workouts. We
get up and eat and hit the road almost immediately. You'll
blow me away in a race when I get back, that's for sure.

But give me time. I'll be ready by summer, for sure.

Emily's eyes clouded, but she smiled anyway. As if Justin
could ever really be out of shape. He cared too much about giving his best to let that happen. She scrolled down.

So, yeah. This is the part I hate, the end part. I sit here
and all I can see is you, the way your eyes looked on the
boat that day and at your dorm afterwards. I don't hear the
wind howling outside, or the sound of gunfire and explo-
sions, but your voice, asking me to take you with me, beg-
ging me not to go. I feel your face beneath my fingers, your
lips against mine.

I miss you, Emily. A little more with every breath. Keep
praying. All my love, all the time ... Justin.

She read the letter through again, and when she reached the end, there was nothing she could do to stop the tears from burning two hot little trails down her cheeks. She printed the letter and then hit the reply button.

Dear Justin ...

You're famous! I'm attaching a link to the story in Time *magazine, and I'm saving you a copy. But I have to warn you. You'll be signing autographs by the time you get back here. Your picture's bigger than life. And obviously I know about you running into my mom. Wait till you read her story.*

Emily kept typing. She told him about the magazine piece and her conversation with her father. She told him about her time at the teen center and the reaction of the kids when they saw the article.

At first, Bo couldn't stop smiling. He said something about you being his homeboy, out there saving the world. But the longer he looked, the more his expression changed. Bo didn't want me to see, but he got tears in his eyes, you know? He told me to tell you that he's proud of you, that you're doing the right thing. But he and the guys need you more.

There, I told you.

She went on, giving the details of her soccer games and the weather and her plans to go to Kelso on Sunday to visit Buster.

Don't worry, Justin. I won't let him kiss me. My lips are off-limits until you come back. And then ... well, let's just say we better keep away from private places, okay?

She told him about her panic attack at the library, how she almost let fear swallow her whole.

I get like that sometimes, when I think of you out there on the streets of Baghdad. But God grabbed hold of me before I stopped breathing altogether. He sort of tapped me on the shoulder and was like, "Uh, Emily ... I think you're forgetting about My peace." And I was like, "Right. How could I forget?"

Anyway, I can't wait for you to read the article. It's a pretty good picture of you. I can't wait to hear what the rest of the team says when they see it. They keep asking if you've got a friend or a brother—someone they could meet. I'll have to tell them about Joe. Maybe he could get some email, after all.

I know what you mean about remembering that last day. Sometimes I'm walking across campus, looking at the changing leaves, and I feel your breath on my skin, as close as if you were walking beside me. I'm hanging on, Justin. But only barely. So be safe. I'll be praying, and when I'm not praying, I'll be missing you. I love you, Emily.

She hit the send button and sat back, watching her letter disappear from the screen. As they often did, her fingers found the heart around her neck and she rubbed her thumb across it. All she could think as she signed out, collected the printed email, and headed back to her room, was that Bo was right. They were all proud of Justin and the work he was doing. After today, all of America couldn't help but be proud. But no matter what he accomplished in Iraq, he was needed more back home. By his family and Buster and the Veterans and the schoolkids. By Bo and the guys at the teen center.

And most of all, by her.

SEVENTEEN

Angela Anderson closed the cover of *Time* magazine and moved to the front window of her new town house. She wouldn't call it a premonition, but her heart felt unsettled, the way it had so long ago when she and Bill and the Galanters made the decision to separate Lauren and Shane.

Now here she was, widowed and living near the Galanters. Everything had worked out for everyone—except the two kids who had loved each other more than life. At first, after their reunion, she had been certain that Lauren's decision to live in Fallon meant everything would end happily for her daughter and Shane. Lauren had been touched by her father's death, softened by the restoration of friendship between them and the Galanters.

But every time Angela talked to Lauren, she felt it coming, felt her daughter pulling away. Lauren wouldn't be boxed in, not now anymore than when she was a girl. Back then all four of the adults in her life had figured it was best for her and Shane to be apart.

Lauren had shown them.

She had done such a great job of disappearing that none of their attempts to locate her had amounted to more than disappointment. Until Emily stepped in.

Angela held the magazine to her chest and studied the street below. Children played in a grassy field across the way, a game that looked like kickball. Two of the kids—a boy and girl, maybe twelve or thirteen—seemed particularly close, the way Lauren and Shane had been back when they were kids.

Maybe that's all this feeling was, the sense of guilt and shame over what she and her husband and the Galanters had done. They'd manipulated Lauren and Shane, and in the process denied them of a life together. At least last winter, when Emily found her parents and brought them together for a final week with Bill, it had looked like their future could still be salvaged.

But there was no way to get back the years they'd lost, no way to relive the decades that should've belonged to them alone, decades that might've been golden if the parents in their lives had trusted that Shane and Lauren could actually know real love when they held it in their hands.

Angela sighed.

She missed Bill more on days like this, days when it would've been good to talk through her feelings. He would have told her they couldn't waste today regretting yesterday. Their energy would be better spent making tomorrow so good, the glow of it cast bright light even on the dark shadows of the past.

Something poetic like that.

She could call Sheila Galanter, and she would. Later. But for now she needed to talk to God more than anyone else. Because she didn't fully understand why she was feeling this way. The article should've brought smiles for the rest of the day. Lauren's viewpoints seemed to be softening, and Justin Baker was perfect for Emily, a shining example of young patriotism, the sort of boy who gave the older generation hope for the future.

So what was the problem?

The longer she dwelt on her unease, the more it seemed like a sense of impending doom. Maybe it was because Lauren had placed herself in such a dangerous place. Journalists were not immune to the violence in a war-torn place like Baghdad. The news told the stories every month or so of how a journalist was captured and tortured or held for a few weeks and then beheaded.

Angela shuddered. If that happened to Lauren, then how could she live another day out from under the cloud of guilt? That very minute, Lauren should've been living with Shane, happily married for twenty years, parents to a houseful of kids, with Emily the oldest.

None of that had happened. But now—if the article was any indication—Lauren's heart was changing. Her viewpoints were broadening. Which meant everything was going to be okay—hopefully sooner than later. Lauren could ask her editor if she could work from Fallon once again.

War was no place for her daughter, not when she'd spent two decades unable to find true happiness. Angela turned and set the magazine down on a lace doily that covered a small round end table. She was tired, more than usual. Fear was probably eating away her energy.

She sat down in the upholstered chair near the window, leaned back, and closed her eyes. *God ... what is it I'm feeling? Is it guilt? Is it Bill, another day of missing him?* She waited, but there was no response, nothing but the sound of the children playing outside.

Lord, I beg You. Bring Lauren home to Shane, where she belongs. Please ... use the stories and events in Iraq to turn her heart around, and once that's happened, make her feet turn around too. Bring her home safely. And please, God—keep using Justin Baker.

When she finished praying, she sat for a while, savoring the sound of the children across the street. Where had the years gone, the ones where Shane and Lauren would play out back for hours and hours? Hadn't it seemed like life would go on that way forever? And maybe it would have, if only she and the others had been more forgiving.

The way the Lord had so graciously forgiven her.

By the time she went to the kitchen and put a chicken in the oven for dinner, she had a much better outlook. There was no need to worry. Lauren was going to come home, she and Shane were finally going to marry and find happiness, and Justin Baker was going to keep winning the war in Iraq. They'd had enough sorrow in their lives. Surely God wouldn't allow more. The unsettled feeling was just left over from all that had come before. But here, today, life was going to be just fine. Even more than the nagging sense of dread, Angela could feel it with everything in her being.

EIGHTEEN

They were halfway through November, and Justin was more homesick than ever. The stretch between Thanksgiving and Christmas loomed like a terrible period of exile. It was late at night, and the task that lay ahead the next morning was a considerable one.

Justin rolled onto his side. He needed his sleep. But he needed to hear Emily's voice more.

For a crazy minute, he thought about finding his commander and asking to make an emergency call. Only there wasn't an emergency, not really. Just the fact that his heart hurt from missing her. He flopped onto his back and stared at the dark ceiling.

Next to him, Joe was snoring. Rumbling like a slow freight train. Justin closed his eyes and tried to find that calm place in his mind. The one he needed to find every night before he could fall asleep. He and Joe had read the Bible that night, the book of John, chapter sixteen. In it was the verse Justin thought about often when they were out in Baghdad: "In this world you will have trouble. But take heart! I have overcome the world." Indeed. God's peace and grace and strength were all that got him through.

Two more U.S. soldiers had died that week. Two guys Justin knew from holding operations around the city's polling centers. They'd been traveling in a caravan from one location to another, when a car loaded with explosives and traveling the opposite direction crossed the middle line and drove straight into them.

Justin and his company had seen the fireball from a mile away. Suicide bombers. More terrorists. More insurgents.

A long sigh pressed through his lips. They should have twice as many troops in Baghdad and around every hot spot in Iraq.

Additional surveillance equipment should be brought in, and the army and marines should be given the green light to do whatever it took to get the insurgents. He hated that they seemed so often to be sitting ducks, always on the defensive and never making the first move.

But how could they increase their efforts unless the people of the United States got behind them fully, completely?

He flicked on the light overhead. Sleep was useless. Maybe he'd find some peace if he spent time with the scrapbook, the place where Emily lived. Her letters had been like air to him lately. Everything she had to say gave him hope and brought him another reason to count down the days, to long for home.

Not that he minded serving in Iraq. If he had it to do again, he'd still choose a second tour. But he hadn't thought the holiday season would hit him with such a longing for home.

He studied the photo of Emily and him, the one on the front cover of the scrapbook. She was so beautiful. On the outside, yes. But that wasn't what he saw when he looked into her eyes. He saw the person she was on the inside, her soul. She was taking sociology courses, she'd told him, so she could "be like him when she grew up."

He smiled at the thought. *Emily* ... He ran his thumb over the image of her face. *You don't need to be like anyone but yourself.* The schedule she'd been keeping was enough to make him tired. Soccer and schoolwork and weekly visits to his parents in Kelso. He teased her about Buster, but secretly Justin was thrilled. How great that she was taking time with his dog. That, and the fact that his parents and his sister looked forward to her visits. They all mentioned her when they wrote.

But the thing that made him most grateful was that she'd been dropping by the teen center. Guys like Bo and Dexter were easy prey for the corner drug dealer, boys without fathers, kids whose culture centered around narcotics and violence. Teens like that needed a reason to come to the center, a regular face they looked forward to.

Emily had become that face.

One time, Bo wrote him an email. *Look out, homeboy. When you come home, your pretty mama might belong to me.* Justin chuckled softly. Bo's letter was cocky and brash, but no question the kid expressed a sense of security in hanging out with Emily each week. Almost as if by seeing her, they were assured that one day, when his six months were up, Justin would walk through the door of the center with her.

He yawned and turned the pages slowly, taking in the light that came from Emily's eyes, her smile. She thought he was a hero, a guy who had no faults. But that wasn't true. Every day it was an effort to head out to the streets of Baghdad knowing that something could happen to him, something that would keep him from ever seeing her again.

That was his secret, the little fear that never quite went away. The secret only she knew about. He smiled at the final photo, the one he'd added into the book their last night together, after he'd gotten back to the fort. It was the picture the old man had taken on the pier, the one with the ship in the background. What had the guy said? *Someday, when you're old and gray like us, you'll look back on that picture and understand about the passing of time. Don't blink, young people. Enjoy every minute.*

The first time Joe looked at the scrapbook, he stopped at that picture and shook his head. "You'd never know you were hours from saying good-bye. The two of you look about as happy as any couple I've ever known."

It was true. That's what being with Emily did to him. Her presence, her happy heart that day, made him forget the hard times just ahead. And that's what looking at her pictures did for him now.

He yawned again. The elusive calm filled his mind. *Okay, that's all I needed, God. Thanks for reminding me how lucky I am.*

He put the scrapbook away, turned off his light, and in what felt like five minutes, he heard Joe's voice in his ear.

"Come on, you bum. Get up!" Joe was in his boxers, one leg in his fatigues, one foot trying to find the other leg hole. "We're late."

"Late?" Justin shot up in bed. "What about the alarm?"

"Didn't go off. A few guys from down the hall pounded on the door." He jumped a few times in place and pulled his fatigues all the way up. "All I know is we have ten minutes before the caravan takes off."

Ten minutes? Justin groaned. He was up and dressed in seconds, and he rummaged through the bottom drawer of his dresser for one of the protein bars he'd brought from home. Instant energy for moments like this.

"You sharing?" Joe had his shirt buttoned, and he was perched at the edge of his bed, tugging his boot onto his right foot.

Justin grabbed another one and tossed it. "You owe me."

"Always."

With a minute to spare, they hurried outside and jumped into their spots in their military vehicle. Ace, the driver, turned around and raised a brow. "Cuttin' it kind of close today, hey guys?"

"Yeah, well—" Joe was still tucking his pant legs into his boots—"lover boy here kept the lights on all night."

"Not all night." Justin fastened his chest gear.

"Girl trouble, huh?" Ace waited until the car in front of him pulled out, and then he gave a burst of gas and their vehicle fell into line. "Forget about her, Baker. Distractions are never good."

"She's not a distraction." He mouthed a sarcastic thank-you in Joe's direction. "Things are great between us."

"Right. He can't fall asleep until he's hung out in the pages of his scrapbook for half an hour." Joe elbowed him, his eyes dancing.

"How sweet." Ace steered the vehicle with one hand. "Did you get briefed on the mission today?"

"Last night, same as everyone else." Justin settled back against the seat, ignoring the way the bumpy road jarred his back.

"We're checking out another abandoned building, right?" Joe leaned his head against the doorframe and closed his eyes. "If we can stay awake."

"You better stay awake. These are the big dogs, pal." Ace kept his eyes on the road. Ahead of them the caravan of cars was hard to see through the cloud of dust coming up off the road.

The big dogs. Justin let the words roll around in his mind, his soul. How many times had they done this? Gotten a tip that gunfire or bombs had come from a specific location, and then gone in, kicking down doors and breaking up another bunch of bad guys? Too many times to count. Medics willing to work the front lines were always needed.

God ... give us Your eyes, Your ears.

He heard no response, but he could feel the Lord with him. The way he always felt it. He stifled another yawn and slid his fingers down the back of his boot. He pulled up her photograph.

Even on a hurried day like today, he'd remembered. Her picture was part of his uniform now. When he printed the photos from their lunch cruise that last day, he made a copy of one particularly good shot of Emily. Then he found someone with keys to the public information office, and he laminated it. That way he could keep it with him, and no amount of dirt or sweat would hurt it.

Most of the time out in the field, he didn't have time to look at it, to pull it up from the back of his boot and feel the strength it gave him. But today they were traveling from one end of Baghdad to the other, and a half hour in the car meant plenty of time to think about Emily. Sometimes, he liked to picture his homecoming, and how the spring and summer would play out.

He knew where he would ask her the question, the one he could hardly wait to ask. He closed his eyes and imagined it all taking place. He would get the ring, the solitaire she'd admired once when they went to Pacific Place.

I like simple rings, he could hear her saying. *A simple band and a simple diamond.*

"You're too easy." He had poked her in the ribs, laughing with her.

"Not really." She raised her brow, her eyes dancing. "Only when it comes to rings."

Anyway, he'd get the ring. Then he'd take her down to the waterfront and he'd find the same cruise ship, the lunch cruise. And they'd go to their private spot on the top deck, and there — out on the water — he'd ask her to marry him.

He could see her eyes, feel the wind against his face. He cupped the laminated photo tight in his palm. She would hug his neck and tell him yes, over and over and over again. And they'd talk about churches and flowers and colors and bridesmaids. And the months would pass and they'd hold the wedding somewhere with walls of windows and light coming in from every possible angle.

She would look like an angel in her wedding dress, and he would stand there trying to breathe as she made her way down the aisle and —

The explosion happened so fast he didn't have time to react. One second he was standing in a church somewhere in Tacoma, dressed to the nines, watching his bride walk down the aisle toward him, and the next ...

Nothing had been louder in all his life. It shook him and mixed with the sound of breaking glass and disintegrating metal. The pain hit then, ripping through him with a heat and intensity that left him dazed. He couldn't draw a breath, couldn't feel his legs, couldn't see anything but deep wet red and muddy brown, and fire and smoke.

"Emily!"

He screamed her name because maybe this was part of the dream. Maybe he'd fallen asleep and the sliver of fear, the one that never quite went away, had magnified a thousand times over and created a hellish nightmare. Yes, that had to be it. *"Emily?"*

He was shouting her name, but he couldn't hear himself, couldn't make the words loud enough to actually be heard. And then, in a rush, the explosion faded, the noise stopped, and he felt himself land hard against the road.

That's when he realized what was happening. He wasn't dreaming. Ace must've hit a roadside bomb. Somehow the cars in front of them missed it, and theirs ...

Theirs had taken the hit.

The hot feeling grew worse with every attempt he made at breathing. And what about his legs? Why couldn't he feel them? He opened his eyes, struggled to see even a sliver of light. *God ... no, not now. Please ... don't let me die here. I need to talk to Emily.*

Emily! Again the sound of his own voice wouldn't quite clear his throat. *Emily, baby, I'm sorry ... I never meant for this to happen ...*

There were feet shuffling near his head, feet and the shouts of voices. "Justin!" It was Joe; he'd know his voice anywhere.

"Joe?" He blinked hard, once, twice, and finally ... finally opened his eyes. His buddy was kneeling over him, his uniform and his face were splattered with blood and dirt. And something else. Tears. "Joe ... what ..." He coughed. Couldn't catch his breath. "What happened?"

Joe clenched his fists and leaned his head back. "Help! Someone get us help over here! Now!"

"Joe ..." His strength was leaving him. The burning feeling was worse, but now it felt like his lungs were filling up, like he was drowning, only there wasn't any water and his mouth was parched. He held out his hand. "Talk to me, Joe."

"Justin, hang on, buddy." Joe dropped to his knees and took his hand. "They're coming, okay?"

"What ... about my legs?"

"Don't look, man. Keep your eyes on me, okay?" He looked over his shoulder, and the intensity in his scream was frightening. "*Hurry!* We need help, now!"

Justin turned his head just a little and there was Ace, his body ripped to shreds. A roadside bomb. That must've been it. Ace was gone. No one was hovering over him, no one looking to help him.

So that meant he still had a chance, right? He was alive ... Joe was calling for help. But what about his legs? He and Ace had been sitting on the same side of the car. And Joe ... what about Joe?

"Joe, man ... you okay?" Justin's eyes were closed again, and he fought to open them. Was that blood trickling down the right side of Joe's face? "You're cut, buddy ... put ... put pressure on that thing."

"No!" Joe sounded panicked. He shook his head hard and lay his entire body across Justin's, across the upper part of his legs just above his knees. "We gotta stop the bleeding." He shouted again. "We gotta stop the bleeding. Someone ... someone, help!"

Justin wanted to say something, but he felt drugged, like he was in the middle of an intense sleep and nothing—nothing at all—could wake him. He was getting married, wasn't he? Watching Emily walk down the aisle toward him?

"Hang in there, Justin!" Joe was crying now. Joe, the big oaf who never took anything very seriously, was crying. "Don't leave me! Please, Justin, don't leave me!"

"Okay ..." He ran his tongue over his lower lip. "Joe ... buddy ... pray."

Joe nodded, his motions quick and jerky, frantic. "God!" He stared up at the sky. "God ... help us! Please!"

Justin gave the slightest nod. He wanted to say something, but his mouth wouldn't work. Maybe he just needed to rest a bit, work up the strength to get the words out. But wait. There was something in his hand. Not the hand Joe was holding, the other hand. He ran his fingertips over it and then he remembered. Emily's picture. He still had Emily's picture in his hand. With all his might he tried to lift it, and finally, barely, he did.

He couldn't draw a full breath. The heaviness, the heat pulsing through him was too great. *God ... let me see her. Please ...* He tried once more, and this time he squinted against the bright blue sky. *Ah ... there. Thank You, God ...*

He could see. He turned his head—and there she was.

His Emily. Smiling at him, willing him to be strong, to fight hard even now. *Emily, baby ... I'm sorry.*

"Justin!" Joe was crying harder. "Here, give it to me." He took the photograph and held it up close. "She's waiting for you, man. Don't quit on me."

Running feet came up from a couple directions and he could hear other voices.

"Too much blood loss ..."

"There's nothing to save ..."

"Get him on a stretcher ..."

"He's still breathing ... we have to try."

The words and sentences blended together, but they told Justin what he already suspected. His legs were gone. Joe was lying across him, and that's all that had kept him from bleeding to death. Just like Ace.

They were trying to move him now, but he didn't want to go. Not until he could talk to Joe. He squinted, and black circles rolled around in his vision. "Joe ..."

"I'm here, buddy." His friend was kneeling beside him, Emily's picture still upright in his hand, still stretched out close so Justin could see it. So he could savor it.

"Joe ... tell her ... I love her."

"*You* tell her, Baker." Joe dragged his free hand across his cheeks. His nose was runny, and his tears mixed with the blood on his face. "She's your girl."

Justin was out of air, out of strength. His life was draining away, so the only reason he could talk now was because God was giving him this time, this moment. He looked at the picture of Emily and then at Joe. "Be her friend ... for me." He winced, because the pain was worse, exploding through his body the way the bomb had exploded through their vehicle.

"Don't!" Anger flashed in Joe's eyes. "Don't talk that way."

At that moment, one of the medics came up and put his hand on Joe's shoulder. He shook his head and gave Joe a couple hard pats. Joe seemed to understand what the guy meant, same as Justin did. There was no point. Justin had a minute left, maybe less. Too much damage, too much blood loss.

He felt dizzy, desperate to close his eyes and get back to the dream, the one where Emily was walking toward him, his beautiful bride. But he needed something from Joe. He forced himself to think, to concentrate. What was it?

Then it hit him. He needed Joe's word. "Promise me ... promise you'll be her friend." Because when this day was done, she'd need a friend in the worst way. He was sure of it.

Joe hung his head and sobbed. He still held out the picture of Emily, kept it positioned so Justin could see it. "No, God! Please!" Joe tightened the hold he had on Justin's hand, and he lifted his chin. Lifted it just enough so their eyes could meet. Then he said the words that looked almost impossible for him to say. "I promise. Whatever you want."

Relief flooded through Justin and his eyelids closed. The pain was unbearable, the heaviness and burning and heat that filled his body. But now there was a peace ... a peace from God, one that passed all understanding. Joe would tell her. He'd be her friend, because he'd given his word.

Justin could feel himself falling, falling fast and far, away from the streets of Baghdad, away from the carnage of bodies and broken car pieces that lay strewn around him. *Once more, God ... let me see her one more time. Please ...*

And then, with no strength left at all, he opened his eyes. He looked at Joe and felt the corners of his mouth lift ever so slightly. "Thanks, man. Keep ... keep praying." What else? There was something else he wanted to say. He concentrated with all that remained in him. "Tell them I ... I wanted to be here. Tell them to win ... this thing."

"I will." Tears streamed down Joe's face, but he wasn't shouting, wasn't screaming for help. "I love you, man. Save me a spot up there, okay?"

Justin felt himself smile. "I will. You ... and my family ... and my guys at the center. And Emily." His eyes found her picture. "I'll save ... a spot for her—"

Deep inside him, he felt his heart struggle. *Beat ... beat.* Long pause. Another beat. His pulse was slowing down, fading. *Emily ... don't be mad at me, baby.*

Her face, her deep blue eyes, were the last thing he saw.

His thoughts blurred and his eyes closed, and in the flash of an instant, the darkness was filled with a million shining moments. He and Emily meeting for the first time at the public information office, and Vonda saying, *He wants to run the place one day*, and he was grinning at Emily and telling her, *Not yet. Not just yet.* And Vonda was shaking her head and clucking her tongue. *Looks like we got us a pair of smitten youngsters. Don't fight it, Emily ... don't fight it.*

And Emily was raising an eyebrow at him and asking, *Mr. Smooth, huh?* And they were walking along Puget Sound and their arms were touching and he was thinking he'd never felt like this in all his life. And suddenly he was on a soccer field, jerking his shirt from his body and bandaging up the girl's leg, and Emily was looking in his eyes and saying, *You're my hero, Justin. You'll always be my hero.*

The scene changed and they were hiking in the hills east of Tacoma, and she was a few feet ahead of him and she tripped and fell into his arms, and she was begging him, *Just stay behind me, okay? You never know when I might need you to catch me.* And they were walking but the path became a pier and there was a cruise ship in the distance and a little old couple and the woman was saying, *Oh, dear, aren't they the most adorable couple? Just like you and me at that age.*

And he was standing at the foot of the steps of her residence hall and Emily was crying. She was crying and he couldn't make her stop, no matter what he said. And she was whispering, *Please ... don't go. Don't leave me.* And he was running his hands down her back, her arms. *Baby ... I'll come back. I promise. Everything's going to be okay.*

And suddenly her arms were around his neck and he could feel her body against his, taste her tears in his lips, and through her tears she was saying, *Take me with you. Wherever you go ... I wanna be there too.*

And he was reminding her that he would take her if he could, but in the meantime ... in the meantime she would have his heart. She would always have his heart. And the picture changed again. He was sitting in his bunk at the barracks, looking at the scrapbook and being jolted awake and rushing to the car, to the caravan. And he was resting his head and picturing her, the way she would look when she walked down the aisle, his cherished bride ...

Finally, the images faded, and all that remained was warmth. Warmth and light and a sense of hope and peace and perfection. And one lingering thought. He hadn't kept his promise. Because he wasn't going back at all, and so what was she going to think? *Don't be mad, Emily ... I love you ... I'll always love you.*

The sadness faded along with her image as the reality set in. *I'll save a place for you ... save a place for you ...* The light was golden now and beyond it a great city, shining and perfect. And he knew—he absolutely knew—that there would be no more tears, no more dying, no more destruction or devastation.

The pain was gone.

He could feel his legs again, strong and healthy, moving beneath him. He wasn't going back, he was going somewhere better. The place he was created for, the place where he belonged. Where his family and Joe and the teens, where the Veterans and the schoolkids, and where Emily one day would join him.

He was going home.

NINETEEN

Carol Baker knew before she opened the door.

She heard the car outside and came to the entryway. And through the window in the door she watched the pair of uniformed soldiers get out and stop, their eyes fixed on her house. She saw them start up the walkway. Her mind raced. When was the last time they'd talked, the last time they'd heard from Justin? And what was the news yesterday?

Three soldiers killed in a roadside bomb.

Same as always, the story stopped her in her tracks. The soldiers remained unnamed pending notification of family—

There was a knock at the door, and she shook her head. No ... not her family. The notification belonged somewhere else.

"Gary!" She shouted her husband's name. He was in the back den, watching football highlights from the weekend games. How stupid they were! They should have been trying to call Justin. Because that was where he was stationed. Right there, where the roadside bomb struck. "Gary, please!"

She heard footsteps in the hall. "Honey, what—" His voice dropped off. Through the window in the door he must've seen what she'd seen. The army green, the shadowy figures of soldiers. His eyes met hers, but he didn't say a word. She could see the blood draining from his face, but he was silent as he came to her, one slow step after another.

Her heart pounded so hard she expected it to give out on the spot. Because if her Justin was gone, then she would be gone.

Even if her heart continued to beat for another forty years. "Not Justin ..." She whispered the words and moved aside.

A second knock sounded, so loud it seemed to shake the house, shake her foundation, her core. *God ... not Justin.*

Gary swallowed—swallowed so hard she could hear him. Then he did what people do in a situation like this. He opened the door. And all she could think was that this was how it happened, how people were notified. This scene played out all the time, as long as war had been going on.

But she'd never pictured it happening to her. Imagining such a thing would've been to live in constant fear, hounded by it, hunted by it, suffocated by it. She never could've let Justin go if she'd thought for a minute that this was how it would end.

Everything seemed to happen in slow motion. Gary opened the door, and the soldiers on the front step hung their heads. Hung them for what seemed like forever.

She wanted to scream ... *What? Why are you here? And why so down? My Justin is the toughest soldier in Iraq. He isn't dead. There's no way he's dead.*

"Can ... can we help you?" Gary sounded frozen, like he hadn't had time to catch his breath. He held the door handle so tight his knuckles turned white.

The soldiers looked up, and one of them had tears in his eyes. She could hear Justin, five or six years old, running inside with a skinned knee ... and she was getting a cloth, something to wash away the blood, and he was saying, *It's okay, Mommy ... soldiers don't cry ... soldiers don't cry ...*

But they do. They did. Because he had cried at the airport when he said good-bye. Not hard or long, but the tears were there for both of them. All of them. That's when she remembered Jill, their daughter. She was at an all-day dance camp. She wouldn't be home until late that night. How were they going to tell her that her brother was gone?

Finally, one of the soldiers handed Gary a letter. "I'm sorry, sir. Your son ... he was killed yesterday in Iraq. Victim of a roadside bomb." He nodded to the letter. "The details are all there."

With every hateful word, she felt her knees giving way. As they apologized one more time and turned around, she spun to Gary and collapsed in his arms. "No!" Her voice wasn't the slightest bit familiar. It was a guttural scream, high-pitched and desperate. The sobs hit her, and she wailed like a crazy woman. "No, Gary! Not Justin! Never Justin!"

Gary held her, clung to her, almost as if he needed her support as much as she needed his. "God ... we can't do this. We beg You to hold us." He sounded on the verge of collapse. "We have no ability to get through what lies ahead for us." Desperate, cavernous sorrow overflowed his words. "Please, God ... hold us."

Carol wanted to shout that it was too late. God had already taken their son. But she couldn't because she didn't believe it. She exhaled and slowly, sadly, her world began to right itself. Screaming and yelling wouldn't do anything now. Justin was gone, dead. Struck down doing what he felt so strongly about.

"We need ... to read the letter." Gary cradled the back of her head in his hand and kissed her forehead. Then he led her to the couch. He opened the envelope and read the first line out loud, the line every military family member dreaded reading. "We regret to inform you that your son, Lieutenant Justin Baker, was killed in action ..."

He read the whole thing, the part about Justin's courage and great attitude, the fact that he would be remembered as a role model for other soldiers, for all U.S. citizens, and then the details of that day. The caravan had been heading to the far side of Baghdad, intent on finding insurgents, when the car Justin was riding in hit a roadside bomb. One soldier in the car in front of them was killed. In Justin's car, he and the driver had died.

His body would be shipped home within the week.

There were no real facts, nothing that gave them a glimpse of Justin's final moments. When Gary finished reading, he folded the letter and set it on the sofa beside him. Then he pulled Carol into his arms and together, locked in the saddest embrace, they wept. The anger and shock were still there, but they had grown dim, overshadowed by a vast consuming sorrow that would never go away.

Not as long as either of them lived.

Minutes became an hour, and still they sat there, weeping for the son they would never hold again, never laugh with or share a meal with. Finally, as the numbness and panic faded, memories mixed with Carol's tears. Because Justin had been born to be a soldier. When other kindergarten boys played baseball or ran cement trucks through the dirt, Justin wanted nothing more than a child-sized army uniform.

Carol leaned back against the sofa. Her sobs were quieter now, but they were constant. So many tears, more than she knew she could cry. And a million memories. "Remember … that Christmas when he was six?" she looked straight ahead, seeing the room as it had been at Christmastime sixteen years earlier. "He opened that uniform and he couldn't wait to put it on."

"'I'm gonna be a Ranger one day, Daddy!' That's what he told me." Gary's voice held a smile leftover from that day. "'I'm gonna fight the bad guys.'"

When his playmates came over, Justin would give them one of his green plastic guns and they'd play war games. His fascination never waned, not through junior high or high school. Not as he kept his commitment to ROTC through college, and not after he enlisted.

She turned and looked at her husband. "There was never any life for him other than the military."

"No." Gary squeezed his eyes shut.

Carol put her hand on his shoulder. Her husband, the man who had been Justin's closest friend. What was he thinking? That Justin had just written to them the other day, or that he'd sounded so upbeat, so alive? How could they even consider planning a funeral for their sunshine boy, the son who had been everything to them?

Gary looked at her, and the tears came harder. "He would've been … the best commander." He tightened his hands into fists and pressed them hard against his knees. "God knows he would've been the best."

Her husband was right. How could God need Justin more in heaven than the world needed him right here? Than *they* needed him. And suddenly she gasped. Because only then did it hit her. "Emily."

Gary hung his head, and his tears became sobs, sobs that came from a bottomless ocean of grief that would never, ever go away. When he finally regained control, he looked up. "We have to tell her. In person, Carol. Today."

She tried to speak, but she couldn't. Suddenly twenty-two years fell away and Justin was minutes old, cradled in Gary's arms. And her husband was looking at her with those same teary eyes. Where had the years gone? Each one dropping off like so many summer days. Through it all, nothing could've prepared them for this.

He was right. Emily needed to know. She closed her eyes, but the tears came anyway. Streams of them. Poor Emily. Carol let the sobs come, let them wash over her reminding her that the nightmare was real. Way too real. She brought her hand to her face. How would she find the strength even to move? Once a long time ago, she'd heard a talk by Elisabeth Elliot, the famous wife of Jim Elliot, the murdered missionary. One thing she'd said had stuck all these years. *Sometimes, life is so hard you can only do the next thing. Whatever that is, just do the next thing. God will meet you there.*

No matter how hard it would be, telling Emily was the next thing. Carol stood, and it took every bit of her energy to walk across the room and into the kitchen. She needed her purse. Gary followed, but before she found the bag, she spotted Buster at the back door. At his feet, crumpled in a ball, was Justin's sweatshirt. She stared at the dog, just stared at him. Because the longer she looked, the more she didn't see the sweatshirt, but Justin. Age fifteen, and sixteen, and seventeen—sitting outside on the patio petting Buster or brushing him or hooking up his leash for a walk.

As if the dog somehow knew, he began to whine, whimpering and pawing at the door. Gary exchanged a look with her. A look that said every step, everything they had to do that day and the next and the day after that, would be all but impossible.

He went to the door, opened it, and crouched down. "It's okay, Buster. It's okay."

But it wasn't, because Buster would never see his master walk through the door again. Carol ached for the sadness inside her. The tears would never stop, because it would take forever to cry the river of sorrow raging inside her. Gary led Buster back to his doghouse and tucked Justin's sweatshirt in close beside him. "There, Buster. Go to sleep."

Carol watched, unable to move, unable to do anything but breathe and cry and wish with every breath that she had one more chance, one more time to hug her child and look at him and marvel over the boy she'd raised. The soldier, the friend, the son. The hero.

Gary grabbed his car keys and his wallet. "Let's go."

She nodded. It was time to do the next thing. Now she could only pray that Elisabeth Elliot was right, that somehow they'd survive the coming hours.

Because God Himself would meet them there.

$\mathscr{T}$WENTY

$\mathbf{E}$mily had finished her last class of the day and was heading back to her room when her cell phone rang. It was email day, time to get her weekly letter from Justin. That alone had made it a good morning—that and the fact that the recent rains had let up just enough to allow a few glimpses of blue on the PLU campus. The air was colder than it had been all fall, and snow was forecast for Thanksgiving.

She grabbed her phone from the side pocket of her backpack and checked the Caller ID. Strange. She didn't recognize the number.

"Hello?" She kicked at a loose pile of fallen leaves and smiled at a passing student, a girl whose room was down the hall from her own.

On the other end, the caller wasn't saying anything.

"Hello? Is anyone there?"

"Emily?" The man's voice was familiar, but he sounded upset, his words thick and muffled so she couldn't quite pinpoint it.

Her heart hesitated. Who could be calling her so upset he could barely talk? "Yes? Who's this?"

"Gary Baker."

Emily stopped cold in the middle of the walkway. "Mr. Baker? What's wrong?"

"Honey, we're here at your campus. Carol and I. In the parking lot. Can we meet you somewhere?"

What was this? Justin's parents were in the parking lot? And his father sounded like he'd been crying? Her entire world rocked hard to one side. She looked for a place to sit down, but there was none. The bench. They could meet at the bench, the same one where she and Justin had spent so many late hours talking before he said good-night and headed back to his base. "By the stairs," she managed to say. "Meet me at the bench."

She snapped her phone shut without saying good-bye, without asking any of the questions that shook her mind, her senses. What had happened? What terrible thing would cause Justin's parents to drive an hour north without calling first? She ordered her feet to start moving, and they obeyed. But her head was spinning, even as she walked.

One of the kids in her sociology class had the paper out that morning, but what had it said? Three soldiers dead ... another roadside bomb. At the time, Emily had chided herself. Usually she checked the news—either at night or before heading off for class. But she'd had a game the day before and spent a few hours at the teen center. Between her busy schedule and her homework and daydreaming about Justin, she hadn't had time to think about anything else.

Not even the war.

Justin had been gone nearly two months. Four more and he'd be home. She'd stopped getting sick over every report of a casualty. There were thousands and thousands of soldiers in Iraq; Justin would be fine. He'd promised. Her feet moved faster. She was imagining things. All she needed to do was meet the Bakers at the bench and look in their eyes, and then she'd know that his promise was still good.

He was fine.

So why are they here, sounding so upset?

Okay, maybe he was hurt. Maybe he was coming home early. But so what? She'd be there to meet him, and whatever help he needed getting better, getting back on his feet, she'd be there for him. Whatever he needed.

Once she saw the Bakers, she'd know.

Or maybe something had happened to Buster. He was an old dog, after all. If Buster died while Justin was away fighting, he'd never forgive himself. Yes, that made sense. If something had happened to Buster, the Bakers wouldn't want to tell her over the phone. They'd need to talk about it in person, so that they could come up with the right words, the right way to tell Justin.

She walked faster, and there, up ahead, she could see them. Mr. and Mrs. Baker, standing near the bench, the one that belonged to her and Justin. From far away, it seemed strange seeing Justin's father there. The two looked so alike, and if she didn't know better, she'd think it was Justin himself. The way he might look in a few decades, when they were looking back at the picture they'd taken that day on the pier, knowing that what the old couple had said about the passing of time was all too true.

But it wasn't Justin.

It was his father and his mother, and they were watching for her, staring at her. She took shallow breaths, all that her lungs would allow. Her heart banged against her chest. She wanted to stop, turn around, and run the other direction. But she couldn't. Whatever this was about, she had to know. Now, before another minute passed. She began to jog — and then to run.

She reached them breathless, and that's when she saw the tear stains on their faces. The red in their swollen eyes. "What ..." She leaned over her knees and waited until she could breathe again. Then she straightened. "What's going on?"

Justin's mother held out her arms. "Emily ... I'm so sorry, honey."

Emily shook her head. She didn't want to be hugged. She was a competitor, not a meek person who would fall apart when the game momentum turned on her. She took the woman's hand, but she held her ground. "Tell me."

His father took a step forward. "He's gone, Emily. He was killed in battle yesterday."

The moment his words were out, a wall threw itself up between the person standing in her shoes and the person who so loved Justin Baker. A wall made of thick cement and razor wire. The sort of wall no emotions were ever going to get around.

She shook her head and took a step backward. "No." She held up her hand. "No, it's not true."

"Emily ..." His mother began to cry. "We just found out. We had to tell you in person."

Justin's father crossed his arms, and tears forged two trails down his cheeks. "He was on his way across Baghdad, and his car ... the car hit a roadside bomb."

A roadside bomb? The one mentioned on the front page? Were they trying to tell her that Justin had been one of the three soldiers killed? She began to tremble. Her coat was too thin for winter weather. She pulled it tightly around her waist and shook her hair free from the collar. Why were they standing here like this, crying? Justin wasn't dead.

She needed to tell them. "I heard from him ... just the other day. I probably have an email—" she pointed toward the residence hall and her hand shook hard—"right up there. His letter is right up there waiting f-f-for me."

"Honey." Justin's mother put her hand on Emily's shoulder. "Please ... I know this is hard for you. Our daughter's at a dance camp, but we got her a message to leave early. She'll be home later tonight. We tried to call your father, but he was out." Her voice cracked. "It's hard for all of us."

They tried to call her father? Emily stood a little straighter. Whatever bad information Justin's parents had gotten, they didn't need to all stand outside in the cold. She wasn't being the least bit hospitable. She tried to smile, but her lips wouldn't lift. "Mrs. Baker, Mr. Baker ... you've come a long way." Her voice was calm, because they were wrong. Of course they were wrong. "Why don't you come in and wait in my room. That'll give me time to check my email."

Gary Baker nodded and put his arm around his wife's shoulders. "We'll follow you."

"Good." She led the way up the stairs. "How's Buster?"

Justin's mother exchanged a look with her husband. Then Mr. Baker said, "We can talk about him later. Let's get inside."

She moved through the entryway and down the hall to her room. Pam was gone for the afternoon, so she used her key and opened it. "You can sit there." Emily motioned to a single sofa that sat against the wall between the two beds. Again she'd forgotten her manners. "Can I get you water, anything to eat?" She moved past them and opened a small cupboard. "We have fruit leather."

Justin's parents wore looks of astonishment, and his mother seemed on the verge of a breakdown. They took their places on the sofa and Mr. Baker shook his head. "No. We'll ... we'll wait here, Emily."

Good. She didn't want to hear anything else about Justin, not when they were completely wrong. He was fine. His letters told her that he knew what he was doing, defending the various ethnic groups in Iraq, the ones in favor of freedom and democracy. He'd done this before, that's what he told her. He knew his way out of the battlefield. Just four months. Sixteen weeks and he'd be home again.

She ran up the stairs to the computer station and signed on. *God ... help the Bakers. They're so upset.* She felt arms behind her, arms that were holding her up. But even that was strange, because she wasn't about to fall. She only needed to check her email and find the letter from Justin.

The screen came to life and there it was. A brand-new letter. Hah! Just like she'd known it would be there. The subject said the same thing it always said, "Missing you." She opened it, but she refused to read it. Not here. Not with his parents sitting in her room certain that Justin was dead.

Dead, of all things! The idea was ludicrous! While his letter was printing, she stared at the Internet Explorer button and warned herself not to look. It wasn't possible. The wall was firmly in place. No matter what the Bakers believed, they were wrong. She could run a check on the Internet and then she'd know.

Don't do it! A voice deep in her heart warned her. *Don't look. You're right; his email is enough.*

But she had to look, because if she could find the story, if she could find the names, then she could make a printout of that too and take it to his parents. Then they could hug each other and smile and thank God that they were wrong.

And they could talk about Buster and how sixteen weeks wasn't really all that long, and they could go home where they belonged. Yes, that was a good idea. The letter was still printing, so she'd run the search real quick. The Internet was always helping her find things.

That was how she'd found her parents, how she'd first made contact with them and brought them back together. Yes, the Internet would know, and then she could tell Justin's parents. Everything was fine. Justin was fine. Her heart thudded harder, her breaths quick and raspy.

She called up Explorer, and then opened Google. With her fingers shaking so hard she could barely type, she went to the search box and typed in the words, "roadside bomb, three soldiers." Despite the part of her heart that was desperate for her to stop the search, she hit enter. Then she waited.

The first story was one dated that day. The source was CNN. Fine, CNN would have the facts. Especially if the story was dated that day. She called it up, and as she did, she told herself she wouldn't actually read it. She would print it out, and she and the

Bakers could read it together. She hit print, but as she did, her eyes betrayed her.

They scanned the story, and that's when she saw it.

A blur of names, and there in the middle of them ...

"Justin Baker, 22, from Fort Lewis."

"No." She slid back her chair and jerked to her feet, staring at the screen. "You're wrong. You're all wrong!" The wall was crumbling, but Emily wouldn't let it. Not all the way. She was in a match for her life, down 3–0 with the championship on the line. *Be tough, Emily*, she could hear her coach shouting at her. *Be tough!*

And she would be.

She grabbed the pieces of paper from the printer, ran back to her room, and snatched up her purse and car keys.

"Emily ..." Mr. Baker was on his feet. "Where are you—?"

She held up her hand, stopping him. "I can't ... I'll be back." Then she ran as fast as her feet would take her, out into the hall, down the stairs, and into the parking lot. Her car was parked in the back row, and that was good. The running felt right, something she could do to get her head back in the game.

God ... guide my hands. I can't think, can't breathe, so guide my hands. She climbed into her car and took off, out of the parking lot and onto the freeway. Not until she took the exit did she really understand where she was going, where her car was taking her.

The Sound, of course. Puget Sound, the place where she'd come so many times with Justin. She folded the printouts. Then she stuffed them into her jacket pocket and put her keys in the other. Overhead, the clouds were gathering again, threatening to break open just like her heart. But not yet, not until she reached the water's edge.

She kept running, ignoring the way her ribs ached, the way her lungs burned from the effort. And finally, finally she reached the metal railing. She tilted her head back, gasping for her next breath. The boardwalk was empty, deserted on this cloudy mid-November afternoon. Her sides heaved, and she leaned on the railing, leaned on it the same way she and Justin always did whenever they came here.

But this time she didn't look out at the water; she bent almost all the way over. *Fill up, lungs, come on.* And after a minute, they did what she asked of them. She straightened and tried to remember what she was doing. The Bakers had come up from Kelso and they'd been crying.

Be tough, Emily ... be tough.

She needed to read the papers in her pocket, but which one first? She knew before she took another breath. The letter of course. The letter that would fill her heart and mind and soul with Justin's voice, his laughter and wisdom, his compassion and love. She was still shaking, even harder than before. She took the papers from her jacket and figured out which was which.

In a rush, she thrust the CNN article back in her pocket. Then she opened the other page, slowly, reverently. And suddenly her hands weren't shaking anymore, and the breeze felt like his breath, his touch. *Talk to me, Justin ... talk to me ...*

She scanned the top of the email. It was dated three days ago. She swallowed hard and tried to ignore that single detail. The date didn't matter; this was Justin, alive and talking to her. Her eyes found the place where the letter began.

Dear Emily,

I can't believe it! I read the article finally, and, well ... I mean, I believed you, of course. But wow! Your mom! Are you sure she wrote that story? Just kidding, but still ... you and your dad are right. Something's happening in her heart, no doubt.

Emily closed her eyes. She clutched the letter with both hands, picturing him. This was something new—he'd read the article. She opened her eyes and kept reading.

I'll never forget that day. Talk lately is that the Iraqi people are afraid to come out of their houses. I don't know. I guess that might be true in some regions, but around here they come out. Even the kids. Obviously. And you know why?

Because we're here. Maybe your mom is seeing that too.

Emily smiled. *Yes, Justin, you're right.*

She was halfway through the letter, so she slowed down. As long as the letter was in her hands, as long as Justin's words were echoing through her mind and her heart, then he wasn't gone. No matter what the next piece of paper told her. She found her place.

Anyway, enough about that.

Did I tell you I carry your picture with me? Because I do. I know, it's a little sappy, but how else can I survive another four months without you? Joe thinks I'm going soft, but I told him the same thing I told him before. He's just jealous.

So yeah, I took one of the pictures from the cruise and I laminated it. I keep it in my boot so that if there's ever enough time, I can take it out and look at it. I figure there you are back in Tacoma drinking lattes out of my mug and looking at our pictures. I need something to look at too. Even if I'm thousands of miles away from my next cup of Starbucks.

Something else has been helping me lately.

Emily closed her eyes. *Slow down ... you have to slow down.* What would she do if by some crazy chance the Bakers were right, or if her eyes really had seen Justin's name in the CNN article?

Then this would be her last time to hear him, the last time she would feel his arm next to hers leaning against the railing overlooking Puget Sound. *Okay.* She drew a steady breath. *Slower.*

> *Something else has been helping me lately. Whenever I get tired of all the dust and grime and desert, when the violence seems like it's never going to end, I let myself do a little dreaming. Even in the middle of the day. I can picture myself coming home and finding you that ring. The simple one.*
>
> *You're smiling, I know it.*
>
> *Okay, so then I take it a step further, and I can see the wedding, Emily. The tux and the dress and the people filling the pews, and I can hear the doors of the church open, and there you are. Stunning. My precious bride. I can feel you in my arms, dancing that first dance and knowing that if I have my way, I'll never leave you again. Not ever. And there it is. One more way I can stay sane until I see you again.*
>
> *You know how I thought last summer was amazing? Well ... it'll be nothing compared to this one. I can't wait, Emily. To see you, to touch you, to hold you. You're with me always. You have my heart. I love you, Justin.*

Emily refused to take her eyes from the page. She could read that last part a thousand times and it would never be enough. *You're with me always ... you have my heart ... I love you.*

And then, somewhere deep inside her heart, the wall began to fall. It didn't happen slowly, but all at once. Like the Twin Towers.

She lifted her head and looked out at the Sound, as far out as she could see. And suddenly, as surely as she knew her name, she knew it was true. She didn't need to read the CNN article. It was there all along.

Justin was gone.

Rain started to fall, and it mixed with her tears, as if God Himself were there beside her, weeping over Justin the way He'd wept over Lazarus. She didn't want Justin's letter getting wet, so she slid it back into her pocket.

Sobs didn't come, not right away, and she wasn't surprised. They would come later, but for now she couldn't picture him lying on a street in Baghdad, couldn't picture him torn apart. Because that wasn't the Justin she knew, the one she would keep forever alive in her heart.

The ocean breeze sent the rain sideways and it washed against her face, against her silent stream of tears. What was it? Had he been too good to be true, was that it? She wasn't sure, but she couldn't consider the depth and breadth of his loss. Not fully. He was gone, and that was enough for now. As if she was only being given a small peek into the pain and sorrow that lay ahead.

If only she hadn't finished reading the letter. She would've pulled it out and read it again, but she didn't want it to get wet. Instead she had everything else about him alive and within her. His voice and his smile, the smell of his cologne. It hit her then, why she wasn't falling apart. Because in every possible way, Justin was still alive, real and good and whole and strong.

There was too much good about Justin Baker to feel only sadness, even with the knowledge that he was gone. Before she could mourn his loss, or even imagine it, she had to celebrate him. Her eyes lifted, beyond the water to the sky. The rain was still falling, but there in the distance, was a break in the clouds and a section of the purest blue.

He was there. Somewhere beyond the clouds.

God … You're so lucky. She smiled and the slightest laugh sounded on her lips. She could imagine a heavenly version of Vonda, introducing Justin to the rest of the gang and shaking her head. *You know Justin. Wants to run the whole place someday.*

Her smile faded. *God ... You must have big plans for him. Because if he can do more up there for You than he could down here, well ... that would be something. And I know he will. Because ...* Her eyes filled with another layer of tears. *Because You wouldn't have taken him otherwise.*

Countless questions lined up around the perimeter of her heart, peering in at her, making themselves known. What would happen to Buster, and who would talk to the Veterans, and how would a generation of schoolkids learn about the good things soldiers were doing in Iraq?

And what about the teens?

But she couldn't face any of the questions. Not yet.

She could see her coach's face again. *Be tough, Emily. Be tough.* But this wasn't the time to be tough. By loving a soldier, this was the risk she'd taken. That one day, this moment might come and his name would join the thousands of others on a military tombstone. No matter what she told herself, she'd always known this could happen.

She wiped her nose, wiped the rain from her cheeks and her chin. Never mind the end, she would've fallen for him all over again if she had the chance, spent the summer dreaming with him and playing with him and figuring out for herself everything her mother had ever said about love.

But still ...

She hugged herself and watched the patch of blue, watched it until the clouds swallowed it up and the sky became all cloudy gray once more. She needed to go, needed to get back to her room and fall into Justin's mother's arms. But she couldn't pull herself away. As long as she was here, as long as she had his last letter in her pocket, then she didn't have to think about the questions storming the edges of her heart. Here she could look at Pier 55 and at the cruise ship. The very same cruise ship where he'd promised her his heart. And she could feel the rain on her skin the way she'd felt his touch that day.

She looked out at the water again. *Talk to me, Justin … talk to me.*

And his words were there, as close as her next heartbeat. *I can't wait, Emily. To see you, to touch you, to hold you. You're with me always. You have my heart. I love you.*

There was much she had to do, and she would do it proudly, with strength. The way Justin would've wanted her to do it. She'd take care of everything he would've taken care of, and when the tears became sobs and she couldn't breathe for the pain, she would know it was okay to fall apart.

Because God would do what Justin had done for her that summer.

He would walk beside her, and when she fell, He would be there to catch her.

With that knowledge, she pulled away from the metal railing and walked back to her car, her feet moving slowly along the cobblestone roads, remembering every time she'd walked them with Justin. Somehow she made it to her car and shut the door. She held the steering wheel with both hands, but it was an effort even to start the engine. As she pulled away, she could barely see the road for her tears, but it wasn't until she walked into her room, until her eyes met Mrs. Baker's, and then Mr. Baker's, that she felt the full force of Justin's loss.

"Justin …" That was all she could say. She stumbled across the room and collapsed into his father's arms.

"It's okay, honey." The man stroked her back, rocked her as if she were his daughter. "We're going to get through this."

"I can't …" she sobbed against his chest, her body reeling from the loss. Justin was dead? How could it be? His email was still in her pocket. "I don't … I don't think I can …"

She felt his mother come up alongside her, and the three of them stayed that way for a long time, hugging, holding onto each other, and doing what they could to convince each other that Justin's dad was right.

Somehow they were going to survive without him.

And deep inside, Emily knew they would. They would survive, but without Justin, how were they ever going to *live*? And that was the question that shouted at her the loudest, more than any of the others.

The question only God could answer.

$\mathscr{T}$WENTY-$\mathscr{O}$NE

Lauren hadn't left her cramped quarters at the journalists' compound for two days. Fighting had picked up, and her editors had asked her and Scanlon to stay put. Better to do the wrap-up story, the what-happened story, than to wind up in the middle of the action.

That sort of coverage was for dailies and television news, not *Time* magazine. And so she'd used her time to work on an opinion piece and catch up on her email. That, and sit by her window looking out at the desert and wondering about the stories she'd seen play out since she'd come to Iraq.

Apparently Scanlon could sense the change in her. He was in her room now, sitting in the chair across from her bed. There was no escaping the suspicion in his eyes. He drummed his fingers on his knees. "Okay, look." His hands went still. "I know what you're thinking."

"What?" She had her laptop open, but she set it down beside her. "I'm not turning soft, if that's what this is about."

"No, not soft. Just ..." Scanlon took hold of the arms of the chair and surveyed her. "Different."

"Okay, so sue me. I'm different." Lauren hated her tone. Clear proof she hadn't taken the time she needed to actually process the things she'd seen. Sure, she'd had fleeting thoughts of regret or remorse. Doubts about her opinions of the past, whether she'd led Americans to the wrong conclusion about the war. But she and Scanlon had been too busy to really think things through.

Scanlon looked hurt by her response. He leaned over his knees. "I'm your friend, remember? I'm out there with you. I see the same things you see, hear the same stories. I have my doubts too, okay?" He sighed. "I just wanted to hear it from you, what you're thinking. What you're feeling."

What was she feeling? Antsy. Ready to get on the next flight home, that's how she felt. Crazy for how badly she missed Shane. That everything she'd thought was written on her heart in ink was now only sketched in fading pencil. But how could she say that? "I don't know, Scanlon." She reached into her dresser drawer. "Emily sent me this." She held out a folded piece of paper.

Scanlon stood, crossed the room, and took it. "What's it say?"

"Read it." Lauren swung her feet over the edge of the bed and walked to the window. She could hear Scanlon opening the paper. She remembered the way she felt when she first read the email a few weeks ago. Emily had copied a section of Lauren's long-ago journal right into her letter.

Here, Mom, the email said, *read it and see if you remember loving Dad like this.* And then it began. A whole section Lauren wrote on love, back when Shane was everything to her. Some of the lines were profound, much deeper than she remembered feeling. But since reading those long-ago words, she couldn't shake them. Couldn't get them out of her head, even if she wanted to.

The letter was all she needed for a whole parade of memories to return. Even the memory of making chocolate chip cookies. Shane was her best friend back then, and she lost him. The loss had changed her, darkened her entire existence. She vowed to find him, to love him, no matter how long she had to search.

Behind her, she heard Scanlon lower the paper. "Profound."

"Yes." She turned around and folded her arms. "I miss him."

"You knew you would. That was never the question." Scanlon lowered himself to the chair again. "The question was whether you could *agree* with him."

Scanlon was right. Missing him was never the question. And yes, they'd been busy, but she knew the answer, didn't she? It wasn't an easy one, wasn't one she even knew how to live with yet, but slowly, assuredly, she nodded. "Yes." Her voice held a fear she hadn't known before. The fear that possibly she'd been wrong. "Yes, Scanlon. I think I can agree with him now. About some very big things."

Frustration flashed in Scanlon's face, but only for an instant. He stood and brought the letter back to her. "I wish you would've said so."

Now it was her turn to feel frustrated. She tossed the letter on her bed. "I wasn't sure. I'm *still* not sure." She looked out the window again. "I watch people falling in the streets and write about soldiers being ripped apart by roadside bombs, and I hate this war more than anyone ever could hate it."

Scanlon was quiet for a moment. "You hate it ... but you understand it." His voice dropped a notch. "Is that it?"

"I think so." She faced him again and leaned on the windowsill. "What if we'd never declared war on Afghanistan or Iraq?" She made a sound that was part laugh, part dawning realization. "Can you imagine? I mean, I never thought about it that way. War is wrong. Period. That was my mantra."

A mantra Shane had responded to that first night when they were together at her parents' house in Wheaton. She remembered his words and repeated them now. Not because Shane had said them, but because she was starting to understand them. And believe them. "What happened on September 11, Scanlon, that was only the beginning. Everyone knows that now. The terrorists' plans were beyond anything we can begin to fathom, even now."

Scanlon exhaled hard.

"Don't dismiss me." She stood, angry. "You said you're my friend. Then listen to me. I'm not talking rhetoric here, I'm talking firsthand observation."

He frowned. "Meaning what?"

"How can we think anything but the obvious? It's been five years, and the terrorists haven't harmed a single American on U.S. soil. So the war must be working, right? Is there any other conclusion?"

"Maybe it worked at first, when we made the air attacks, but what about now?" He waved his hand toward the window. "All that violence out there can't be doing any good."

"So what's the answer?" The debate had raged inside her ever since she spotted Justin Baker playing with the Iraqi children. It felt wonderful to finally put words to her feelings. She waved her hands in the air. "Just walk away and hope things work out for the people here? 'Cause you and I both know what would happen if we did that. The terrorists would recruit another generation of kids, and new cells would start up, and a dictator would rise to power. And before you know, we'd be staring into the rubble of another catastrophe, wondering what went wrong."

He stuck his hands in his pockets and his shoulders fell an inch or so. "I don't want to fight with you, Lauren." His eyes told her he was astonished, amazed at the things she was saying. "Is this really how you feel?"

His question hit straight at her soul. "I'm not sure. But it's starting to make sense, starting to make me wonder if maybe Shane and Justin Baker are right."

Scanlon looked skeptical. "About what?"

"That what this war needs is more support, more financing. So we can finish the job right and *then* get home."

He was about to respond when the phone on her desk rang. Lauren looked at it, startled. The line was for incoming and local calls only, something her editors at *Time* had established for her. Cell phone reception was spotty, so the landline was the best way to keep open communication. She hesitated. Maybe it was

Bob Maine giving them the all clear to hit the streets and find the stories in the recent wave of violence.

She crossed the room and lifted the receiver. "Hello?" Her eyes were on Scanlon. She didn't want to offend him or scare him off, but what was she supposed to do with her feelings?

"Lauren … it's Bob."

"Hey, let me guess. It's okay to step outdoors again."

"No." He was a serious man, but his tone was heavier than usual, sad almost. "That's not why I'm calling."

She dropped to the edge of the bed. "Talk to me, Bob. What's going on?" Had something big happened in the U.S., some event she'd missed by being there in Iraq?

"I'm calling with a special request from Shane Galanter."

Shane …? Her heart skipped a beat and slammed into double time. "What … what request?" Scanlon was still watching her, but now she looked away, found a spot on the floor so she could concentrate.

"Lauren, the three soldiers who were killed?"

"Yes." Her mind raced. How did the violence in the streets of Baghdad affect Shane? Was he that worried about her, that he'd called her editor? "I'm aware of that."

Bob sighed, and the sound rattled over the phone lines. "One of the soldiers was Justin Baker." He paused. "I'm sorry."

The news hit her like a physical blow. She closed her eyes and turned her head from the receiver. *No, not Justin. No, God …*

"Lauren … are you there?" Gruff old Bob sounded worried about her, brokenhearted for her.

She gripped the phone and forced herself to speak. "Yes." She looked up and motioned for Scanlon to leave. Her eyes begged him to understand that she needed to be alone. Needed to process whether the conversation with Bob was even taking place.

Scanlon mouthed the words, "Everything okay?"

She shook her head and closed her eyes again. She waited until she heard him leave, heard the door close behind him. Then she found her voice once more. "Are you sure, Bob? Justin Baker?"

"Yes." Her editor hesitated. "Officer Galanter would like you to contact the army headquarters there and accompany the soldier's body back to the United States." He exhaled hard. "Oh, man ... I hate this, Lauren. I really hate this." He sounded like he was fighting tears. "Shane and your daughter will be waiting for you."

Lauren felt a flood of tears gathering in her heart. She was a reporter, a veteran of war correspondence. Tears didn't come often or easily. But all she could picture were those Iraqi kids, grinning and laughing and playing catch with a soldier who would lay down his life for them. *No, God ... not Justin.*

"Lauren, what should I tell Officer Galanter?"

She steeled herself. This was part of her job, wasn't it? Reporting the casualties, surrounding herself with the reality of war? She would get through this, and she would do it for Emily and Shane, for the Bakers. She would fly home with their son's body, and she wouldn't leave his side for a moment. "Yes. Tell Shane yes. I'll contact headquarters as soon as I get off the phone."

"Okay." Bob's tone was quieter, defeated. "I'm sorry, Lauren."

"Me too." She thanked him for calling and then, before her emotions overtook her, she made the next call. For the purpose of her stories, she was often in touch with officials at the army headquarters. She had the number written on a card beside her phone.

In a matter of minutes the plans came together. They'd be shipping Justin's body stateside in the morning. By special request, they'd agreed to allow her to accompany the body home. Justin's friend, a soldier named Joe Greenwald, who was injured by the same bomb, would make the trip with her.

Blindly, like a person in a trance, she hung up the phone and walked down the hall to tell Scanlon. He listened, then came to hug her. "I'm sorry."

As she stepped back, she knew what he was thinking. She gritted her teeth, anger rising within her, taking place of the shock. "Everything I said a minute ago?" She searched his eyes. "I was wrong." Justin's face came into view again, and she shook her head. "There can never, *ever* be a reason for losing a kid like Justin Baker. Not ever."

The tears didn't come until she was back in her room.

How in the world was Emily taking the news? The guy had been everything to her, her first taste of real love—the way Shane had been Lauren's first taste. Lauren had watched them together and known as Shane had known. What Emily and Justin shared was strong and real. Neither Lauren nor Shane had any doubts that one day, when Justin returned from Iraq, he would pledge his life to their daughter.

Emily had already started talking about the wedding.

Lauren put her head in her hands. Her mind was racing. What about what she'd just told Scanlon? Was that really how she felt? Now that one of the victims was someone she knew, she couldn't possibly find it in herself to support the war effort? Was that right?

She curled up on her bed, closed her eyes, and buried her face in her pillow. She had come here asking God for wisdom, that she might see things the way He saw them, think about them the way He thought about them. So what was she supposed to make of *this*? That there were no easy answers, no right sides and wrong sides, was that it?

She didn't know, and her heart hurt too badly to try to figure it out. *God ... Lord ... if there's wisdom to be gained in the next week, let me find it. Because I don't understand. It's my job to have educated opinions, to know the facts. But I don't understand this.*

The prayer swirled in her head over and over as she laid there. She wept for the family whose son was gone forever, and for the Iraqi children who looked up to him, and for her precious daughter who would never again kiss him or hold him. Never marry him.

No, she didn't understand any of it.

And the most terrifying thought was the one she fell asleep with.

Maybe she never would.

TWENTY-TWO

As it turned out, Justin's parents didn't know even half of what he was involved in. Emily traveled back to Kelso with them that night, the night she learned of his death, and when his sister Jill came home, Emily sat in the other room so her parents could break the news to her in private.

Later, when the wailing had died down, they all sat in the living room, and Emily told them she would take care of letting everyone know, all the groups he was involved with.

"Groups?" His mother's cheeks had been wet all evening. She clung to her husband's arm, barely strong enough to be curious.

"Yes." She looked at Justin's father and then at Jill. Their faces were blank also. "He volunteers a lot of his time." She realized she was still using present tense, but that was okay. It was too soon to talk about Justin in anything but present tense.

His mother raised her chin and sniffed. "He ... he used to do volunteer work here. When he was in high school. But I didn't know ..."

"He didn't like talking about the things he did for other people." Justin's dad sat up a little straighter. "What all did he do?"

That was one of the few highlights of the day. When Emily had the chance to tell them about Justin's work. She told them about the Veterans, and how Justin believed it was no big deal. "He used to tell me someone needs to hear their stories, to keep their legacy alive." She held a damp tissue in her hand and caught her tears as they fell. But her voice remained clear as she continued. She told them how he visited local classrooms, telling school children about the good the U.S. soldiers were doing over in Iraq.

And she told them about the teen center.

"My goodness ..." His mother looked at her husband and then back at Emily. There was a catch in her voice. "Someone has to tell those boys."

Emily nodded. "I will. Justin would've wanted me to do it."

She stayed at the Bakers' house that night, and she heard from her dad. Her mom was going to fly home with Justin's body. And after the connecting flight through the air base in Germany, they were scheduled to arrive in two days. Plans for Justin's memorial service came together sometime around midnight, and by one in the morning they were all drained. Sleep was restless that night, and several times she woke up, sobbing, her pillow soaked. But as morning dawned—as she gradually faced the day, and as the reality of Justin's death hit her again—Emily knew it was time. She would drive back to Tacoma and break the news to the teens and the Veterans. Everyone he spent time with.

When she reached her residence hall again, when she was controlled enough to speak, she sat at a table and picked up the phone. The person at the school district would be the easiest of all. She took a deep breath, begged God for strength, and dialed the number. When she was connected to the right person, she explained she was a friend of Lieutenant Justin Baker.

"Yes, we know Justin." The woman sounded all sunshine and smiles. "Several of our classes are writing cards and letters for him. They've taken up a collection of Jelly Bellies." She laughed. "Every time Justin ever came to talk to a class, he brought Jelly Bellies."

Emily exhaled. *God ... what am I supposed to say?* She pinched the bridge of her nose and searched for the words. "Yes, well, I'm afraid I don't have good news, ma'am."

"No?" Gradual alarm filled the woman's tone. "Did something ... is he okay?"

"No ... he isn't. He was killed this week in Iraq."

The woman on the other end gasped. It was a long time before she said anything. "I'm so sorry."

"We all are." She had promised herself, promised God, that she wouldn't break down today. The people who knew Justin needed her to be strong. But there was no getting around the sorrow. It seeped from every pore, grew with every breath.

"When ... when is the service?"

Emily gave her the details and asked her to pass on the news to the teachers and kids who knew him. She hung up the phone, then hesitated.

Her next task wouldn't be as easy.

The rain hadn't let up since the day before, so she wore her jacket. The one Justin liked best because it made her blue eyes stand out.

The Veterans met every day after lunch at the American Legion hall. They played bingo and poker or just sat around the table telling stories of the old days. War stories, mostly. Emily had only been with Justin once when he visited them. She thought it would be good for her writing someday to watch Justin interact with the old guys.

But their time that day had given her an even greater appreciation of the man she loved. He sat there in their midst, every bit a part of the group, and there was no getting around the pride that filled the room.

Justin wasn't like other kids his age. He was a throwback. Hope existed for the entire generation if there could be one young soldier like Justin Baker, that's what the Veterans thought of him. And they loved him for taking the time to remember them.

When Emily and Justin left that day, one of the men, an old guy in a baseball cap covered with military patches and hunched over in a wheelchair, his jacket not quite straight on his shoulders, pointed a finger in Justin's direction. "I know you're shipping out, but you be careful now, young man." He patted the place on the table beside him. "We'll keep your spot open."

Emily tried not to think about the image as she drove to the hall that day. The old guy couldn't have been serious about saving Justin a spot. Not with all the Veterans looking to get in on a conversation or a game of cards. Table space seemed to be at a premium. She drove without ever really seeing the roads or the stoplights, her body moving in a sort of automatic motion so that her heart and mind were free to think about Justin.

She pulled into the parking lot, walked up the flower-lined sidewalk, and peered into the window. The place was packed, but there at the table ...

The old guy with the jacket was there, and beside him was an empty space. The place set aside for the young soldier, the one who had brought them hours of joy. *Okay, God ... hold me up.*

When the lump in her throat subsided, she pushed her way to the door and went inside. The action around the table and in chairs and sofas along the walls all stopped.

"Hey!" A big jovial guy waved at her, beckoning her to come closer. "You're Justin Baker's girl!"

What was she supposed to do? How could she say it, when every time ... every time she heard the words cross her lips, they felt more shocking than the last? Justin Baker ... dead? Even now she had his email in her pocket.

The men were smiling at her, waiting for her to join them. The guy in the jacket patted the empty spot beside him. "I'm Vern. You tell that young soldier of yours we're keeping his spot open. Just like we said we would."

"I'm ..." Her tears cut her off midsentence. She hung her head for a moment, willing herself to find even a sliver of control. When she looked up, the expressions on all their faces had changed.

The jovial guy stood and came to her. He put his hand on her shoulder. "What is it, darling? Tell us."

She dabbed at her tears and looked at him. Maybe if she said the words in a hurry, all at once … She took a breath. "Justin was killed in Iraq this week. A … a roadside bomb."

The reaction hit them in slow motion. Beside her, the old guy took his hand from her shoulder — then removed his hat and held it over his heart. Around the room, the others did the same thing, taking off embroidered military baseball caps and holding them over their chests.

One of the men asked about the service, and Emily pulled out a few cards with the information. A muffled round of condolences came from the group, and she realized that their reaction was different than most. They'd been there, witnessed the destruction of war firsthand.

For the most part, the men's eyes were dry. But before she left, Vern straightened his jacket and looked at her. His eyes brimmed with tears. "As long as I'm here, I'll save him a spot. Just so you know."

Emily nodded. She looked around the room, hoping they could see that she couldn't speak or she'd break down, collapse right there on the floor. She left, and for a long time she sat in her car, her head on her steering wheel. *Why, God … why?* She'd asked the question over and over, but she never sensed an answer. She didn't need one. It was enough to know that God held the number of their days, and that if He'd taken Justin, then it was Justin's time.

But still she asked.

And she tried to convince herself that it was really true, that when he came home in the morning it wouldn't be with a running embrace and whispers of love. It would be in a pine box, with an American flag draped across the top.

Now she had one more stop. The hardest of all.

The teen center wasn't far from Puget Sound, located in the tougher part of downtown Tacoma. This was their afternoon, the one day a week when she showed up and mixed with Bo and Dexter and the guys, playing ping-pong and telling them the latest news from Justin.

They'd be expecting her.

As she made her way there, her eyes grew dry. Fear masked the sorrow, because how in the world was she going to walk into that teen center and tell them Justin was gone? And how would they react once she told them? What was she supposed to do with eight teenage boys being dealt one more blow, one more harsh bit of reality?

When she found a parking spot, she pursed her lips and forced the air from her lungs. Justin had been reading Philippians, chapter four. That's what he told her. That meant he'd been focusing on the very thing she desperately needed if she was going to have the strength to leave her car, the strength to walk through the doors of the center.

Peace.

Please, God ... breathe Your peace into me now. I can't do this otherwise ...

With her very next heartbeat, she felt God's presence surround her. She could almost hear Him saying, *My daughter, ask and you shall receive.* His peace permeated her fear and sorrow, filling her with the promise of new life. One day the dark clouds of this time would lift, because morning always came. No matter how long and dark the night.

That was God's promise.

She braced herself and forced her feet from the car and on in through the front doors. Bo and Dexter were playing a hot game of ping-pong when she walked in. They must've sensed something different about her, something in her eyes or on her face, because the smile that flashed on Bo's face faded almost as soon as she took a step forward. He caught the little white ball in his hand and leaned his fists on the table. "Why you looking like that, pretty mama?"

Fear rang through every word, undermining the machismo he tried to put off. The others picked up on it, because they stepped away from the foosball table and the pop machine in the corner and drew close. Slowly, they gathered around Bo, their eyes on her.

She could feel God moving her forward, taking her closer to them. But all she could see was Bo taking his sweaty T-shirt off, wadding it up and throwing it on the ground that far-off summer day when Justin told them he was leaving. That, and the tears in the boy's eyes when he looked at Justin's picture in *Time* magazine. *Tell him we need him more ... tell him we need him more.*

Bo tucked the ball in his pocket and took quick steps around the table, his eyes never leaving hers. "Emily ..."

Her name sounded strange on his lips. He'd never called her that. Justin's girl, pretty girl, hot mama, yes. But not Emily. He came to her and put his hands on her shoulders. He searched her eyes, his lips slightly open. "Talk to me ... why you lookin' like that?"

Dexter came up, and then the guys who were planning to enlist, followed by the others. She covered Bo's hand with her own and shook her head. "He's dead, Bo. He's dead."

"*What?*" Bo swore under his breath and jerked away from her. "Don't *say* that stuff, girl. Don't say that about my homeboy."

This was what she was afraid of. That the emotions these kids had bottled up would explode in a burst of anger once they knew about Justin's death. She needed to be strong for them, but now—from nowhere—a wave of sorrow knocked her to her knees. She covered her face with her hands and began to weep.

Because Bo was right.

These guys needed Justin more than anyone in Iraq needed him. And now he was never coming back, never going to play another game of hoops with them again, never sit on the steps of the center and shoot the breeze about girls and school and the reason he believed in God.

She didn't dare look. Didn't open her eyes to see how the guys were reacting. She heard someone slam their fist on the table, and another boy kick a trash can. At least that's what it sounded like. And that's when she knew she had to look, because she was doing this for Justin. He wouldn't have run from the raw pain that filled the room.

He would've embraced it.

She opened her eyes and looked around. They'd all scattered. Bo stood, face to the wall, his hands behind his head. Softly, he hit his forehead against the brick again and again and again. She could hear him saying, "No way ... not my homeboy."

In the other corner, two guys had dropped to a pair of chairs, their heads all the way back, eyes focused on the ceiling. No tears, no anger, no emotion. Nothing. She shifted her attention. Dexter was gripping the trash can. He picked it up with both hands and slammed it against the cement floor. Other guys were responding like Bo, their faces to the brick wall, shutting out the world.

She knew where to start. She went to Bo, and when she was close enough, she put her hand on his shoulder. She had no idea how he would respond, whether he would spin around and shout at her or knock her hand off him and run from the building. *God ... the peace You've given me, give it to Bo. Let me show it to him. Please, God ...*

She dropped her voice so only he could hear her. "Bo?"

Slowly, she felt the tension leave his shoulder, and then the rest of his body. He turned around, and she saw that he'd skinned his forehead on the bricks. But that wasn't all. He was crying, weeping like a little boy who'd lost his best friend. Or the only dad figure he'd ever known. Anger twisted his features again, and he thumped his chest, ignoring the tears streaming down his face. "I *told* him not to go."

"I'm so sorry." She didn't give him a chance to push her away. He was a tall kid, almost a foot taller than her, but she didn't hesitate. She put her arms around his waist and embraced him.

At first she thought he might pull back, but then what was left of his hard exterior fell away. He hung his head on her shoulder and wept. "Why? Why him?"

Emily couldn't turn around and see how the others were handling this, the sight of their leader breaking down. But she didn't have to. She heard footsteps behind her, and first Dexter, then the two future enlistees, came up and put their arms around her and Bo. A minute passed and the others joined them, so that she was surrounded by a group of crying tough guys whose whole world had come undone in as much time as it took her to tell them Justin was dead.

When the crying subsided, when she was sure they were at least stable, she took a step back and pulled a handful of cards from her coat pocket. "The service is Saturday."

Bo took a card and fresh tears spilled from his eyes, angry tears. He shoved the piece of paper back at her, his words so many rocks. "I ain't got no car, pretty girl."

"Yeah. How we supposed to get there?" Dexter let his card hang limp in his hand.

Emily hadn't thought about that. She looked over her shoulder at the office. Through a window, she could see a man working there, but apparently he was only filling in — someone displaced from a desk job at the city. Not someone passionate about the kids. Never had she heard about him interacting with the teens. Justin had told her the guy was there more for security than anything else, at least until they could find a full-time counselor. Still, he was in charge. Maybe he would have an answer.

"Can you all be here that day, meet here three hours before the service? Say at about ten o'clock?" She hoped so. The idea that they wanted to come meant more than they could know. Further proof of Justin's impact on their lives.

The guys looked at each other and a few of them shrugged. "Yeah ... of course."

"Okay, just a minute." She hurried to the office door, knocked, and then entered before being asked. She explained the situation and asked if the man could provide a city van or a bus, some way for the kids to get to Justin's service.

The man behind the desk looked at her, his face blank. "For a funeral?" He set his pencil down and gave a sad laugh. He pointed out his office window at the kids huddled together near the ping-pong table. "Those kids see more death than you want to know about. Drug wars and gang fights. One more day, one more funeral." He shook his head. "I wish I could help, but my hands are tied. They cut the budget again this year. Cut the pay for counselors— which is why we can't get someone in here to work with the kids." He frowned. "No way I can get a van or a bus." He looked back at whatever he'd been working on. "Sorry 'bout that."

She ground her teeth together and stared at the man. That was it? No offer to make a phone call or see if there was money somewhere to help the guys? How did people get so calloused? And no wonder the teens looked forward to Justin's visits. At first she'd figured he was probably one of lots of volunteers, another great role model for the teens. But she was beginning to under-stand. He was probably the only role model they had. And now he was dead.

Without saying another word, she whipped around and shut the door behind her. The guys were watching, waiting for an an-swer. The sketchy hope in their eyes broke her heart. She locked eyes with Bo. "A van will be here at ten o'clock." She looked at each tear-stained face, one at a time. "For sure."

Before she left, she took one more risk. "Justin's death has left a lot of hurt behind. I wonder—" she held her hands out to either side—"I wonder if all of us could just take a minute and pray."

Dexter smiled, even though his eyes were swimming in tears. "Justin was always trying to get us to pray, man."

"Yeah." Another stepped forward and took Emily's hand. "Too bad it took this to make it happen."

With only the hint of reluctance, the others stepped forward. Bo took one hand, and the rest fell in and formed a circle. He squeezed her fingers. "Can I say it … can I try, I mean?"

Emily could almost picture Justin, somewhere in heaven, getting a front-row seat for this. She couldn't talk, so she did what she could. She squeezed Bo's fingers and nodded.

He closed his eyes and hung his head, and around the circle the others did the same thing. Emily kept her eyes open. She wanted to savor this, the way Justin would've done if he were here.

Bo cleared his throat. "Okay, God, so like … we're all here and we're really ticked off. Ticked don't even cut it." He sounded like he was talking through a clenched jaw. "I just have to ask if You'd please let people know what a good guy Justin was. He was our homeboy, and, I don't know." He sniffed. "Like a brother, I guess. I know he never shoulda gone, but he did. And now he's with You." His voice broke, and for a moment there was only the sound of his muffled sobs. "Take good care of him. Give him a hoops game like we used to play. With some good comp. And be with his girl. Because she's being strong for us guys, but inside I know her heart's breaking in half." Another sob stopped him, and he struggled to find control. "Heck, all our hearts is breaking in half."

He released Emily's hand and wiped his cheeks. Then he took hold of her fingers once more. "Thanks for helping him find his way here in the first place. None of us'll ever be the same. You know, gangstas and stuff. Justin wanted better for us than that." He paused, as if he wasn't sure how to end the prayer. "That's all. Amen."

Emily had attended church all her life. She'd grown up active in Sunday services and Sunday school and midweek Bible studies. In her twenty years she'd heard hundreds of beautiful, eloquent prayers.

But none had ever made her feel as close to God as this one.

The prayer of a grieving teenager whose first words to God came from a heart that was broken in half.

TWENTY-THREE

Lauren had never covered the sending-off of a dead soldier back to the States before. She'd seen the pictures, of course. Her magazine once ran a special about how bodies were lined up unceremoniously in the bellies of planes and brought back to the States in what amounted to covert operations. As if the commanding officers were trying to keep the picture of human loss from the public eye.

As she stood on the tarmac, with Justin's company lined up on either side of the walkway, she had no choice but to admit the obvious. If this was a typical send-off, they'd gotten that story wrong. The reason the military hadn't paraded reporters in for a closer look at flag-covered coffins wasn't because there was something to hide.

It was out of respect.

Every fallen soldier, every body that left the Middle East in the cargo compartment of a plane, in a box with a flag over the top, mattered deeply to the military. She could see that much simply by watching the proceedings taking place.

A color guard made the presentation of the flag, and every eye in the company was on the red, white, and blue. Then, when the flag had been properly presented, a group of Justin's closest friends carried the coffin to the far end of the aisle. On either side, soldiers moved in unison, their fingers lifting to their brows and staying that way. In a frozen salute.

Lauren studied them, the look in their eyes as they bid their comrade farewell. How could the United States be anything but

239

supportive of these young men? If they needed more supplies or more manpower, then someone better get on the ball and get it to them. She caught herself. If she meant that, then what about the comment she'd made to Scanlon?

An ache spread through her chest.

Why did everything about the war have to be so complicated? All along she'd thought it was either her way or Shane's. A person could either be for the war or against it. But now neither answer seemed right. The only thing she'd really decided was that every U.S. citizen should support the young men fighting for freedom in the Middle East.

Every single citizen.

And if even a single American felt disdain for soldiers because of a story she'd written, then shame on her.

The procession started to move, and Lauren could barely watch.

Joe Greenwald, Justin's bunk mate, held the front end of the coffin. Lauren had met him earlier, when she first arrived. Joe was a big teddy bear of a guy, but there was no denying the wetness on his cheeks. When the coffin had passed by, when the men had carried it up the stairs and into the plane, they went for the next one, and finally the third. Each body was going back to a different base, but the first leg of the journey started here.

Finally, Joe was given his release orders, papers stating that because of his injury, a gash in his head that had taken nearly thirty stitches, he wasn't required to return to Iraq. Lauren found out that this was Joe's second tour. Same as Justin. Now he would go back to the base and decide whether he wanted to enlist for another four years—make the military a career choice, the way Justin had decided to do.

Not until they were on the plane and the doors were shut, did Lauren take her seat next to Joe and say the words that had been building in her heart ever since she arrived at the base. She turned and studied the young man's face, the pain in his eyes. "I'm sorry, Joe. About Justin."

"Yeah." The soldier's lower lip quivered. "Me too."

"You and he were good friends?"

Joe nodded. He looked across to the window on the other side of the plane, and for a single instant, he glanced over his shoulder at the flag-draped casket a few feet away. "Best friend I ever had."

"I wish I'd known him better." She turned to face him. "You were with him that day, with all the Iraqi kids, weren't you?"

Joe managed the hint of a smile. "Which day?" He chuckled and soothed his finger and thumb along his brow. "Oh, that Justin. There were never enough hours."

"My daughter says he was like that at home too."

"The volunteer work." Joe shook his head. "If I wasn't his roomie, I would've thought he was an angel or something."

"Messy?" Lauren winced.

"The worst. Dirty shirts hanging from his bed, stuffed in the drawers." He shifted positions and looked straight ahead, seeing into the past. "I'd tell him, come on, man. Isn't it easier just to wash the clothes rather than work so hard to hide 'em?"

They were quiet for a while as the plane gathered altitude and settled in. Lauren wouldn't talk to him the whole time. He needed rest, no doubt. Time to think and grieve. But she wanted him to know her thoughts — in case he had any preconceived ideas. "My daughter, Emily ... she loved him very much."

"I know." He leaned back, his eyes distant. "He'd read me her emails. I'm not sure I can face her."

"She's hurting, but she's strong. She's had a lot of loss in her life already. Things that happened when she was just a baby, when her father and I were separated."

"Right." He looked straight ahead again. "Emily talked about some of that in her letters."

"Really?"

"All about you and her dad and stuff." Joe looked at her. "Justin was happy for you, Ms. Gibbs. He thought maybe God was changing you, softening you. Something like that."

"He has been." Lauren still didn't have all the answers, but her response was an honest one. "It started that day when I saw the two of you handing out bags and tossing a ball with those kids. I kept thinking, 'Why isn't that the picture I have in my head when I think about soldiers?'"

He gave a sad nod. "Lots of people have the wrong picture."

"My stories lately ... I hope they're helping some readers see things more clearly." She fell quiet. Then she remembered something Joe had said a few minutes ago. "What you said earlier, about facing Emily ... I'm not sure she knows you're coming. We never talked about it."

"Good." He made a tight line with his lips, and his eyes grew watery. "That'll give me more time to figure out what to say."

Lauren tilted her head. "What to say?"

Joe opened his mouth to speak, but no words came. He shaded his face with his hand and looked down at his lap. When he finally lifted his eyes, the pain there was so strong, she could feel it.

"Joe?" She didn't know if he needed a hug or a touch, but neither one seemed right.

"Justin ... he was lying there ... dying." He twisted his face up, fighting the tears, angry. "He made me promise to talk to her, to ... to be her friend." He swallowed hard. "Only ... how am I supposed to do that when every time I look at her, I'm going to see the other part of the picture?"

Again Lauren wasn't sure what he meant.

In light of her confused look, Joe reached down and pulled a red book from his bag. "This." He handed it to her. "Emily made him a scrapbook." His emotions took the upper hand for a few seconds. "Every night ... Justin would look at it. I mean every night. He musta showed it to me a dozen times, until finally I opted out."

Lauren looked at the book in her lap and stared at the picture on the front page. It had dirt smudges and worn areas. Joe wasn't exaggerating. Justin must've spent hours in the book for it to look this way.

"See?" He pointed to the photo on the front. "Every time I look at her, I'll just see the other half of the picture. Justin. Because he's supposed to be the one coming home to her."

Lauren tried to absorb it all. Her heart was heavy for the young man beside her. He'd been through so much in the last few days. Riding along beside his best friend, a routine trip across the city, and suddenly being cast into the street, his vehicle ripped apart, bodies lying all around. He'd knelt there and watched Justin's life drain away and then he'd made a promise. A promise he had no idea how to keep.

"Something else." Joe reached into his bag again and pulled out a smaller object, a photograph. He held it out so she could see it. "He had this thing laminated, crazy guy." He laughed, but it came out more like a sob. "Carried it with him in his boot. And wouldn't you know ... he was holding it when we hit the bomb." Joe pulled the photo closer and looked at it. "Had it in his hand the whole time he was dying, only ..." He hung his head, too distraught to speak.

This time Lauren didn't hold back. She took gentle hold of his arm, fighting the sadness in her own heart. The scene the young soldier was describing was gut wrenching, but more than that, it gave her a window to how much Justin Baker had loved Emily.

Joe's shoulders shook for a time, and then he exhaled hard and looked up. "Sorry. I think I'm getting past it and then ... I don't know." He looked dazed, his eyes numb. "So Justin was losing strength fast and ... I took the picture from him, held it up so he could see it." Joe looked at the photo once more. "It was the last thing he saw before he died." He brushed his knuckles rough and hard beneath his eyes. "Right after I promised to talk to her, to be her friend."

Lauren took the picture from Joe and studied it. The lamination had kept it intact, but even so, it was slightly bent and smudged. The single thing Justin had kept with him to give him hope about the future, about a time when he would be back in Tacoma, taking Emily on dates to Puget Sound and living the life of any other twenty-two-year-old kid.

But that was just it. She ran her thumb over the photo. Justin wasn't any other kid—or any other soldier. And nothing she could say would ease the pain of his loss. She returned the picture to Joe and settled back in her seat to look through the scrapbook.

In the brief year that she'd known her daughter, Emily had always seemed mature for her age. Almost more like the adult than either she or Shane or their parents. It was Emily who doggedly hunted down information about Lauren and Shane, determined never to give up until she found them. It was Emily standing strong beside the two of them in the hospital room when her grandpa—Lauren's father—was dying of cancer last December. Emily was a planner, an organizer, a peacemaker.

But she was a girl too. A girl so in love with Justin that she'd taken time to add paper flowers and cutout hearts to the pages of the scrapbook. And silly things, bits of jokes and memories that only the two of them could understand. *Just call me klutz*, near the picture of the two of them hiking, and *I'm not that simple*, and *Tell me about ever after*.

It all spoke of laughter and frivolity, the kind that was perfectly fitting for a girl her age. And now ...

Lauren breathed in hard through her nose. Now Joe would have to find a way to give the scrapbook back, and Emily ... all Emily would have to remind her of that beautiful summer with Justin Baker were a handful of photographs and paper memories.

Lauren gave the book back to Joe and turned toward the window.

The rest of the flight she said little. Every now and then she could feel Joe crying beside her, and she didn't want to intrude. Didn't want to turn and look at the casket either. For a while she actually slept, but as she did, she dreamed about Shane. The two of them running in the seventh-grade Olympics and she tripping over her shoelace and falling flat on her face.

She missed him so much, and even that made her feel bad. Because Shane was meeting up with Emily and Justin's family, and she'd see all of them at the end of the trip. In less than a day, she'd be safe in Shane Galanter's arms one more time.

But Emily would have no one.

That's when she remembered Joe. Poor, dear Joe sitting beside her. *God ... maybe You could help him keep the promise to Justin ... Please, let them find a friendship in each other.*

The flight continued and they made a change of planes in Germany. They slept most of the next leg, and in what felt like only a few hours, they were landing, and suddenly Lauren's stomach hurt. How could she face them? She'd been wrong to report the war as she had, that much was clear. Where the lines between right and wrong lay, she still wasn't sure. Maybe there wasn't a line.

But one thing was certain. What she'd seen in the past few months had changed her heart. Wonderful things — and terrible things too. But nothing was going to hurt as much as stepping off this plane and seeing the devastation in her daughter's eyes. Emily was so young. How could she even begin to survive the days ahead?

Slowly, a realization struck. For all that Emily was mature for her age, for all the ways she seemed more together than Lauren, losing Justin had probably brought her to her knees. Emily needed love and support and someone to hold her, someone to stroke her hair and convince her that somehow everything was going to be alright. Someone to hold her even if she needed to cry all day long. Yes, it was time for Lauren to be more than an item on her daughter's prayer list.

It was time for her to be a mother.

TWENTY-FOUR

Shane was dressed in uniform, his back straight as he stood between his daughter and his friend, Gary Baker. The rain had let up, but the air was damp and the sky over Tacoma was a lifeless gray. Shane had his arm around Emily, though neither of them spoke. Other than the rumble of planes landing and taking off, the only sound was the quiet muffle of tears.

Constant tears.

The return of a dead soldier was handled different ways. But in this case, they'd been given access to meet the plane on the tarmac. Justin's body would be carried from the plane to a waiting hearse while a color guard stood by. The transfer would be brief, after which time the hearse would take his body to the funeral home in Kelso, where it would stay until the funeral two days from now.

Shane watched the plane come into view, probably the one they were looking for. Right on time. He willed himself to stand strong, to stay strong. The people on either side of him needed his strength. But inside—in the place a soldier always kept but rarely showed—Shane had no idea how he was going to survive what was coming.

He kept his eyes on the plane, because that's what military men did when a fallen soldier returned home. But his mind drifted back to the moment when he first found out. He'd been at his desk, minutes away from observing a pilot on a testing mission, when the phone rang.

It was Gary, and for the first few seconds he said nothing. Finally, Carol took the phone. She sounded terrible, like she was fighting the flu. But somehow she managed to tell him the news. Justin was dead. One of the three soldiers killed in the most recent roadside bombing.

Death was part of life for the military. Shane had known that ever since he shied away from his father's push toward banking and business and instead enlisted in the navy. The Gulf War brought news like this, as had the wars in Afghanistan and Iraq. But no matter how often it happened, the news never came easily.

The phone call was short. Shane managed only to say he was sorry, and that he'd fly out in the morning, that he'd be there for them and take care of what they needed. When he hung up, he stood, shut his office door, and walked to the bank of windows behind his desk.

Of all the enemies a soldier faced, only one could ever truly threaten him: Futility. Soldiers were men of faith and family and conviction. They took the risks willingly, believing with every breath in the cause they defended. But futility could cut a soldier's legs out from under him, take away his purpose and his passion all at the same time.

Shane looked to the distant sky, the clear blue over the mountains of Fallon. That was the problem in Vietnam. Young men who signed up to defend their country wound up in a war without support from the government or the nation. Futility. That terrible sense of waking up in a war-torn village, looking around at the broken men and thinking of the missing men—and having just one question.

What's the point?

There had to be a purpose to military strength, and as long as Shane had been in the navy, he'd had one. Defending U.S. soil had never seemed more necessary than it had in the past decade.

Especially for fighter pilots. The ones who swept in and eliminated an enemy in a twelve-hour campaign, the ones who left news anchors shrugging their shoulders and reporting to Americans that all the fear and worry about the men on the front lines was for naught.

Sometimes, fighter pilots finished the job before the ground battle even got started.

That's the way it was with the Gulf War, and that's the way the United States citizens expected it to go with the wars in Afghanistan and Iraq. Quick and easy, a bombardment by U.S. fighter pilots, a dusting off of the hands, and everyone could notch another victory.

But the problem in the Middle East was more complicated than that. The enemy didn't wave a flag or stay in one place. They were insidious and cowardly, hiding in clusters and striking in ways that were almost impossible to stop. It was like trying to eliminate fire ants in Texas or Oklahoma. They went underground, and when they surfaced—with a roadside bomb or a suicide attack—it was too late.

Even so, the war in Iraq did have a purpose, and with purpose came passion. The passion he took to work with him every day. The passion Justin Baker lived by.

But that day, standing there with trembling knees trying to absorb the news, looking out onto the airfield at the naval training academy, Shane pictured Justin—the photograph in *Time* magazine of the young soldier playing with the Iraqi children, pictured him playing hoops with the guys at the teen center and holding his daughter's hand. Justin was everything good about the U.S. military, and now he was gone. And in that moment, Shane felt futility like he'd never felt before.

What *was* the point? Maybe Lauren had been right all along. They were spending millions of dollars and losing lives every day, and for what? If so many Iraqi people were still bent on fighting

249

against freedom, then fine. Let them live in their mess, and let's get the American boys home. Safe where they belonged. So that not another Justin Baker would ever return to his family and loved ones in a coffin.

And so he stood there, futility breathing its ugly, putrid breath down the back of his neck. During the Gulf War, Shane was in terrible firefights, times when he and his wingman barely made it out alive. He'd taken part in wicked combat, dodging tracer missiles and ground-to-air rockets. But no battle ever felt more fierce than the one he fought in that moment.

The one taking place inside him.

Lord ... He hung his head, the claws of futility sharp around his neck. *Give me my purpose back. Give me a reason to wear this uniform, please ... Everything I've done, everything Justin fought for, it can't all be for nothing, can it?*

Then — slowly at first, but then fast like a music video — images ran through his mind. God's people fighting for righteousness time and time and time again. Joshua and the battle of Jericho, Moses leading his people from captivity in Egypt, David and Goliath ... Every time men took a stand for what was right, God had given them the strength to prevail.

He stood straighter, held his head higher.

It was wrong to hijack a plane and fly it into a building full of people. Wrong for any possible reason. It was wrong to strap on explosives and walk into a crowd of people, and wrong to plant roadside bombs along the streets of Baghdad in a cowardly attempt at killing U.S. soldiers.

The war against Iraq wasn't a battle of wills, wasn't a matter of differing opinions. It was the United States stepping up to the plate and taking on a form of evil that threatened to destroy anything in its way. He felt God's presence around him, inside him, and futility slouched its way to the corner of his office.

There was a purpose in what they were doing. If the United States didn't take action against countries of terror, the whole world would pay the price. And if along the way it cost the life of someone good and golden, someone like Justin Baker, then the fight would become all the more dear, all the more full of purpose.

Because the cost was so high.

Shane felt the victory that day, minutes after Gary's phone call, felt all sense of futility leave him and his office and the job all of them were doing on behalf of the United States. He drew in a full breath and pushed his shoulders back. He would wear his uniform proudly, standing strong for the Bakers and his daughter, and for everyone who would attend the funeral. Everyone who would feel the loss of the young soldier.

He would be strong, but he would carry Justin's loss with him until the day he died. Because in Justin's loss, there was purpose all by itself. To accomplish what the boy had set out to accomplish. Victory and freedom and a world without terror.

Shane blinked, and the memory of that day faded. The jet plane came to a stop a safe distance away, and airport security officers motioned for the small group to come forward. He was right; it was the plane they were waiting for.

"Dad ..." Emily clutched his arm. "I can't do this ..."

He braced her, held her up and pressed her to his side. "We'll do it together."

Gary and Carol huddled around their daughter Jill, the three of them taking slow steps toward the place where the hearse had pulled up and the color guard now stood. Justin's family reached their places, and Shane and Emily stood beside them. After a minute, the door to the plane opened. For what felt like an eternity, there was no movement.

Then, a lone figure appeared near the door, and then a second. Both were soldiers, and they exited the plane holding the front end of a coffin. The soldiers saluted the color guard, the flag, and then moved the coffin through the door and onto the plank.

Tears poured down Emily's cheeks and her body shook, racked by sobs. She didn't cry out or wail, but in her whimpers Shane could hear what she was saying. "Justin … No, God … not Justin."

The loudest one in their midst was Jill Baker. She was a senior that year and busy at school. Gary had told Shane that Jill had deep regrets for not taking time to drive up to Fort Lewis more often. For not making a habit that year of sharing lunch or a conversation with Justin.

"My brother!" She wailed and held out her hand toward the coffin. "Just one more day, God … why can't I have one more day?"

Shane fought tears, stiffening his back until he saw the person trailing the coffin, holding up the far right corner.

Lauren, his only love, her eyes downcast.

Everything about her looked different. She was broken. He could see it in the way she held herself, the way she hung her head. And even from where he stood, Shane could see that she was weeping.

His eyes clouded over and he tightened his hold on Emily. Somehow in that moment, he knew Lauren truly had changed. It wasn't just the way she'd been reporting on the war lately. The change must have been in her heart—and he had the strongest sense that sometime that week he would know his prayers had been answered.

Lauren lifted her head and looked around, and then their eyes met. She hesitated, but only for an instant. Her cheeks were red and tear stained, but she focused on the task ahead, staying with the coffin, walking behind it. When the procession was halfway to the hearse, the soldiers stopped. The color guard approached the casket, performed a salute, and then retreated to a spot near the hearse again.

Shane could almost feel Emily straining against his arm, wanting to break free and go to him, to the young soldier she loved. But that wasn't protocol, and Emily knew it. Instead she pressed her head against Shane's shoulder, and between low sobs she whispered, "This ... this wasn't how it was supposed to be."

Shane turned his focus to the coffin, to the flag draped across the top. If futility was going to have something else to say, this would be the moment. The moment when reality stood before him, looming as large as the pine box. Instead Shane felt his heart swell with pride. The red, white, and blue had been what prompted a kid like Justin Baker to enlist in the first place. Shane had heard the stories from his buddy, knew about the patriotism that ran deep in Justin from the time he was a young boy.

And Justin was right to believe in the meaning of the flag, same as Shane was right and every American who held pride for the red, white, and blue was right. Because with all its flaws and differing opinions, the United States really was the greatest country on earth — the birthplace of freedom.

The flag would always evoke a sense of purpose and passion and pride in Shane, whether it was flown in front of a school or government building, waved at a high school football game, tattered in battle, or planted on a heap of rubble where once a towering office building stood.

Or whether it was draped across a coffin.

He watched as they reached the hearse, and Shane noticed that one of the soldiers, the one at the front right corner of the casket, was crying. A big guy with a bandaged forehead. Then Shane remembered. Gary had said something about a kid named Joe, a soldier who had been Justin's best friend, a guy who had been riding with him and survived the bombing.

The soldier at the front of the casket had to be Joe.

When they slid the coffin into the hearse, the color guard retired the flag and the hearse pulled away. Beside him, Emily's sobs shook her body, and finally, when she could no longer see the funeral car, she turned and buried her face against his chest. Shane stroked her back and watched as Lauren and Joe said something to the other three soldiers. The three nodded, shook hands with Joe, and headed for a waiting car.

Lauren and the wounded soldier walked slowly, reverently toward Shane and the others.

As he watched her, he felt a surge in his heart. The body in the coffin could just as easily have been hers, she'd been in that much danger. He wanted to run to her, take her in his arms, and breathe in the nearness of her, the reality of her. She was here, and she was home!

But Emily needed him, so he waited. Lauren came closer and her eyes held his. When she reached them, she put her hand on Emily's shoulder. "Honey ..."

Emily eased away from him and turned around. For a few seconds she looked at her mother, her eyes flooded with tears. A mix of emotions played on her face, and Shane understood. There was hurt and grief and even a little anger. Maybe because of the way Lauren had viewed the war last time they were all together.

Whatever her hesitation, it fell away and she melted into Lauren's arms. "Mom ..."

Shane folded his arms, his feet shoulder-width apart, the stance of a soldier. But he couldn't tear his eyes off them, mother and daughter, grieving together. He had been there for Emily, no doubt. After she'd broken the news to the people in Tacoma, they'd had almost a full day to talk about Justin and for her to cry in his arms.

But she needed her mother.

After a long time, Lauren released Emily and put her hand on the shoulder of the soldier, the boy standing awkwardly a few feet away. "Emily ... this is Joe Greenwald."

Apparently no other introduction was needed. Emily's face twisted in a fresh wave of grief, and she moved from Lauren's embrace into the wounded soldier's open arms. "He … he loved you, Joe."

Joe squeezed his eyes shut, and his body shook. Before he released her, he said, "He loved you too."

Gary and Carol and Jill came closer, moving as one unit. "Let's go back to the house." Gary looked shaken, but there was a strength in him that couldn't be denied. The retired soldier, the police officer. He would draw his strength from God, even as his family drew their strength from him.

Shane turned to Lauren and Emily, and only then did Lauren reach out to him. With one arm still securely around their daughter, she drew him close, and in her eyes Shane saw what he hadn't seen since they reunited a year ago.

Faith and love and forever, and something else.

Common ground.

Twenty-Five

E mily borrowed the twelve-passenger van from her soccer coach. It wasn't registered to the school, but rather to the team, so there was no legal reason why she couldn't drive it. At nine-thirty that morning, under skies that had cleared overnight to a surreal blue, she drove the van onto the freeway and headed north, toward the teen center.

Strange how the planning and preparations for this day felt something like a wedding. The wedding she and Justin would never have. There was the church and the white roses and the special music and the close friends and family who would share from the pulpit. People would wear nice dresses and dark suits, and afterward there would be a reception in the church hall. There was a guest book and even several hundred printed programs, small booklets that had kept Justin's mother and her working late into the night, folding and stapling each one.

Everything but Justin.

The memory of the casket, of the soldiers carrying his body down the ramp, and of Joe — straight and stoic, tears coursing down his face — would never leave her. She couldn't go five minutes without seeing it play again in her mind. From the moment Justin picked her up that day at her residence hall and told her the news — that he had a deployment date — she'd pictured his homecoming.

Pictured, as clear as day, flags and confetti and people cheering. And Justin — back straight and proud, walking off a plane and into her arms.

That was the homecoming he should have had. Not this.

Never this.

She checked her features in the rearview mirror. Her eyes had been dry all day so far, but fear ran in the small lines near the corners of her eyes. From the moment she climbed out of the guest-room bed in the Bakers' house until now, every minute, every step, every heartbeat took her closer to one o'clock. The hour Justin's funeral would begin.

The drive north from Kelso had been filled with song. She'd made several CDs in the days since hearing about Justin. One was all praise music — songs like "I Still Believe" and "Walk by Faith," by Jeremy Camp; and "Dare You to Move" by Switchfoot. On it she had written in permanent ink just one word: "Help." Because singing to God, praising Him in the midst of this, her darkest hour, was sometimes the only way she could get through.

Last night, after the funeral programs were made and stacked in a box, she lay in bed reading her Bible. She read 2 Chronicles, chapter 20 — the scene where God's people had come under attack. In it the Lord promised that He would fight the battle. But not until the people joined hearts and voices in praise to Him did victory come.

And so she sang.

Another CD held songs that were special to her and Justin, and songs about losing someone. She played it when the only way to let the sadness out was to weep. Today, when she still had so much ahead of her, she didn't dare play that one.

Now she was minutes from the teen center. The guys didn't know she was coming to get them, and from their reactions the day she told them the news, they probably thought she'd arranged some sort of public transportation. And at the time, Emily wasn't sure how she was going to pull this off. Just that she was.

Because God would make sure those kids had a way to Justin's funeral.

The minutes passed, and she reached the center exactly at ten. She took a parking spot on the street adjacent to the small building, and that's when she saw them. Emily uttered a small gasp. The scene waiting for her brought with it the first tears of the day. Clustered just outside the front door of the center were the boys, the tough teenagers, who but for Justin, might've been running with a gang that day. Bo and Dexter and the rest, all dressed in what had to be their nicest clothes. Baggy belted jeans and dress shirts, their hair neatly combed. They looked sad and scared and out of sorts, their hands deep in their pockets.

Before they had time to notice that she was driving the van, and that the van was for them, something caught her eye. One of the boys who had been missing from the group darted out of a secondhand store with a bag in his hand. As he reached the others, he pulled a buttoned-down from the bag, jerked off his T-shirt, and slipped into the new shirt.

Emily bit her lip. So that was it. The boys—most of them anyway—must've scraped together a few dollars and gone to the secondhand store. So they would look appropriate at Justin's service. She pressed her fingers to her eyes. "No. No crying. Not now."

Bo noticed her then. He led the others, sulking closer, his eyes confused, suspicious. She rolled down the window that separated them, and he pointed to the van. "What'd you do? Steal it?"

"No." She laughed, and the release felt wonderful. "Crazy kid, get in before I leave without you."

They piled in, admiring the van's paint job and the upholstery on the inside. She could imagine that in normal circumstances, a car trip with these boys might be a bit wild. They'd ask for loud rap music and wave at pretty girls along the way. But not this time.

Each of them found a seat, and what little conversation there was died down before she hit the freeway. She played her "Help" CD and the guys were quiet the rest of the way. Along the drive,

Emily wondered if any of them had even been out of the city. They were a mixed group, some black, some Hispanic, some white — but all of them had that tough inner-city look, and all of them were bound to feel out of place in a small town like Kelso.

But they'd come anyway. They'd come in their secondhand dress shirts, trusting that somehow a ride would show up for them at ten o'clock. All for the love of Justin. Emily tried not to dwell on it. Otherwise, her eyes would be swollen shut before the funeral.

The church the Bakers attended was on the south side of town, and Cowlitz View Memorial Gardens, on the north. She reached the church just after twelve noon, and already a crowd of people stood outside, waiting for the doors to open. Emily parked the van and stared wide-eyed at the people gathered there.

They were all ages, older couples and young children, families and groups of high school kids. Many of them held flags, and some held signs. *Justin, We'll Miss You!* and *Stay Strong America* and *Justin Believed in the U.S.A.*

Emily blinked back tears.

"Wow." Bo's voice held a level of awe that hadn't been there before. "Looks like he was their homeboy too."

Uniforms dotted the crowd, some worn by white-haired men and others by young Boy Scouts. That's when she saw them. A group of uniformed Veterans near the back of the crowd, one of them in a wheelchair with a jacket that wasn't quite straight on his shoulders.

They'd come. The Veterans Justin had befriended had traveled south for his service. Emily caught two tears and brushed them off her cheeks. Not yet, she couldn't cry yet. She turned around and sized up her group of teens. "We're early."

Dexter pointed at the crowd. "Or not."

"We are." She nodded. "I want you to follow me. We'll go in through the back, and you can find seats."

"The front row." Bo lifted his chin. "I wanna be in the front row." His chin shook a little. "As close as I can be."

"Well …" Emily wanted to hug him. She held her breath and tried to find her voice. "The … the first row is usually for family."

Bo plucked at his shirt and nodded at his friends. "*We're* family." His face twisted and it looked like he might cry. "Look—" he sat up straighter, his eyes flashing anger. "I ain't never met my dad, and my mama's in prison. When I was eight I tried to knock off a liquor store jus' so I could be with her." He clenched his jaw. "My grandma died when I was ten, and my aunt … she's gonna kick me out when I turn eighteen." The anger left as quickly as it had come, and something in his eyes made him look like the child he still was. He pressed his lips together. "Justin's all the family I got."

"Bo …" The heartbreak all around her was more than she could take. "You can sit where you want. Whatever you think's best."

Dexter looked from Bo to her, and back again. "What she means is, the first row's for his mom and dad and stuff." He gave Emily a sad but understanding smile. "I get it."

"Fine." Bo wasn't backing down. "Second row, then."

They filed out of the van, an unlikely procession, and went around the crowd to the back of the church. Bo led the way, but he stopped when they walked inside. The casket was already there, positioned at the front of the church, the flag draped over it like before.

Emily knew it would be there, but the teens …

Bo shook his head and buried his face in the crook of his arm. He stifled a sob while the others stood behind him, not sure what to do next. Those with baseball caps removed them, and after a while, Bo lowered his arm. He looked at the casket. "Man … why'd you have to get yourself killed? I told you we needed you more."

He walked down the aisle, his eyes never leaving the coffin. When he reached the second row, he kept walking. Emily followed behind with the others, glad they were early. She was a little worried about what Bo might do next. But Justin would've wanted the guys to have this time, this chance to express their feelings.

Bo reached the casket, stopped, and crossed himself. Then he took a tightly folded piece of lined notebook paper from his pocket, and put it on the casket. He kept his hand there, leaning on the coffin, and he hung his head. "I shoulda been there too, man. I shoulda had your back, the way you always ... always had mine."

Dexter joined him, and then, one at a time, the others did the same. They surrounded the casket, placing their hands on the flag and uttering quiet, heartbreaking good-byes. After several minutes, Bo left the note, took a step back, and saluted. He didn't use two fingers, he used all five, and it wasn't the crisp military salute that would mark the rest of the day. But it was the one Emily would remember long after the service was over.

Bo moved into the second row, first spot near the aisle, and the others filled up the seats beside him. They were set, so Emily excused herself—and that's when she saw the lone soldier on the other side of the church, sitting in the back, his hat in his hands.

Joe Greenwald.

Emily steadied herself and headed in his direction. When she reached the pew where he was sitting, she took the seat next to him. "How you doing?"

"Not so good." His eyes were bloodshot, and he looked dazed, as if he hadn't quite figured out how a few days ago he and Justin were teasing each other about dirty clothes stuck beneath the bed and now he was at a church in Kelso about to tell him good-bye.

Emily covered his hand with her own. "At Justin's parents' house ... the other night. You said you needed to talk to me?"

"Yes." He opened his mouth but no words came out, and he made an exasperated sound as he hung his head.

She wouldn't push him, not now. Joe had been with Justin when the bomb went off, he had knelt by him in his final moments. When the time was right, she wanted to hear the details, what Justin had said, his last thoughts. She patted Joe's hand and eased back. "Maybe later, okay?"

"Okay." He didn't look up, didn't make eye contact.

She stood quietly, giving him his space, and went to find her parents and the Bakers. After a round of hugs and quiet words, she opened the church doors so the crowd could file in. Then she worked her way through the people until she reached the old Veterans.

She bent down and gave the white-haired man in the wheelchair a hug. "Sir ... Justin would've been honored that you came."

The man sat tall and straight in his chair. "We would've driven all day to be here." He straightened his jacket. "We loved that boy."

"Yes." Emily nodded. "Me too."

She stayed with the group of Vets, and by the time they were inside, the church was almost full. A military contingency in dress uniform filled the front of the church, standing guard near the casket and on both sides of the pulpit area. Joe Greenwald was one of them.

For a single moment, Emily stopped. Until she blinked, until she took a closer look, any one of the soldiers might've been Justin. And she realized he would have been standing there if the fallen soldier had been someone else. An ache greater than she'd ever known filled her heart. The soldiers up front were so real, so alive. If only she could've had one more chance to be with Justin, even just in the same room the way she was in the same room with these soldiers. To hug him and hold him and hear his voice close beside her.

Just one more time.

That's when Emily saw what was happening. People were placing things near the casket. Everyone seemed to have something for Justin, a card or a letter, a flower or a teddy bear. Joining Bo's simple folded note now were so many items, it was impossible to see the flag.

Emily hurried to find Justin's mother, and the two of them found a stack of wicker baskets in one of the church closets. They returned to the sanctuary and set them on the floor around the casket. Then, carefully, they placed every item into one of the baskets.

"Thank you." Carol took her hand as they finished the job. "I want to take these home."

Just then a group of parents entered the church with thirty-some schoolkids between them. The children all wore shirts that said Elmwood Elementary. The school where Justin volunteered his time talking to the students. Emily whispered an explanation to Justin's mother, and then together they went to meet them.

"I'm Emily. I spoke with your principal." She shook the adults' hands.

One of the men stepped forward. In his arms was a box. "The kids made cards and letters for Justin a few weeks ago." The man wasn't crying, but his eyes were damp. "We were getting a package together to send him for Christmas. The kids ... the kids collected twenty-three pounds of Jelly Bellies for him and his buddies." He held it out. "Is there some place we can put it?"

Justin's mother covered her mouth, too shocked to speak. Emily slipped her arm around the woman, hugged her, and then motioned for the man to follow them. The box was placed next to the last of the baskets. Emily looked inside it. Dozens and dozens of letters and cards and Jelly Bellies.

Further proof of the lives Justin had touched.

That's the way it went as the church filled and overflowed out into the courtyard, everyone coming with a different gift, a different reason why Justin had mattered in his or her life. There was a group of Kelso football players, guys who knew about Justin and planned to be career military men because of him, and a cluster of teachers who had taught Justin when he was in high school.

Neighbors and church members and a hundred soldiers from Fort Lewis. One of the last people to file in was Vonda. She wore a dress and held an embroidered handkerchief. Emily went to her and the two embraced.

Vonda didn't hold back her tears any more than she had held back her opinions. She looked at Emily straight on. "That boy was crazy in love the moment he laid eyes on you."

Emily couldn't fight off the tears another moment. They came like constant reminders of all she had lost, all she would never have again. "I know."

"Now don't go tellin' yourself that things didn't work out." Vonda's tone was strained, her words hard to understand through her muffled weeping. "They worked out, you hear? Because one day with a boy like Justin Baker woulda been worth all this sadness." She took two quick breaths. "Mr. Smooth Talker."

Emily couldn't speak, so she nodded, never breaking eye contact with Vonda.

Her voice fell to a painful whisper. "He was gonna run the place, remember?"

"I know." She held onto the woman again. "I know."

Vonda touched her handkerchief to her eyes and gave a single shake of her head. "I'm gonna miss that boy something fierce."

"Me too."

Vonda turned away and found her seat, and just like that it was time for the service to begin. Emily took her place in the front row between her parents; on the other side of the aisle, the Bakers huddled together. Only then did Emily realize that her grandparents were there also. All three of them. Emily gave each of them a sad smile and then turned her attention to the front of the church.

The service passed in a blur. Most of the time Emily couldn't take her eyes off the coffin and the large portrait of Justin his father had set there. The eyes, the smile, the charisma coming from the picture almost made it feel like Justin was there, looking over all of them, urging them to believe that he was fine, happy and whole and anxious to see them again one day.

A pianist started the ceremony by playing and singing a song from MercyMe, "I Can Only Imagine." The song moved the entire room, and by the time it was over, after the final refrain built to the place of wondering whether upon his death a person would fall to his knees or dance before Jesus, everyone was weeping.

Now it was time for sharing. The first person to speak was Joe Greenwald.

Emily had heard him and Justin's dad talking about the funeral the other night at the Bakers' house, but she wasn't sure if Joe was actually going to get up. The way he'd looked before the service, she was pretty sure he'd declined. But now, walking stiffly in his uniform, Joe moved up the few stairs and took his place behind the podium.

"I'm Lieutenant Joe Greenwald." He leaned into the microphone, and a squawk sounded from the PA system. He eased back, his discomfort as plain as his army dress greens. He pulled a piece of paper from his pocket, unfolded it, and looked at it. Ten painful seconds passed, and then he exhaled hard and slid the paper back into his pocket.

He looked at the crowd, and his eyes welled up. "I'm here for Justin." He blinked twice and steadied himself. "He ... he asked me to tell you something."

Emily's heart went out to the guy, the one Justin had considered a comrade and brother, a believer and friend. He seemed quieter than Justin, but the compassion in his expression, the honesty in his eyes, was hauntingly familiar. No question the two shared a kindred spirit. Emily closed her eyes for a brief moment. *God, give him the words. Hold him up the way You've been holding me.*

Joe swallowed hard. "He wanted to be in Iraq; he believed in what we're doing over there — no matter how complicated."

Silently Emily cheered on Justin's friend. He was standing straighter now, conviction taking over where fear and sadness had reigned only an instant ago.

"He didn't want to die." Pride rang in his voice. He pressed his lips hard together, struggling. "He didn't want anyone to die. But he believed that ... that all men have the right to be free. To live without fear." He gripped the podium and took a half step back, hanging his head, overcome for the moment. When he looked up, there were tears on his cheeks. "I love Justin. And I know you love him too. There is ... no way to measure his loss."

Emily rested her head on her dad's shoulder and took a tissue from her mother. She pressed it against one cheek and then the other, her eyes never leaving the gripping scene playing out at the front of the church.

Joe inhaled and seemed to hold his breath. He looked slowly at every one of the Fort Lewis soldiers standing at attention around the front of the room. "He told me to tell you to win this thing!" He nodded at one group of soldiers and then the other. "Win this thing for Justin Baker."

One soldier in the middle, a clean-cut black guy, slowly brought his right hand to his brow, and with an intensity that matched the tears in his eyes, he saluted Joe. And all around him, down the line on either side, the other soldiers did the same. Ignoring his wet cheeks or the way his eyes filled with fresh sorrow, Joe returned the salute.

Emily could feel something happening behind her. She turned and looked, and around the room, first one soldier, then two more, then dozens from each side of the church, stood and saluted Joe in silent compliance with Justin's dying request. And before Emily could absorb the show of support, others began to stand — retired military and current military, no doubt.

Then from a row near the back, Justin's Veteran friends stood. It took them longer. Three used their canes for support, one had a walker. The white-haired man in the crooked jacket sat a little straighter in his wheelchair, and each of them also saluted.

Joe held his salute, his mouth tight, stoic in the face of the dramatic show of support. Finally, he raised his hand toward the heavens and said, "They heard you, buddy. They heard you." Then he leaned toward the microphone and gave a last look at the crowd. "Thank you."

Emily wasn't sure who made the first move. It was quiet at first, and then it built in intensity. Applause from people in the room. Again Emily turned around. First on his feet was Bo, and with a look, the other teens joined him. Then, all over the church, people rose from their seats, hands clapping. Not the way they'd applaud if this gathering were to welcome home the troops, but loud and long in a show of support that couldn't have been stronger.

Across the aisle, Emily caught a look at the Bakers. Justin's parents sat on either side of Jill. All three clung to each other, weeping, clearly touched by the outpouring. Justin's dad stood, turned, and gave a single wave to each side of the congregation, silently thanking them for caring, for understanding the sacrifice their son had made on behalf of his country.

On behalf of them.

Joe joined the applause, and when after a minute it died down, he returned to his place in line with the other soldiers.

After that, Pastor Kirby did most of the talking. Speaking with a smile and a sparkle in his eyes, he told about a freckle-faced kid who one time brought a water gun to Sunday school along with a wadded up pair of socks. Quiet laughter sounded around the church.

"You see—" the pastor motioned toward the mourners—-"those of you who knew Justin best are nodding." More laughter. "And some of you probably know the story. Mrs. Ellis, the Sunday school teacher, pulled him aside and asked him what he'd brought." The pastor paused, his eyes smiling. "'A gun and a hand grenade,' Justin told her."

The pastor raised his brow, and a few more ripples of laughter came from the congregation. "'Why in the world would you need a gun and a hand grenade at Sunday school?' Mrs. Ellis asked. Well, you know that way Justin had of grinning and making you forget he'd done anything wrong? That's what he did. Just grinned at Mrs. Ellis and said, 'If the bad guys attack our class, I'll keep it safe.'"

Emily hadn't heard the story before. There were more. Stories from Justin's days as a Boy Scout, and how he'd earned his Eagle award a year ahead of schedule. "It wasn't that long ago we gathered right here in this building as Justin accepted his Eagle badge—something only a few young men ever accomplish."

Surprise filled Emily's heart, and she looked across the aisle at Justin's parents. She had known he was a Scout, but an Eagle Scout? He hadn't told her, same way he hadn't told her at first about his volunteer work.

Pastor Kirby was going on. "Justin stood right here—" he pointed to the spot next to the pulpit—"and promised to uphold the Scouting tradition, to be a person of principle and integrity and virtue." He gave a confident nod. "Justin was that young man everywhere he went, right until his very last moments."

As the pastor finished talking about Justin, he commented on the lives Justin had touched. "I'll bet we could spend a week in this room, letting each of you come up and tell what Justin meant to you."

Emily glanced across the aisle to the second row. Bo and Dexter were nodding.

"And so we must do the thing Justin would want us to do. We look to the flag and believe in its worth." A few "amens" rose up from the crowd. "And we must look to the cross, to the ultimate sacrifice, the true source of our hope. Where Justin's hope came from." Pastor Kirby smiled, but he hesitated. His face twisted up just enough for all of them to know. He too was struggling that day. "He would not want us to walk away from this room weeping and mourning. There is a time for that, yes." He sniffed. "But today Justin would want us to walk away celebrating his life, happy for all that he brought to us, and he would want us to be determined. Determined to live our lives the way he lived. With passion and purpose, with his eyes on the flag, and his arms outstretched to the cross."

Pride filled Emily's heart, and she linked hands with her parents. Justin was everything people said about him. And none of them—none of them—would ever be the same now that he was gone. But the pastor was right. Justin's was a life worth celebrating. And in that instant, Emily made a decision. She would cry when the tears came, and she would mourn. But she would not rest there, not stay there. Justin would not have wanted her to live in a dark place, grieving the days his death had taken from her. He would've wanted her to smile at his memory. Celebrating every single day they'd been given.

She had lost much, so much. But with Justin, she could never look at his loss without also looking at the incredible gift she'd been given, the gift of knowing him, of loving him.

No matter how short the time.

TWENTY-SIX

L auren survived most of the service with only a few tears. Not that she wasn't grieving Justin's loss same as everyone else. But her heart and mind and soul couldn't seem to land on the same page. Every moment of the memorial was a reminder that Justin was no longer with them, that the nation had lost someone golden, one of its very best.

And for what?

She had seen the good things American soldiers were doing, and for the most part she'd come to trust the military public information office press releases—whereas before she'd disregarded them out-of-hand. Despite warring ethnic groups and the threat of civil war throughout Iraq, she'd also seen the desperate desire on the part of most of the people for freedom without violence, the need for democracy for themselves and their children.

In addition, she'd been privy in recent months to details of terrorist plans that truly would've made the events of September 11 seem small in comparison. The war efforts in the Middle East and the covert operations taking place on U.S. soil had prevented those, no doubt.

But was anything worth losing a young man like Justin? Could America really support a war where thousands of soldiers had lost their lives? She was just one reporter, after all. Without support from the media and the masses, the war in Iraq really might be pointless, right?

And everything she read—even from reporters she knew well and trusted—said that support for the war was at an all-time low. So where did that leave guys like Justin? Lauren wasn't sure, but she couldn't clear her head of the thoughts, couldn't feel quite right about any part of the funeral service.

The only certainty was the sadness, because it filled every heart, every pair of eyes in the room. None of them, of course, sadder than her precious daughter's. Emily had wept through the service, taking a fresh tissue every few minutes. Lauren felt a mix of heartbreak and protection, responsibility and sacrifice as she and Shane sheltered their daughter, feeling the way the sobs shook her slim frame.

What if Emily hadn't found Shane and her? How could she have gotten through this morning without them? She would've had her grandmother, of course. Lauren's mother. But still, Lauren found herself thanking God throughout the memorial, grateful that though she'd missed Emily's first steps and first smile, first words and first day at kindergarten, she was here for this: to hold her up as she walked through a season of grief that would no doubt change her forever. Emily would always have a special relationship with her grandma. But here, on a day when she was being forced to say good-bye to the only boy she'd ever loved, she needed her mom and dad.

When the service was over, Gary Baker asked them to be second in line in the motorcade procession to the cemetery. When they filed out of the church, Emily looked at Shane and then at her. "Let's get to the car, okay?"

Lauren understood. With all the emotion of the afternoon so far, she didn't want to talk to mourners, not yet. She wanted to take her place in the procession — the hearse, the Bakers, and then the three of them. As close to Justin's body as possible. Behind their car, Joe Greenwald had agreed to drive the van with the teens from the center.

"We're family," Bo had said. "We go after you."

There were no arguments.

Shane took Lauren's hand and led the way. She melted a little more each time he looked back at her and Emily. Shane Galanter, who knew her better than anyone and loved her anyway. The love in his eyes was something no other man had ever shown her, even after she'd left him again. He would've laid down his life for her, he loved her that much. A love she had spent a lifetime searching for. A love that would resonate in her heart as long as she lived.

But would he want her now? After all the grief she'd caused him?

Lauren held Emily's hand as they followed Shane through the milling crowd. This wasn't the time to think about Shane. That would come later.

They were driving a rental SUV, and the three of them climbed in, Lauren in the passenger seat and Emily in the back. As soon as they were situated, Shane reached over and wove his fingers between hers. The feeling reminded Lauren that she was still alive. They both were. She breathed in and felt new life stir inside her soul. After this dark day — if God would give them a miracle — they might finally find the life together they'd always dreamed of sharing.

Shane pulled up behind the Bakers' car, and in the side mirror, Lauren watched Joe steer the van into place, and after that, a convoy of military vehicles fell in behind them. Lauren wasn't sure what to say, and she decided on nothing. The moment seemed to demand quiet — a deep, honoring silence. She stared out the window and replayed yesterday evening, the hours they spent at the Bakers' house.

Carol had brought out Justin's keepsake book from his first tour in Iraq. "I think I'll set it up at the service. In the back." She angled her head and studied the book in her hands, then held it out toward Lauren. "Here. Emily's already seen it."

Panic tried to bury her, but Lauren resisted. Looking at the book would remind her of the cost of war, but it would also remind her that in some ways she'd contributed to that cost.

She took the keepsake book from Carol Baker and drew a slow breath. Then she took the book to the Bakers' sofa. Carol followed and sat on one side, Emily on the other.

The cover was adorned with fancy stick-on letters spelling out *Lieutenant Justin Baker — One Soldier's Journey*.

Lauren studied Justin's picture, his striking face and the grin that lit up his eyes. But all she could see was the young soldier playing catch with Iraqi children in an empty lot fifty yards down the street from a mob of protestors. A young soldier whose love and care for those kids had stopped her cold.

"He always wanted to be a soldier." Carol leaned in so she could see the pages better. "I remember," her eyes grew distant, "he was seven years old, and once in a while he'd still wake up frightened in the middle of the night. He was such a sweet little guy." The corners of her lips came up in a sad smile. "Anyway, one night we woke up with him in the middle, and as he opened his eyes, fresh from sleep, he looked at me and said, 'I had a dream, Mommy.'" She looked at her son's photo again. "I asked him what he dreamt about and he said, 'I got to try out for the army.'" A tender laugh rippled from her throat. "He told me, 'I did drills and pushups and running!'"

Lauren and Emily listened, imagining the scene.

"His older cousin had just been in a play, and the night before we'd talked about how they staged tryouts and picked the best actors to be on stage. And I told him that—" she looked up—"you know, you don't have to really *try out* for the army. They take every healthy, law-abiding guy who signs up."

Carol's voice grew soft, and she looked off. "And I'll never forget. He said, 'But you *should* have to try out, Mommy, because only the very best boys should get to fight for America.'" Her voice broke. "Only the very best."

Emily reached across the book and took hold of Carol's hand for a moment. Her daughter wasn't shaking or sobbing like at other times in the days since Lauren had been back, but her face was wet, her eyes never leaving the photograph. Then she linked her arm through Lauren's and laid her head on her shoulder.

Pictures danced to life in Lauren's mind, the little boy, blond back then, tanned and green-eyed, waking up with his bed-head and telling his mom about his dream. And that same boy running out to the soccer field, ready to help the fallen player. "Carol ..." Lauren could barely eke out the words. "If there were tryouts, he would've been first picked."

"Thanks." She nodded. "I know. He was born to wear the uniform."

They spent the next hour looking through the keepsake book. With every page, every layout, Lauren felt her views leaning hard in the other direction again. Justin had sent home photos of him and Joe and a few other soldiers from his company surrounded by Iraqi men. Men grinning and cheering and waving Iraqi flags and American flags all at the same time.

Several photos, with different groups taken on different days.

Beneath, his mother had included emails Justin sent home. One of them read, *It's an amazing feeling, Mom. Helping these people find a freedom they've only dreamed about. It makes every minute here worth it.*

There was a photo of Justin and a teary-eyed Iraqi man, their arms around each other's necks. Below the picture, Justin's letter said:

This is Ali-Abdul. He's a young father here in Baghdad, a guy with four kids. We were protecting the market where he gets his food, and he came up and gave me his change. I don't know, a bunch of coins worth maybe a dollar or so. But I got the feeling it was all the guy had. He wouldn't take it back either. Wouldn't hear of it. I mean, Mom, I really tried to give the guy his money. But he started crying, then he shook his head and started to walk away. You know me with my camera. I had to get his picture. He told me he would die a thankful man for what Americans have done for his country. Wow. I mean, I know there's lots of bad over here, because war is always bad. Always. The sacrifice is unspeakable. But this is what I see time and time and time again. People like Ali-Abdul. No matter what you read in the papers, this is what's going on over here.

Taped to the page next to that layout were six Iraqi coins. The change from Ali-Abdul.

Lauren played Justin's last line over in her heart. *No matter what you read in the papers . . .* Or in a magazine, right? The sorts of stories she had churned out every week without ever thinking about the repercussions. Because repercussions weren't her problem. War was wrong for any reason, and she had a right to say so. That's how she'd always felt.

Until the last few months.

She turned the page to photos of children waving and people working in makeshift marketplaces, all signs of a new sort of freedom. Only a few letters talked about Justin's fear, his realization that he wasn't merely on some kind of humanitarian expedition.

There is an insurgent group here in Baghdad that hates us, Mom. I studied this stuff in college, and I understand. At the root of this war is a spiritual battle that has been waged against mankind and against God's people since the beginning of time. But still . . . it's weird, you know? Being here and knowing that hiding just about everywhere are people who hate me enough to kill me.

Just because I'm an American.

A couple of the photos showed a more playful side to Justin, and it reminded Lauren that he really wasn't much older than a kid. A picture of him and Joe sitting on the dirt outside a tent, a small basin of water between them. They each had a toy sailboat, and like a couple of little boys, they were sailing them across the surface of the water. Under the photo, his email read in part, *I won the sailboat race, in case you have to ask. I mean, look at my tricked out boat. And yes, the water was wonderful.*

Emily laughed, but it mixed with the sound of a stifled sob. "He loved being on the water. We sailed on the Puget Sound before he left." Her smile faded. "We were … going to take a cruise to the Bahamas."

What impressed Lauren most about the keepsake wasn't any one picture, but the preponderance of them. The message — from Justin's emails and from Ali-Abdul's coins and especially from the photographs — was loud and clear. The war in Iraq was more complicated than she'd ever wanted to see.

When they finished looking at the book, they moved to the kitchen table and Carol showed them that day's newspaper, the one with a front-page tribute to Justin. The headline read, "Kelso to Honor Local Fallen Hero." The article started on the front and moved inside with an entire page dedicated to the story and photos of Justin and his days growing up in Kelso.

One photo showed him at school — second grade, maybe third — dressed in a child's mock army uniform, saluting a teacher. Another was a close-up of him and his sister Jill a few years later, freckle-faced and suntanned, each of them holding a string of fish. There were photos of Justin in his Kelso High basketball uniform, and a photo of him the day he graduated from college, proud and tall in his cap and gown.

The pictures told the story. The sweet, sometimes mischievous, little guy he'd been, and the genuine young man he'd become. Lauren put her arm around Emily's waist as they stood side by side and looked at the photos Carol had chosen for the article. They studied the newspaper tribute quietly, each lost in their own memories of the young man. Carol finally ran her fingers over the photo of him in uniform. The rest of the night Lauren caught Carol looking at the picture a number of times.

There was a knock at Shane's window, and the memories lifted. Lauren turned to find a soldier—one of those who had stood near the front of the church.

"Sir, we're asking everyone in the procession to keep their headlights on. We'll have a police escort, so we should be able to stay together."

Again the thought had hit her. Was it unpatriotic to disagree with a war that had taken a kid like Justin? Could a person support the troops without supporting the government's decision to stay in a war? Or had Shane been right when he'd said that while no one wanted war, sometimes it was unavoidable—for the defense of the nation or the support of a people struggling for freedom? In that case, it was a matter of fighting for what was right and making a commitment to sacrifice, whatever the cost, for the sake of victory.

But could the people truly continue to support a war that had gone on so long? Even one that was netting positive results for the U.S. and Iraq? Lauren looked at Shane, at his strong jaw and the way he kept his eyes straight ahead, not on the Bakers' car, but on the hearse in front of it. He had been shaken by Justin's death. They'd talked about his battle with futility, and his realization that as long as the United States was free, there would always be a purpose in defending her.

Shane was as good and golden as Justin. And she'd been willing to walk away from him. Suddenly, as she looked at him, her heart filled with love, and a dawning happened in her. When the sadness of this day had dimmed, before they made a decision about what came next, she would talk to Shane. She would tell him that life was too short to live without the sort of love they felt for each other. The love they'd always felt toward each other.

The cars in front of them began to move, and Shane set their vehicle into motion. A wave of cold fear and sorrow hit Lauren, dissolving her thoughts. How could they be here, part of a procession to lay Justin Baker to rest? He was just standing there, a few feet in front of her, tossing a football with those kids, right? Just the other day. A part of her still refused to believe that he was in the flag-covered box in the hearse ahead of them.

Eight miles of two-lane roadway separated Kelso Community Church from the cemetery on the far end of town. They headed out of the church parking lot and turned right. The sight of the hearse put a lump in her throat, and she looked down. How would the Bakers possibly get through this day? She leaned on Shane's shoulder, drawing strength from him, relying on him.

He kissed her forehead. "I'm praying for Gary and Carol." His voice was soft, a caress against her battered conscience.

"Yes." She could do that too. Talk to God about the Bakers.

She was just getting started when Emily let out a soft gasp from the backseat. "Look!"

Lauren sat up. "What?" She turned her attention to the roadway and then saw for herself.

As the procession slowly moved forward, they saw people lined along the sidewalks on either side of the road—all of them holding American flags. These were not mourners, but Kelso citizens who had turned out to pay final respects to one of their own. Lauren watched, mesmerized as they passed a gray-haired couple. The frail, bent-over woman held a small flag, and the man, his hat over his heart, saluted. Next they came upon a pickup truck with ten teenage guys standing in the bed, hands on their hearts. A full-size flag flew from a pole planted in the ground beside them.

Shane said nothing, but his eyes looked wetter than before and the muscles in his jaw flexed as he drove. Lauren and Emily were silent, stunned. Lauren studied the people, saw the pride in their eyes. The line of them didn't seem to have an end.

They passed a group of handicapped adults, flags flying from their wheelchairs and walkers. Auto mechanics still in their uniforms, office workers in ties and suits. An entire Girl Scout troop came next, and even from the car, Lauren could see that several had tears on their cheeks.

Next was a group of medical workers in scrubs, together holding a single flag; and then what looked like most of the Kelso football team, all in uniform, their helmets tucked beneath their arms. There were entire families, some with babies in strollers, some with kids on bikes. And a Little League team standing wide-eyed along the curb.

Lauren looked back as block after block, mile after mile, the show of support continued, unlike anything she'd ever seen. She'd witnessed her share of parade routes and people gathered three deep along a stretch of road. But this was different. A parade route had people laughing and moving about.

These people stood motionless. Even the children had their attention entirely turned to the procession. Lauren wouldn't have believed if she hadn't seen it, this deep respect for Justin—for all soldiers.

Suddenly she realized she was crying, and it occurred to her what was happening.

God was giving her one final bit of wisdom on the topic she'd wrestled with for nearly a year.

He'd taught her to temper her views, shown her another side to the war—just as she'd asked. And now He was dealing with her final question. Could Americans still support a war effort that had gone on so long? That had cost so dearly?

The answer lined the streets all the way from the church to the cemetery. It was hard to imagine Kelso even had so many citizens, and yet they'd found a way to come, to support Justin and his family and his country for eight solid miles. Lauren took a tissue from her purse and pressed it to her cheeks. They pulled into the cemetery, and she felt overwhelmed with the desire to let Shane and Emily know how she was feeling.

She sniffed and turned so she could see them both at the same time. "Before we get out, I want to ... to tell you something."

Shane had her hand. His eyes met hers, and she felt his compassion all the way to the center of her soul. She made her living as a writer, but now she had to search for the words. "When I left Fallon, I prayed for understanding, for wisdom. But ... I didn't really expect to learn anything, because, well, I knew I was right." She sniffed. Her confession released a landslide of emotion she hadn't known was there. Because this was the first time she'd shared any of her new feelings with the two people she loved most.

"It's okay." Shane's tone was kind beyond understanding. "We don't have to talk about it now."

"I want to." Lauren searched his eyes. "Please."

Shane looked hesitant. Clearly he had no idea where she was going with this.

"Today ... now ... I can't go another minute without telling you that God has changed me." Her eyes blurred, but she stayed strong, as if by telling them, she could lend some sort of purpose to the sadness. "He's shown me time and again that my one-sided views were wrong. Shane—" she looked at him—"you were right. War is complicated and no one wants it. No one wants a young man like Justin to die." She pressed her fingers to her upper lip, fighting for control. "Yes, it's okay to question, and all of us wish there was a better way. But in the end—" she looked out the windshield at the hearse—"it comes down to supporting the troops. Even if you don't agree with everything about the war."

Emily looked down.

"So I want to apologize." She waited until she had Emily's attention again. "I'm sorry, Emily. And I'm sorry, Shane." The grief and regret caught up to her. It blanketed her and made it hard to breathe. She covered her eyes with one hand and fought her emotions.

"Mom..."

Lauren looked up.

Emily touched her shoulder, rested her hand there. "I wrestle with all this too." Her eyes were dry. "I think of what the world just lost." Her voice grew tight. "What *I* lost." She looked at the soldiers filing along either side of the line of cars, ready to take the casket to its final resting place.

Emily shook her head. "I can't think of a single cause that would've been worth losing Justin. But here's the thing." The look in her eyes grew intense and she searched Lauren's face, then Shane's. "Justin believed in it. He was over there, he understood what this war's about more than any of us." She looked at Lauren. "Even you, Mom." Peace filled her features again. "He believed in it. That's enough."

"I know." Lauren held her daughter's eyes for a long moment. They filed out of the car then, and Lauren was last out.

She looked ahead to the white tent, the burial site where the procession would wind up. As they started walking, Shane took her hand. Nothing had ever felt so right in all her life. She watched Emily fall in among the teens Justin had visited with every week. Without talking, Joe walked along one side of Emily, and the boy who had declared himself family, on the other.

As they moved toward the tent, Lauren studied her daughter. Controlled and composed, Emily was the picture of strength. It was amazing, really, the maturity she was showing. Where did she get her wisdom? First in finding her parents and playing the diplomat time and time again. And now this. The answer came as soon as she breathed the silent question. Emily's wisdom came from God. Same as the wisdom she, herself, had prayed for.

Lauren replayed her daughter's explanation. Justin was the soldier, the one risking his life in Iraq every day, the one briefed on the missions and the purpose of the battle. He had believed in the war enough to sacrifice his life for it. In that assessment — more than any Lauren had ever done — there was wisdom.

And that was enough.

TWENTY-SEVEN

C arol Baker couldn't take her eyes off the casket.
These were her final minutes, the last moments she'd ever
have with her son. She clutched something in her right hand,
something she'd saved for this time. No telling how many people
filed in around the small white tent, the place where the coffin
would be lowered to the ground. Carol appreciated every one of
them, but she didn't look. Couldn't look.

There was only her and Gary and Jill and Justin. The way
they'd always been for as long as she could remember. Only now,
Justin would never smile at them or joke about Carol's cooking
or ask about Buster or offer to run Jill to Starbucks. Now all they
had was this, their final moments together.

And even then, Carol knew she was wrong. Justin wasn't in
the box. He was free, whole and well, enjoying life the way it was
meant to be enjoyed. Without war or conflict or anything but
constant love. Pure love. Carol liked to think that heaven had a
window, a way for people to look in on the ones they loved still
on earth. But now ... now that seemed impossible.

Because heaven had no tears. And there could be no way for
Justin to look down at his family in this moment without crying.

The graveside service was more formal, shorter than the memorial at the church. When it ended, seven soldiers from Fort
Lewis lined up a short distance away and performed a twenty-
one-gun salute. Emily and her family and the teens sat in the
row behind them. In the front row, Gary sat between her and

Jill. When the first shot rang through the sky, Carol clutched her husband's arm and buried her face in his shoulder.

No, they couldn't be here. The salute couldn't be for Justin.

As the second shot echoed across the cemetery, suddenly she wasn't sitting next to Justin's casket. She was drinking iced tea on the back deck of their house on one of Kelso's endless summer days, and Justin was a nine-year-old towhead running around the corner into the yard, waving a cap-style rifle in the air.

"Take cover, Mom, the bad guys are right behind me."

And she was ducking behind the picnic table until Justin popped out from the bushes. "We won!" And he was coming to her, tossing his gun on the table and throwing his arms around her neck. "I'll always protect you. Okay? Cause I'm gonna be the best soldier in the whole world."

The third shot split the air.

Carol held tighter to the object in her hand. *God, I'll never survive it without You. Never.*

Gary was whispering in her ear, "It's okay ... we'll get through this."

But there was more sadness still ahead. The haunting refrains of taps filled the air, and when the song finished, the American flag was removed from the top of the casket. Two soldiers folded it and handed it to Joe Greenwald. Joe looked at Justin's parents, and never breaking eye contact, he carried the flag over and laid it in Carol Baker's arms.

She looked at it tenderly, longingly — remembering the long ago infant son she'd held in her arms. Then she cradled the flag against her chest, stood, and hugged Joe. Held him for a long time. When she finally let him go, Joe nodded to Justin's sister, exchanged another salute with his friend's father, and then moved a few feet away toward Emily. He stopped at her father, nodded, and then the two of them exchanged a salute. Next he shook hands with Emily's mother, and finally he looked at her.

He took both her hands in his, and she stood and hugged him. As she did, he spoke the words that broke Carol's heart. "He loved you very much, Emily. He … he told me to tell you." Emily couldn't say anything. None of them could.

Joe drew back, took her hands again, holding them so tight his knuckles turned white. He locked eyes with her. "I'm sorry." Joe returned to his place in line with the other soldiers.

After a few minutes, the ceremony was over. Soldiers and commanders came by to pay their respects, and Carol gave the appropriate handshakes and hugs. But all the while, she never strayed more than a few feet from the box, from his body.

Finally, all that remained were a handful of people. Emily and her parents, the teens, and a few old Veterans — the ones Justin would talk to on Tacoma's rainy afternoons. Emily broke away from the group and approached the casket, opposite where Carol and Gary and Jill now stood.

She was a beautiful girl, Emily. Justin wanted to marry her, and he would have. He'd told her so in one of his letters home from Iraq. *I've made my decision*, he'd told them. *She's the one. Now if I can only survive between now and the day I can finally see her again …*

Emily would've made a wonderful wife for Justin. They would've had children and raised them to care about people, to do the right thing. Carol felt another wave of sorrow wash over her. Poor Emily. She loved her son as much as anyone. She had been his first love, and from the beginning, Carol and Gary and Jill had embraced her.

Carol realized the precious girl standing across from her was young. Surely Emily would find love again one day and raise the babies she might've had with Justin. Which meant that the relationship she and Gary had built with her was — for the most part — over.

Emily came another step closer to the grave. Throughout the service, Carol had watched her show deep concern for everyone else. The teens, the Vets, even Justin's friend Joe. Every time Carol looked at Emily during the service, her eyes were on the speaker or the soldiers or the baskets of gifts that stood around the front of the church.

Never on the casket that held the boy she loved.

But now ... the cemetery service was over, and she found her way to the edge of the grave. Finally, without interruption, she stared at the casket. Her hands and knees shook, and after a minute she leaned close and placed her hand on the cool top. Her tears came then, streams of them. She closed her eyes and ran her thumb along the smooth wood.

After a while, she straightened. She kissed her pinky finger and pressed it to the box for a long moment. Then she turned and went to her parents, moving into an embrace from both of them. Off to the side, the rough-looking group of teens stood in a cluster, hands in their pockets, looking unsure about what to do next. The outspoken one came closer. Bo, Carol had heard Emily call him, the one who considered himself family.

He clutched the tent pole as if it might kill him if he took a step closer. But somehow he found the strength, and as he reached the box, he leaned on it with both fists. A single sob ripped at him, grabbed him. "Justin, man ... why?" The words were a whispered cry, desperate and haunting.

Emily pulled herself from her parents' arms when she saw him, this teenage man-child, crying his heart out for the loss of his friend. She went to him and waited three feet away. After a few seconds, the teen pressed his forearm to the casket twice, and then held it out in the air and did a one-sided handshake, maybe the one he and Justin used to do. Finally he pressed his fist to his heart and then pointed heavenward.

Only then did he turn around, notice Emily, and fall into her arms, a big kid looking for someone to love away all the hurt and pain. Carol watched the two of them move toward the others, giving the Bakers their space. Jill and Gary walked the few steps together, and Jill laid a flower on the casket.

Gary hesitated, even after Jill returned to their places near the first row of chairs. He was a strong man, a man much like Justin would've been if he'd had the chance to grow up. But this was a good-bye he'd never intended to make. He laid his hand on the casket, fingers slightly spread. The picture of it reminded Carol of the way her husband's hand had looked a thousand times on their son's shoulder, when the two of them would stand side by side at the end of a church service, or fishing on the edge of a lake.

"Justin—" His voice broke. He squinted and pressed his other fist to his eyes. "I'm so proud of you, son." He waited a minute and then returned to his seat.

And like that it was Carol's turn. She'd been waiting for this moment all day, her chance to be alone with her son. Only now it took everything she had left to make the walk, because she didn't want to say good-bye, couldn't imagine saying good-bye. She reached the edge, and suddenly she could see him lying there, the way he looked stretched out on his bed at night, his green eyes closed, muscled arms flung up onto the pillow.

Picturing him that way made her heart seize up into her throat. She couldn't take a breath or exhale or do anything but stare at the box. They had to get him out of there. He needed air! They both did. The cemetery people couldn't put him into the ground, couldn't leave him here. Because just a minute ago, he was running up and hugging her, telling her all the crazy, danger-ous, tender things that had happened in Iraq. He had never been more alive in all his life, and so how could he be here at all?

She jerked her gaze away from the casket and looked up through the towering evergreens that lined the cemetery at a slice of blue. No. He wasn't sleeping in the box. Slowly she exhaled. That was the only way she could do this, by telling herself the truth. He was climbing mountains outside the city of heaven. Strong and more alive and whole.

A small bit of air filled her lungs, and she reached out and touched the casket. She still had the flag in her arms, and she looked at it. Anything to delay the moment. She ran her fingers over the silky blue and the sewn-on stars. Because blue stood for courage, and no one had ever tackled war more courageously than her son. "You got your wish, Justin." She whispered, so no one—not even Gary and Jill—could hear her. "You were the best, honey. The very best."

Then she took the object, the one she'd been holding in her hand since the graveside service began, and placed it on the casket, a few inches from the flower. The small plastic figurine had been one of Justin's favorites as a boy. He would fall asleep with a handful of them lined up along the side of his bed. They had all known back then which direction his future would go. The only thing Justin ever wanted to do was defend his country.

As she walked away, as she felt the physical force of separation, of leaving her son's body behind, she pulled her eyes away from the casket. The last thing she saw before she turned back to her family was that one small green toy that Justin had given her for Mother's Day a lifetime ago. She still had one on her dresser, where it would stay until the day she died, because it would remind her not of his death, but of his childhood, his boyhood, his teenage years. His life.

A much-loved, well-worn, army green, plastic toy soldier.

The reception would be back at the Bakers' house, but first Emily needed to comfort Bo and Dexter and the other teens. They had held up well through both services, but now it seemed Bo might collapse to the ground. And so she held him until finally his sobs subsided.

"Bo … we need to get going." She looped her arm through his. Joe was standing with the other guys, though none of them were saying much.

The boy sniffed and nodded. "Okay." He looked over his shoulder at the coffin. "He's not there, right? That's what he always told us. Believe in Jesus, and at the end a guy goes to heaven, right?"

Emily smiled. Her eyes were swollen, but she was tired of crying. Justin was gone. Now it was time to celebrate his life—this afternoon and every day she had left to live. "That's right. He's not there."

Bo straightened. "Alright, then." The tough guy image was back, but not like he'd worn it before. Something in his eyes was different, softer and gentler.

Emily prayed it always would be. They met up with Joe and the others, and she and Joe exchanged a look. They still needed to talk, maybe later at the Bakers' house. For now, she appreciated his presence, the fact that having him nearby was—in some strange way—like having Justin there.

In the distance, she saw the Veterans making their way to their cars. Several of them walked with canes, their jackets decorated with dozens of colorful badges and pins, proud to be a part of the brotherhood that Justin belonged to, the brotherhood of soldiers. The man in the wheelchair held up his hand in her direction before his buddies wheeled him toward a cluster of cars—most with handicapped placards.

Emily waved back. This was not the last time she would see the old men. She would go to them, check in on them once in a while and keep them posted about life at Fort Lewis. Because that was one way she could keep Justin's memory alive.

They were almost to the van when Dexter shoved his hands deep in his jeans pockets. "What are we supposed to do now?" His tone was angry, defeated. "What's the point?"

Emily was about to answer him, about to tell him that Justin never would've wanted him to think that way, when Joe cleared his throat. "Hey, man, Justin talked about you guys all the time." Joe kept walking, his steps slow, eyes downcast. "He believed in you." He stopped and looked Dexter straight in the eyes. "And he believed in serving his country."

Two of the guys—the ones with plans to enlist—nodded, silent.

"Listen," Dexter did an exaggerated shrug, "you ain't got no idea what it's like livin' in my shoes, trapped on the streets. No way out." He stuck his chest out and crossed his arms. "Justin ... he knew, man. He knew like nobody." He threw his hands up. "So now what?"

Joe wasn't backing down. He'd never met the guys until today, but clearly he wasn't going to let this moment pass. "Now?" He put his hand firm and hard on Dexter's shoulder. "Now you get your education and you make something of yourself." Joe's lip quivered. "You make Justin proud, because that's what he wanted for you. It's what he believed for you."

Bo took a step forward. His eyes moved around the group to each of the guys, and finally, to Dexter. "The man's right." He looked more composed than he had all day. "Justin believed in us. Maybe ... maybe it's time we believed in us too."

For the first time, the idea seemed to sink in for Dexter. For the others also. Justin had believed in them. Dexter eased his stance. He bit the inside of his lip and gave the slightest nod. "Okay." Then he motioned for the others, and they all started walking toward the van again.

Emily wanted to raise her fist in the air. Here it was, the victory she'd been looking for all day. Justin *wasn't* gone. He wasn't in the casket, about to be lowered into a dark hole in the ground. He was here. He was in the warm smile of a teary-eyed World War II Veteran, and in the innocent eyes of a busload of grade school kids. He was in the firm grip of a soldier named Joe Greenwald, and he was standing beside her, gazing out at Puget Sound. Where he'd always be. But in this moment, maybe most of all, he lived on in the words of a troubled young teenager.

A guy who would forever believe in himself, in his future, in his reason for being alive. And one day—no matter how long or sad the good-bye—they would see him again and know the impact he'd made, the legacy he'd left behind, the lives that had been changed.

All because Justin Baker had lived.

TWENTY-EIGHT

Lauren was standing off by herself, watching Carol Baker grieve, when she saw her mother approaching. She looked older, more tired. Coming to the service was important to Lauren's mom. She'd told them after hearing the news about Justin that she would've come even if she'd had to drive up. Instead she'd flown in yesterday afternoon and shared an early dinner with Emily and Lauren and Shane.

She'd raised Emily, after all. Of course she had come.

"This is the hardest thing my granddaughter's been through," she told Lauren after dinner. "I had to be here."

During the service, she'd given them space, understanding that Emily was struggling in more than one way. She had lost Justin, yes. But unless a miracle happened, she was about to lose any hope of her parents ever reuniting. Lauren took her eyes off her mother and looked at Shane, across the green spread of grass, several rows of tombstones away. He was talking to Gary Baker.

There wasn't much time; Lauren's mother seemed to understand that too. Her return flight was set for tomorrow, and now, as she drew near, Lauren had a feeling she may have come to Tacoma for more than a chance to support Emily.

She stopped a foot away, close enough that Lauren could hear her ragged breathing. "Something in the air here." She gazed at the trees that surrounded the cemetery. "Never had so much trouble drawing a breath."

"You're not sick?" Lauren wasn't used to worrying about her. They'd been out of touch for nearly two decades, long enough that most of the time she forgot she even had a mother. But now that Emily had brought them all back together, Lauren expected to have her mom around for a long time. Especially after losing her father to cancer a week after finding him. Lauren lowered her brow, worried. "You've been getting checkups?"

"I'm fine." Her mother waved her hand, as if she were swatting a fly. "Probably just allergies."

"Could be." She looked at her daughter, climbing into the van full of teens fifty yards away. "Emily says they're bad up here."

Her mother was quiet. When Lauren turned to look at her, she had no doubt. Her mother hadn't walked over to talk about allergies. Lauren turned her back to the rented SUV and tilted her head. "You're coming to the Bakers' house?"

"I am. Haven't had a chance to talk to Emily yet, not the way I want to." Her mother narrowed her eyes, thoughtful. "She's doing well. God's carrying her. I can see it."

Lauren gave a few slow nods. "He is. No way to get through a day like today without faith."

"No." Her mother drew a slow breath. She looked away, but only for a moment. "Lauren, there's something I have to say."

The words reminded her of the semi-speech she'd given Emily and Shane as they arrived at the cemetery. As if death had a way of making people get around to the point, a way of highlighting everything anyone ever said about life being too short. She studied her mom, the woman she'd spent so many years hating. All she could see in the older woman's eyes was love. Lauren gave her a sad smile. "I thought maybe you did."

"Yes." She held Lauren's eyes. "It's about Shane."

Lauren found him again, still talking to his friend. "Shane?"

Her mother looked over her shoulder at the two men, then back. "Don't let him go, Lauren." Her voice sounded suddenly scratchy. "It's ... it's my fault you ever let him go in the first place." She spread her fingers across her chest. "I take full blame. But now ..." She looked at Shane again. "I see the way he looks at you, how he still watches you when you cross the room. The way he used to do all those years ago."

Lauren's heart fluttered. "Really?"

"Honey—" her mother gave her a look that said she knew—- "I'm not wrong about this. Shane loves you as much today as he ever did."

The surprise of her observation was wearing off, and her heart fell back to a normal rhythm. But the thought stirred something deep in Lauren's soul. Shane watched her when she crossed a room? The years fell away and she stared at him, Shane, the only one who could make her feel seventeen again.

"What I want to tell you, Lauren—" her mother took hold of her hand and searched her face—"is that he loves you. He's crazy about you. He'll never love anyone the way he loves you."

"I've been thinking that."

Her mother made a relieved sound. "Good." The familiar guilt and regret cast shadows on her mother's face. "I couldn't bear to see the two of you throw away what you had ... what you still can have ... all because of differing opinions."

"Well ..." Lauren looked at the flag flying near the corner of the cemetery, the way it unfurled in the breeze. The red, white, and blue and all it stood for. "Our opinions are closer than they used to be."

Her mother's brows lifted. She hesitated, absorbing that bit of information, then shifted her gaze to the van just pulling away. "I think of Emily, all she's lost." She had Lauren's hand. "You and Shane still have a chance, honey. Don't ... please don't let him go. Not again."

Lauren was struck by the intensity in her mother's tone. But at the same time, another sort of realization hit hard. Her mother was right. If she didn't do something to stop it, in a few days, she and Shane would both board flights headed for two entirely different locations.

They'd already told Emily they'd stay another week, through Thanksgiving. Long enough to spend time with her, talk to her, and give her space to cry and laugh and remember the crazy, happy months since she'd met Justin. Emily wanted the three of them to visit the Space Needle and Issaquah, Blake Island and Pike Place Market, the spots Justin had taken her.

"If I go back now," she'd told them, "I'll still feel him with me. Before I forget how."

There was no arguing with that, because there was no arguing with grief. A person simply did what her heart led her to do. If that's where Emily wanted to go, how she wanted to spend her days after the funeral, Lauren and Shane would go with her. But at the end of the week, next Saturday, maybe they could spend an hour at the small church Emily had found.

Fallon wasn't so bad now that Lauren understood the military a little better. An entire town full of men and women with the same mind-set as Justin Baker? That wouldn't be such a horrible existence, would it? She and the others could disagree on politics, but some things finally made sense. The idea that a country like Iraq deserved freedom, and the notion that terror — the sort that would fly a plane into a building, or fire a bullet into a sign-waving man named Yusef, or detonate a bomb beneath a vehicle containing a kid who wanted everything good and right — that sort of thinking had to be eradicated. No questions.

Yes, she could live in Fallon now, because it was like an optical illusion. The people who lived and worked around the Top Gun facility used to seem like criminals to her, bullies looking for a fight, wanting to flex their collective muscle. But now she saw them more as police officers, people with the heart and courage to defend and protect.

A strange thing had happened since she wrote that first story about Justin and his fellow soldiers, since she dared to report the war the way so many people in Fallon had talked about it. Other reporters had started doing the same thing. One network correspondent who was interviewed the week before declared her admiration for the men and women of the military, and how it was an honor to risk her life beside them if that's what it took to tell their story. Their real story.

Lauren smiled when she saw the interview.

The press was starting to get it, starting to understand that complicated matters were never entirely one-sided — no matter what a reporter's personal views might be. She could leave the war reporting to the many other capable journalists in the Middle East, and *Time* would find another reporter to pal around with Scanlon.

She was finished, ready to move on with her life.

Shane's face came to mind — his voice and his touch. They'd have their differences, of course. But what couple didn't? And if Lauren returned to the sort of stories she'd been doing before — conducting interviews around the country — she would still have her independence, her time outside of Fallon. Most of all, she would have Shane and she would have peace — not the sort that she had spent her adult years writing about, searching for. But the type of peace that passed all understanding. A peace that could only come from God and His wisdom, and a knowing that she was finally where she belonged.

With Shane, where she had always belonged.

The thought that had hit her a moment ago returned. What about it? An hour in the small church where Emily and Justin had gone, a moment in time to promise forever to the man who had gently taken hold of her heart when he was only a kid. Would he have her? Would he believe that she could share a house with him in Fallon, entertain with him, and understand the people who made up his world?

Or was it too late?

Lauren took her mother's other hand. Patience shone from her mom's eyes, a patience and a persistence that said she wasn't going to leave this conversation without an answer. Lauren looked at her for a long time. "I won't let him go, Mom." Conviction rose within her, a conviction she hadn't fully acknowledged until now. "I know what I want." The words sounded foreign coming from her mouth. She hadn't voiced them to anyone yet, even herself. "Shane and I, well, we had this date all planned, something big set for Christmas Eve in Fallon." Her heart beat harder at the thought. "But I'd do it this week. On Saturday after Thanksgiving … if Shane'll have me." She felt a tentative smile on her lips. "He might say no, because, well … I've been—" she wrinkled her nose—"a little difficult."

"Are you saying—" her mother's face lost a shade of color—- "are you saying you'd marry him this week if he'd take you?"

Only then did she realize the significance of her words. The great and lasting significance. "Yes." No hint of doubt remained. She wanted to marry Shane and grow old with him, love him the way she'd never been able to love him before. "Yes!" She let loose a quiet laugh. "I want to marry him, Mom. That's what I'm saying." Her forehead grew damp, even in the late afternoon breeze. She would marry him that Saturday if he would take her, if he would trust that she was ready to commit her life to him, if he would forego all the fancy planning and flowers and simply hold her hand at the front of the small church and promise her forever.

The way she was suddenly desperate to promise it to him.

Her mother's eyes grew watery. "Well, then that settles it."

"What?" Lauren's heart was still racing within her, the future bright with possibilities that had eluded her all her life.

"I need to change my plane ticket." Her mother squeezed her hands, her eyes glistening. The look on her face said that the wedding was already a done deal, as if she—even better than Lauren—knew without a doubt what Shane would say.

She grinned. "Because I wouldn't miss this for the world."

Twenty-Nine

Funerals were strange.

Emily was amazed how, as the day wore on, the group of family and friends who had known Justin best rode a wave of emotions that seemed to change with every passing hour. What had started at the beginning of the day as resolve had given way to gut-wrenching grief and unending sorrow.

But now that she'd made the round trip to Tacoma to drop off the teens, she joined the others at the Bakers' house. The joy she found there surprised her, but after an hour she was laughing too. A laughter that would've made Justin proud to be a part of them. people told stories about him—the time he rode his bike through the neighbor's freshly paved driveway and denied the charge to his mother.

"I only had to take him outside to see the black tire track leading all the way from Mrs. Johnson's house to ours." Justin's father chuckled. He was sitting in one of the chairs at the kitchen table, his wife and daughter on either side, and Buster sleeping at their feet. Justin's sweatshirt was tucked beneath the dog's paws.

Also sitting around the table with her were her parents and grandmother, and Joe Greenwald along with a few other relatives. The stories kept them there, spellbound, celebrating Justin and every time he'd ever made them smile. Emily savored each one, learning a little more about him with each telling, each round of laughter.

Around seven o'clock, a lull fell over the table. The men moved into the family room, and the women headed to the kitchen to make coffee. Again the atmosphere was familiar. Trays of food on the counter, the smell of barbecued chicken and potato casserole and baked apples, all brought to the house by friends. Flames danced in the fireplace in the next room, and country music played, a soft backdrop for the conversations and occasional rounds of laughter that filled the place.

Emily closed her eyes and breathed in. This could've been any other gathering, a Saturday afternoon when their families had come together for a holiday party. She could picture him beside her, laughing with Joe and teasing his mother for breaking down and letting Buster in the house.

She blinked and the truth was glaringly obvious. Justin *wasn't* there. He never would be again. With the others off to different rooms, she and Joe were the only ones at the table, and she studied him—for the first time since they'd spoken at the church earlier that day. He was staring at his hands, his shoulders stiff, uncomfortable.

Emily's heart hurt for him. How must he feel? Today should've been another attempt at bringing order to the streets of Iraq. Justin should've been beside him in their Humvee, riding through Baghdad and taking care of business, counting the days until their tour was up.

"Joe?" Her voice was soft. "Wanna take a walk?"

He looked up and something crossed his expression, a sense of obligation and inevitability. He didn't break eye contact. "I think we need to."

She stood and found her coat near the front door. He did the same, but he also grabbed his backpack from the floor. Neither of them said anything as they went out the front door and closed it behind them. Darkness had already set, and with the clouds overhead, the only light came from the tall lamps that lined Justin's street.

Emily pulled her coat more tightly around her and stuck her hands in her pockets. Winter was in the air, and rain in the forecast. The breeze was biting, but it made her feel alive, helped lift the stifling sense of death she had carried all day. They hadn't walked too far when Joe stopped and leaned against a tree.

"It should've been me." He breathed in sharply and stared into the darkness. "Justin ... he had everything to live for." Joe looked at her, to the part of her heart that was barely holding on. His eyes pooled with sympathy, empathy. "He loved you, Emily. So much."

This was the moment they'd both put off, and Emily steeled herself against it, willed herself to hear what Joe had to say without falling apart again. "You were with him. When ..."

There was no need to finish her sentence. Joe understood. He slid one foot up against the tree trunk and stared at the ground. "He was sleeping when it hit, dreaming I think. Because an instant after the explosion, he was calling for you."

Tears gathered in her eyes and she held her breath. She didn't want to cry, not now. This was the only chance she'd ever have to hear the details of that terrible hour. But she hadn't expected this. He'd called for her? A moment after the explosion she had been there in his mind? The news filled her with a gratitude and sorrow greater than anything she'd known.

Joe sniffed. "It was like ... like he was talking to you." He lifted his fist to his mouth and waited. "He told you he was sorry, he ... never meant for it to happen."

The story unfolded, how Joe was cut, but alright, and how he crawled out of the mangled vehicle and found Justin on the ground. "His legs ... they were torn up." Joe raked his fingers through his short hair. "I knew he was in trouble. I started calling for help. Justin ... he was pretty dazed. Didn't know what had happened. But right away he started asking about his legs."

Emily didn't want to picture how Justin looked, how bad the scene must've been for Joe. She exhaled. *God ... please get me through this.* She didn't want the details, but she'd wondered about something ever since she got the news. Justin was a medic, and he would've helped a soldier in trouble. But had there been medics on hand in *his* hour of need? Or had he bled to death without any help? A cold bit of wind slipped in through her coat and she hugged herself to ward off the chill. "Were there medics? Nearby?"

"Not at first." Joe narrowed his eyes, which again grew distant, as if the tragedy was playing out again in his mind. "I leaned across him, using my body to stop ..." He shook his head, and anger crept into his tone. "It didn't help. He was bleeding pretty bad."

Emily felt sick, faint. There was a street sign a foot from her, and she leaned against it so she wouldn't fall.

"He didn't ask about his legs after that." The anger faded from his tone. A sad sort of laugh came from him. "He was more worried about me, told me I had a cut over my eye and I needed to get pressure on it. I told him I was fine. I kept ..." His shoulders hunched forward. "I told him to hang on, and he ... told me to pray. So I did, I prayed out loud." His eyes lifted to hers. "I kept telling him you were waiting for him, that he had to hold on for you."

Sadness filled every part of her. She had questions, not for Joe Greenwald. For God. But they would have to wait. She kept her eyes on Joe, willing him to finish.

"The medics came then, and they tried." His face twisted, and he suddenly looked like a young kid, crying because he'd lost his best friend. "It was too much. Too much blood loss, his injuries too bad. There was nothing—" He stopped a sob midway and shook his head hard.

Emily had watched Justin's friend suffer long enough. She took the backpack he was holding and set it on the ground beside him. Then she pulled him into her arms, hugged him the way she'd hug a brother. He clung to her, held on so tight, she could barely breathe. "Emily ... I'm sorry."

"It's okay." She stroked his back, willing him to survive the loss, same as she was willing herself to survive it. "If it's too hard, Joe, you don't have to tell me."

He released her and leaned against the tree once more. "No. I ... I have to. I promised him."

A car drove by on the street a few feet from them. As it passed, Emily lifted her words to God. *Please ... help him through this. Help us both, Lord.* As she silently spoke the words, the chill inside her eased. God was with them, even now, even with her questions and confusion. Emily anchored herself against the street sign and waited.

"That's when I noticed this." He lifted the backpack and held it with one hand. With the other he reached inside, rifled through the contents, and pulled out what looked like a small picture. He handed it to her.

It was a laminated photograph of Emily, one that Justin had taken at the pier that day, just before their cruise. The picture was bent and splattered with dirt. The one he'd written to her about. Emily studied it, remembering that afternoon. Their future had seemed so real and bright. She turned her eyes to Joe. "He told me about this. He kept it in his boot."

"He was holding it when ... when the bomb went off."

Emily stared at the photograph, tried to make out the image of her face through the cloud of fresh tears. If she'd had any doubt about his feelings for her, any doubt about whether she was on his mind in his final moments, this erased them all. He'd been thinking of her, looking at her picture even as his life drained away.

Joe held the backpack to his chest. "He told me to tell you he loved you, but ..." He was more composed now, the sobs having retreated to a place where—like hers—they would never be far away. He squinted. "I told him to tell you himself. You were *his* girl."

A sad smile lifted the corners of Emily's mouth. She appreciated Joe, his heart and his spunk, his willingness to carry out the message for Justin, his determination in those final moments to spur Justin to hold on and fight for every breath.

"I think he knew he didn't have long. He kept his eyes on your picture and—" Joe's expression changed and he swallowed hard. Whatever was coming next, his discomfort was evident. He searched her eyes. "He asked me to be your friend, Emily. That's what he wanted."

Emily folded her fingers around the bent piece of plastic and hung her head. As he lay there dying, Justin's thoughts hadn't only been about her, they'd been *for* her. That she might have a friend to help her survive his loss. She tucked the photo into her pocket and held her coat tighter around her body. *Justin ... how can you be gone?*

Then she remembered Joe, the soldier who had just bared his heart by passing on a request from Justin—a request that clearly made him uneasy. Her silence was bound to feel like rejection. Sure enough, as she lifted her eyes, he was looking at the ground.

"We don't even know each other, Emily. It's okay ... you don't have to ... I mean, I only told you because—"

"Joe." Her tone was tender, but firm. She took hold of his arm and searched his face. This was what Justin wanted, and she was glad. Being friends with Joe would help ease the loneliness, give her someone to listen when all she wanted to do was talk about the love she'd lost. "I want to be your friend."

The awkwardness in his eyes lifted a bit. "Yeah?"

"Yeah." She let go of him and hugged herself again. "I think that'd be nice. You aren't going back to Iraq, right?"

He absently touched the bandage on his forehead. "No. I'll have to do my part from here now."

"Okay, then." They didn't need a plan or a date. They could exchange cell phone numbers and make arrangements to meet for lunch or dinner or for a walk around campus. They would be friends because Justin asked them to be, and because it made sense. Overnight, Justin's loss gave them more in common than they might've found in a year.

Joe reached into his backpack again. "I brought you a few other things." He pulled out the red scrapbook, the one she'd given Justin before he left. With great care he dusted it off and looked at it. "He read the thing every night." His eyes found hers. "I mean, really. He knew every page, knew it by heart." Joe did a sad laugh as he handed it to her. "I think even I memorized it."

Emily's hands shook. She took hold of the book and brought it close. Somehow it smelled like Justin, and she felt her heart breaking again. She had never planned to get it back, never imagined a scene like this one. Joe's words played again in her mind. *He read the thing every night ... knew it by heart.* She held the book tighter. She would look at it later, study each page for signs that Justin had camped there, finger smudges or bits of dirt. She found Joe's eyes. "Thank you. For bringing it to me."

He nodded. "There's more." He pulled out a manila envelope. "All the letters you sent, and a few notebook pages, things he wrote when he couldn't sleep." He handed her the envelope.

Emily tucked it inside the cover of the scrapbook. The night was getting colder, and they needed to get back. Her cheeks were dry now, because the things Joe had told her had eased some of the pain. Almost as if she too had been there beside Justin when he died. "Did he ... say anything else?"

Joe thought for a few seconds. Then his eyes shone with a sweet sadness. "Yes." He looked at the dark sky beyond the trees. "He said he'd save a place for us. For his family and the guys at the teen center, for me—" his eyes found hers again—"and for you. Those were his last words. He was looking at your picture, and he told me he'd save a spot for you."

Another chilly breeze came over them, but a strange warmth made its way through her. She imagined the moment, Justin looking at her picture, wanting to save her a place in heaven. "Did he talk much about the boys, the teens at the center?"

"Mmmhm." Joe eased the backpack onto his right shoulder. "All the time. After missing you, his next concern was for those kids." Joe uttered a soft laugh. "And Buster, of course."

Emily smiled. "Of course." That was Justin, serving in one of the hottest spots in the war and worried more about his dog than his life.

Joe motioned toward the Bakers' house. "We should get back."

"Yes." They began walking, their steps slow, pensive. How strange it was having this mountain of a guy beside her, a new friend she wouldn't have found if it wasn't for a promise between two buddies. "Thanks, Joe. For everything."

He brushed off the thanks and slipped his hands into his coat pockets. Like before, he looked nervous, not quite sure about whatever was coming next. "About those guys at the teen center … maybe we could head out there and hang with 'em once in a while. The way Justin used to do."

This time Emily's smile started deep inside her soul. "I think they'd like that."

As they made the rest of the walk in silence, Emily felt a connection with Joe she hadn't imagined ever feeling. Because Joe wanted to be like Justin, same way Bo and Dexter and all the young guys wanted to be like him. So maybe that would become Justin's legacy, another part of himself he would leave behind. His loss would always be a terrible thing. Emily could live a hundred years and she would never quite heal, never quite get through a day without missing the young soldier who had captured her heart that perfect summer on the shores of Seattle.

But the world would be a different place because of him, a better place. No matter how brief, his life had counted. It had mattered in a deep and lasting way. *This is the bus stop*, she could hear him saying as she took the steps up to his parents' front door. *The great journey is on the other side.* Indeed. Her soul stirred and a new kind of calm came over her. Justin was gone, but he had left behind his wisdom and laughter and a thousand precious memories. And something else. She smiled at Joe as they reached the front door.

He had left her a friend.

*T*HIRTY

*S*hane didn't want to think about saying good-bye. But it was coming. There was no way around the fact. The day after Justin's funeral, Lauren took him up to Seattle's Space Needle. The rest of the week belonged to Emily, she told him. But today it needed to be just the two of them. They rode five hundred feet up to the O Deck and stood against the railing, looking out at the city. After a long while, Lauren turned to him. "Shane ... we need to talk."

The look on her face told him she had something serious to say, and a part of him wanted to stop her. She couldn't give him a farewell speech. Not after all they'd been through that past week. Time and again things between them had seemed better than ever. So why weren't they talking about staying together? Shane steeled himself. "Why do I feel like we've done this before?"

"This is different." She took his hands, and the look in her eyes softened. "In the last few months I've learned a lot. I prayed for wisdom and God gave it to me." Her voice held none of its usual skepticism. "It's easy to step back and see something through the lens of personal bias." She stared at the breathtaking view. "I can stand here and see a harbor or a city or the mountains, and I can think that's what makes up Seattle." She looked at him. "But it's not until I get down from the Space Needle and walk the streets, not until I climb the mountains or find my way to the waterfront, that I can actually know something about the city."

He listened, wanting to draw her into his arms. Hope shone a flashlight on the dark places of his heart. This was the Lauren he had fallen in love with, the one who was levelheaded and careful with her opinions. He let her finish.

"That's what happened to me in Iraq these last few months." She exhaled and looked through the wall of glass again. "I had a chance to walk the streets and talk to the people and watch the soldiers—guys like Justin—and see for myself why this war is important."

He hadn't been sure where she was going with her thoughts, but he was touched. This wasn't the good-bye he'd expected. Not yet, anyway. She'd brought him to the Space Needle so she could tell him how she'd changed, how her eyes had in some ways been opened. But before he could ask her what else was on her mind, what might lay ahead for the two of them, she turned to him and kissed him. Kissed him the way she hadn't done since their first night back together at her parents' house in Chicago a year ago.

"Twice you've asked me to marry you, and twice it hasn't worked out." Her eyes were soft, full of light and love. "Now it's my turn."

For half a second, Shane wondered if he'd slipped into some sort of dream. Then it dawned on him. Maybe this was her way of reacting to Justin's death. If so, he wanted to stop her before she said anything else. "Lauren ... we don't have to decide this now. Last time we rushed the decision and look what hap—"

"Shane." She put her finger to his lips. "I haven't rushed this. I've missed you with every breath, every heartbeat. Almost worse than I missed you the first time we were apart." She slipped her arms around his waist, and her eyes found the way to the most private part of his soul. The place no one else had ever found. "I want to marry you and move to Fallon with you. I want to sleep with you and wake up next to you and share your passion for freedom and safety and for doing what's right—even if that sometimes looks a little different to each of us."

Doubt must've flashed in his eyes because she giggled. "A *little* different, Shane. Not so different that I see white where you see black. Not anymore. I told you … I've changed. God changed me."

He put his hand alongside her face and searched her eyes. This was the scene he'd only dreamed about. "I thought you brought me here to tell me good-bye."

"No. Never again." She moved her arms from his waist to his neck. "I'm done saying good-bye." Her voice trembled. "If … if you'll still have me, then marry me. Marry me this Saturday at Emily's church and let's get started."

He laughed. She was always ready for a project, a purpose. "Get started?"

"Yes." She kissed him again. "On forever."

And that had been that.

The plans came together quickly—almost everyone they wanted to attend was already in town, and his parents were able to catch a last-minute flight. His mother had pulled him aside last night, her eyes teary.

"I've prayed for this for two decades, son." She took his hand. "We were wrong, what we did. But God's ways are better than man's, and now here you are. Here we all are."

Morning took forever to come, and when it did, Shane still couldn't believe it was happening. He wore his dress uniform and stood next to a preacher at the front of a church, the one Emily and Justin had attended just off the base at Fort Lewis. Organ music filled the air, and the faces in the first few rows of the church grinned their approval. And of course, in a few minutes he would do what he'd dreamed of doing since he was a junior in high school.

He would marry Lauren Gibbs Anderson.

The church held everyone who mattered most to them. Emily, who was in the back room with her mother, would be Lauren's maid of honor; and Gary Baker, standing on his other side, sharp in his dark three-piece suit, would act as best man. His parents, who had flown up from California the day before, sat in the second row next to Angela Anderson—Lauren's mother. Carol and Jill Baker were there, as was Joe.

And that was all.

He looked at his parents and then at Lauren's mother. Twenty years ago, the three of them had fought this moment with everything in them. They were wrong back then, and they'd admitted so time and again in the past year. But only this moment—this marriage—could truly free them of the guilt and regret they carried.

Shane smiled. There was no anger now, no residual bitterness. Never mind the years he and Lauren had lost. They had a lifetime ahead of them. Shane caught Gary Baker's eyes, and he gave him a look that said he still couldn't believe this was happening. That a family could survive such terrible, unfathomable grief, and such limitless joy—all in one week.

He stared at the back doors of the church and waited. He and Emily had talked that morning. "Justin's life mattered in a lot of ways, too many to count," she'd told him. "But Daddy, you know what?" Her eyes were soft, full of emotion. "I think his life counted for this too. God used Justin's life to change Mom's heart." Her eyes glistened. "And He used Justin's death to show her that love never has enough time."

Shane smiled. Love never has enough time. Leave it to Emily to sum up the entire situation with one sentence. She was right too.

He heard the music change, heard the beginning refrains of the traditional wedding march begin. Love never had enough time, but what time was left, he would savor. Every single second.

The double doors opened, and there she was, his bride. She wore a striking white dress, her blonde hair swept up in loose curls. But what made her beauty absolutely breathtaking was the look in her eyes. Reporting on the war, spending time with cynical people, being angry much of the time—all of it had taken its toll on Lauren. The entire time she lived in Fallon, he rarely saw her eyes soften, rarely saw her intensity let up.

But now ... she looked seventeen again. She had no chip on her shoulder, nothing to prove. She was simply the tender girl he'd always loved, the girl with a heart bigger than the ocean and a soul full of kindness and love. Finally taking the walk they had both dreamed about.

The walk down the aisle.

Since her father had died the year before, she had explained that she wanted Emily to walk her down the aisle. "She spent a lifetime praying and dreaming about this moment," Lauren had told him. "She's the one who brought us back together. Long after we gave up. I can't imagine anyone else walking with me."

Neither could he.

Emily wore an elegant lavender dress, her dark hair styled much like Lauren's. As she walked next to her mother, Shane caught Joe Greenwald watching her. The two had been together every day since the funeral, and Shane was glad. Emily needed a friend, and because of Justin, she had one.

Lauren was closer now, and their eyes held. Shane had expected to be choked up at this part of the ceremony, watching Lauren walk to him, knowing that finally they had found their way to this moment. But instead he wanted to laugh, wanted to raise his fist in the air and shout for all the world to hear. After searching and longing and praying and crying, here they were.

And nothing would ever separate them again.

~

Lauren had never felt more certain in all her life.

She walked, unblinking, her eyes on Shane's, and inside she celebrated like never before. She was marrying Shane Galanter! They'd agreed to write their own vows, but Lauren didn't have to. She'd written them long ago, when she was a teenager, and she'd been reminded of them just a few months ago by Emily. Always Emily.

Her daughter stood tall, proud beside her. But there was no denying the way she trembled as they walked, arm in arm. Emily had waited for this morning all her life, and now it was here. Even in the darkness of the valley of the shadow of death, this day would cast a light. A brilliant light.

She reached the end of the aisle and the music stopped. The pastor smiled. He had talked with them yesterday morning, asked them and encouraged them about their faith and their determination to keep Christ at the center of their marriage. It was a reminder. They had gotten here by God's grace, and they would stay together the same way. In Christ alone. Even if Lauren was still figuring some of that out.

"Who gives this woman to be married?" The preacher's voice rang clear and strong.

Emily smiled up at her. "I do." She kissed Lauren on the cheek and then took her place to the side.

Lauren turned her eyes to Shane. He looked like a dream, and she felt herself react to his presence. How long had she searched for him? Longed for this day? He walked down the steps, his eyes never leaving hers. Then he took her hand and led her back up the stairs to face the preacher.

"I had a chance to meet with the bride and groom yesterday." The man smiled at the handful of people in attendance and raised his brow. "I must say, normally when a couple wants a wedding to come together quickly, my advice is to wait. But in this case—"

he grinned at Lauren and then at Shane—"the wedding is way overdue." He opened the Bible and read a passage from Colossians and another from 1 Corinthians 13. He focused his talk on love and sacrifice, and how it was impossible to have one without the other.

Lauren glanced at Shane, and he met her smile. The pastor was right. All their lives had been a picture of that truth. Love and sacrifice, and how one couldn't exist without the other.

Finally it was time for the vows. Shane went first. He and Lauren faced each other, and he took her hands in his. "Lauren, I don't know about love except what I've felt for you. I refuse to think about the years we lost, but only about the ones that will begin here, now." He paused, and for a moment they both seemed to forget where they were. There was so much between them, so many memories that only the two of them shared.

Shane took a slow breath. "I promise to be with you, stay with you, love you, and laugh with you. I promise to listen and always look for new ways to show you how much I care." The corners of his lips lifted. "Most of all, I promise to lean on God through life's trials and tragedies and triumphs. Because if I lean on Him, you can always lean on me."

It was her turn. Her throat was thick, and she didn't want to take her eyes off Shane for a single instant. "Shane ... you taught me about love a long time ago. And though I searched, though I became someone even I didn't recognize at times, I never stopped believing in that definition. The one I've held onto since I was seventeen. This is what you taught me." She opened the piece of paper that had been folded tightly in the palm of her hand.

"Real love is this." Her voice rang clear through the church, "Real love waits in the snow on your front porch so you can walk to school together in the fifth grade. It brings you a chocolate bar when you fall and finish last in the seventh grade Olympics." She smiled at him, seeing the way he looked that long ago day. "Real love whispers something in the middle of algebra about your pink fingernail polish so that you don't forget how to smile when you're doing math, and it saves a seat for you in the lunchroom every Friday through high school. Even when the other baseball players think you're stupid."

A few quiet laughs came from the front of the church.

Lauren's chin quivered, but she kept on, looking from the page to Shane and back again. "Real love stays up late on a Saturday making chocolate chip cookies together, flicking flour at you and getting eggshells in the batter and making sure you'll remember that night the rest of your life. And real love thinks you're pretty even when your hair is pulled back in a ponytail and you don't stand perfectly straight."

She folded the paper and handed it to him. His eyes were damp, but he mouthed the words, "I remember."

She smiled and looked to the most tender place in his heart, the place where the teenage Shane still lived. "And this year, you taught me something else. Real love lets you figure out the answers by yourself. It says good-bye for a season and prays for your return. Real love understands about love and sacrifice and is willing to live accordingly." She held onto his hands tighter than before. "Shane, you've spent your life showing me what real love is. I understand now, and I promise to spend the rest of my life loving you like that." She blinked back tears. "As long as we both shall live."

From a few feet away, they both heard Emily stifle a squeal, and again there was laughter.

The pastor stepped closer and took the rings from Emily and Gary. He explained the significance of the unbroken circles, and the promise they would represent for all time. As Shane slipped the band of white gold onto her finger, she felt the greatest sense of rightness. Yes, her life was full before she found Shane again.

She had a career and a purpose. But her life wasn't complete until now.

The rings in place, the pastor nodded to Shane. "You may kiss your bride."

He did so in a way that took her breath and made her anxious for every tomorrow they'd share together. Before they parted, before the pastor could present them as husband and wife, out of the corner of her eye, Lauren saw Emily close her eyes and lift her face skyward.

Their daughter was praying, no doubt. Thanking God, because no matter how hard the journey, they were here. Where they had always belonged. And this time no one and nothing would separate them until death intervened. The bridge to this place had been built with wisdom and prayer and love and sacrifice.

But most of all, it had been built by God.

As Shane drew back, as they shared a smile of sweet expectation and oneness, Lauren was reminded. The miracle God had given them was greater than either of them had imagined possible. Because they had found something they never really believed they'd find, something only God could've given them. A place to start and stand and build upon. A place to love and laugh and live.

Precious, priceless common ground.

Thirty-One

Eighteen Months Later

The haunting sound of taps rang out across the base as the Memorial Day service came to an end. Rain had fallen relentlessly all day, but it stopped an hour earlier, and now only the gray clouds remained.

Emily took the hand of the soldier beside her, and silently they walked to his pickup truck. When they were inside, as Joe Greenwald started the engine and pulled out of the parking lot, Emily turned to him. He still held her hand. "It feels like yesterday."

"I know." He smiled at her, no longer the tentative smile of a young man uncertain about how to proceed. Rather, a smile born of friendship forged in the flames of grief. Friendship ... and something else.

Something deeper.

They had planned this day for a month, knowing what they would do, where they would wind up, and now Joe drove his truck onto the southbound I-5 freeway and settled into a steady pace. They were headed for Kelso, for the place where Justin was buried.

There had been no way to foresee how the past year and a half would unfold, no way of knowing how pain would bring the two of them so close. Emily leaned her head back and closed her eyes. They had been determined to be friends because Justin asked them to be.

But from there, the bond between them took on a life of its own.

It started with the teen center. A month after Justin's death, Joe picked her up at her residence hall and drove her downtown. She had worried that the familiarity of the afternoon would wear her out, leave her emotionally drained. But instead, the time together that day had breathed new life into her. Justin's work, being carried out the way he would've wanted it to be.

Snow fell lightly as they made their way into the center that day, and there they were. The guys who had loved Justin so much. Bo seemed to notice them first. He gave Emily a questioning look, and then he turned to Joe.

"What's up?" The question was loaded, fully defensive and almost threatening.

Joe separated himself from Emily and approached him. "Thought we'd play a little ping-pong." He shrugged. "You know, since there's snow on the court."

Bo crossed his arms and stuck out his chest. He looked at Emily and back to Joe. He began to shake his head, slowly at first and then faster. "Oh, no you don't." He jabbed a finger at Joe. "I know what you're doing."

"Bo ..." Emily took a step forward.

Joe held out his hand, stopping her. "It's okay." He looked at Bo. "I've got this."

"No, you ain't *got* this, man." Bo raised his voice. He gestured hard toward Joe. "You think you can walk in here and take his *place*? Is that it?" He waved off Joe, turned, and paced three steps. Then he stopped, his voice louder than before. "You can't take his place, man. No one can." He pointed to the door. "Get out. We don't want you."

Dexter lifted his chin. The others looked like they felt the same way.

Emily felt tears on her cheeks even before she knew she was crying. Of course they didn't want Joe, they wanted Justin. They all wanted Justin. But he was gone, and Joe was determined to help these kids, to pick up where his buddy had left off. She reminded herself to breathe as she watched Joe.

He laughed, as if Bo's attitude hadn't affected him at all. "Man, I didn't come to babysit you." He crossed his arms. "I came to whip your tail in ping-pong." He held up his hand. "But hey, if you're afraid, that's cool." He looked at Dexter, and then at the others. "Someone's gotta be up for the challenge, right?"

A gradual shift happened among the teens. They glanced at each other and then at Bo, as if to question whether he would really back down from someone calling him afraid. Bo looked angry; he'd been tricked. He gritted his teeth and hissed in Joe's direction. "Someone wants me to beat 'em at pong—" he flicked his shirt, all macho and tough guy again—"then I say bring it."

He walked to the table and picked up a paddle and a ball. "Come on, white boy, bring it."

Joe rolled up his sleeves. "Yeah, that's the Bo I heard about all those nights in Iraq. All talk, no action."

"What?" Bo let his mouth hang open. "I could take Justin any day."

"Fine." Joe practically spat the word. "Let's see what you got."

That first game was one of the fiercest, most intense competitions Emily had ever seen. When it was over, Joe had won more than the game. He had won the respect of every boy at the center. Once a week they began coming, and over time Joe forged a relationship with the guys, a friendship. And at the end of that semester, Bo showed them his report card. Nothing less than a C, even in math and science.

Joe would never be Justin.

But he brought his own brand of loving and learning, and that was more than enough. Emily liked watching him, liked seeing how he was quieter than Justin in some ways, and yet maybe more able to connect with the teens individually. And he was funny. Humor gave Joe a connection the guys hadn't expected.

Half the time Joe was teasing them, and the other half he was telling them how God was the only way off the streets.

Joe's parents lived in Ohio, the Akron area. He was the youngest of six kids, the sometimes quiet one in a loud and fiercely loyal family. Three of them had already decided on military careers. Emily liked hearing stories from Joe's childhood, the growing-up years, how Joe and his brothers would wrestle and chase after each other and stage contests for everything, from eating hot dogs to swimming across the river that ran through town.

His parents thought Joe was headed for a military career too, but he was only serving for a season, getting money for college. Joe wanted to be a doctor. "There's a lot of ways to help people," he had told Emily. "Serving your country in war, or serving your fellow man in a doctor's office."

She agreed with him and found their discussions more fascinating all the time—whether they centered around Iraq, and Joe's thought that the country should be divided into three states—one for the Kurds, one for the Shiites, and one for the Sunnis. Or whether they were talking about the application process for med school. Joe was twenty-one back then, a year older than her, and already he'd taken enough classes between tours in Iraq that he was midway through his sophomore year at the University of Washington.

That same month, when Joe first made contact with the teens at the center, they took the first of several trips down to Kelso. Buster was getting slower. Maybe because he missed Justin, or maybe because he was getting older. Either way, he needed to be walked, and Emily had developed a fondness for him.

Justin's parents welcomed them like long lost friends, though Emily caught his mother looking at her, watching the easy way she had with Joe. That first time, the two of them went outside and hooked Buster to his leash. Justin's old matted sweatshirt was in his doghouse where he had been sleeping.

"Hey, boy ... remember me?" Emily petted him behind his ears, the way Justin had always done.

Buster wagged his tail.

"See that?" She smiled at Joe. "He likes me."

Joe stooped down and patted the dog. "Justin was crazy about him."

Buster hid behind Emily's leg, fearful and maybe a little puzzled over the young man who had some of Justin's mannerisms, but yet wasn't Justin.

They walked Buster through the Bakers' neighborhood, and after an hour, the dog warmed up to Joe. Before they left, Justin's mother pulled Emily aside. "I'm glad you and Joe are ... you know, becoming better friends." She smiled, but tears filled her eyes at the same time. "Justin would've wanted that."

Suddenly Emily understood the haunting looks she'd been giving them since they arrived. She must've thought Emily was developing deeper feelings for Joe, feelings that went beyond friendship. And only one month after Justin's death. Emily shook her head, her voice low so she couldn't be heard by the men in the other room. "Mrs. Baker, there's nothing between us." She shrugged and felt her own eyes tear up. "We have Justin in common, that's all."

Mrs. Baker gave her a sad smile, and she nodded as if to say she understood more than Emily on this matter. "It's okay, Emily. You're young." She put her hand on Emily's shoulder. "No one would expect you to stop living. Especially not Justin."

The conversation stayed with Emily and troubled her. For another three months she worried about what people might think, what they might say. When she talked to her parents—who were happier than ever—she downplayed the time she was spending with Joe.

Meanwhile, she and Joe continued to spend all their free time together. They met with the teens once a week, and every now and then they visited the Vets at the American Legion hall.

"I love this," he told her once, "carrying on in Justin's place." The look in his eyes was deep and sincere. "But there's something I've always wanted to do. Those roadside bombs maim as many guys as they kill. If you'll go with me, I think I'd like to start visiting the VA Hospital."

And so they did that too, spending an afternoon every few weeks hanging out with soldiers who had lost an arm or a leg, or who were recovering from some other sort of war injury. Emily enjoyed the conversations they had with the soldiers, but even more, she liked watching Joe. She was struck by the easy way he had with people, his sense of humor and how it created an almost instant bond with anyone he met.

On the six-month anniversary of Justin's death, they spent a day at Blake Island State Park, a tiny oasis in the middle of Puget Sound, eight miles out from Seattle's waterfront. They hiked the trails and explored Tillicum Village and spotted a pair of bald eagles diving for fish near the shore.

But not until after lunch, when they were sitting on a fallen log staring at the ocean, did Joe turn to her. And suddenly, there it was. The one thing they'd never discussed, never dared to imagine. At first he said nothing, but he didn't have to. His eyes told her that he was feeling the same way she was.

Somewhere along the path of healing and holding onto Justin's memory, a special sort of love had taken root. And now it was deep enough that they could no longer ignore it, no longer spend an afternoon together without somehow acknowledging the feeling.

He took a long breath. "Can you feel it, Emily?" His voice was so soft, it mixed with the ocean breeze and resonated deep in her soul.

She didn't have to ask what he meant. Her eyes held his. "Yes ... I feel it."

A consuming guilt gathered around them, staring them down, daring them to state the obvious. Emily couldn't look at Joe. She let her eyes find a place in the sand near her tennis shoes. How had it happened? Having feelings for Justin's friend was wrong. She'd known when she lost Justin that she would never love the same way again, that no one could ever take his place. So how had they come to this place, to these feelings? And worse, how could they deny their strength, when quietly, beneath the surface, their hearts had already started something too strong to walk away from?

Joe reached for her hand. "We can take it slow, Emily."

The touch of his fingers against hers sent shivers down her spine. She could barely breathe, had to will herself to stay there beside him. What would Justin think? How could they live with themselves for letting this happen? Justin had asked them to be friends, nothing more.

But even so, she didn't let go of his hand. What had he said? They could take it slow? She nodded. "Yes. We ... we have to."

"Look at me, Emily." Again his voice was tender, resigned.

She lifted her eyes and realized that her knees were shaking. It was May, and the weather was still cool. But the chill inside her came from their conversation and not the temperature.

He looked long at her, studying her eyes. "Justin wouldn't be angry with us. He ..." Joe's chin quivered. "He asked us to spend time together. Deep inside—in those last minutes—he had to know."

Emily thought that through. He had to know? Was it possible, that as he lay there dying he had asked Joe to be her friend so that one day she could find a love with him, the love Justin could no longer give her? She swallowed hard. "I don't know." She felt sick, ashamed of herself for being attracted to Joe, for having feelings for him. "It'll take time."

And it had. Their first kiss came seven months later, on Christmas Eve. By then there was no denying the obvious. Through a trail of grief and sorrow, God had forged in them a friendship that would never be broken. Could never be broken.

The bond they shared was deep and anchored in a faith that had survived the most difficult test. Her parents celebrated with her when she told them the news—that she and Joe had moved into a dating relationship. And Justin's parents had rejoiced as well, telling the two of them that it was right and fitting that they find their way together.

"Justin would've wanted this," his mother said. "I saw it coming, Emily. We're happy for you both."

Emily appreciated their support, though she suspected they had shared tears over the situation as well. Same as she and Joe. This wasn't how things were supposed to work out, but they had. Now everyone involved needed to find a way to understand and move on.

Some nights, before she returned to her room, they would sit on the bench—the one she and Justin once sat on—and they would hold hands in silence. Simply missing Justin and all he'd meant to them. But by the time they reached the one-year anniversary of his death, after they took a week over Christmas break and visited her parents in their Fallon home, this much was clear: Justin had brought them together.

There was nothing guilty or shameful about that, and they agreed to let the New Year define a change, an end to the constant grief and sadness, and a tender new beginning for the two of them.

Emily opened her eyes and let the memories of the past eighteen months fade. She had Joe now, and she loved him with everything inside her. No, he would never be Justin, but that was okay. What she and Joe shared would always—in some ways—be deeper, stronger, because of the painful journey they'd traveled together.

It was fitting, really. That the trail of tears they'd walked would end and begin here on this day, Memorial Day, the day when Justin would always be first in their minds. As long as she lived she would remember their summer together. He had given her happily, but he had promised her more.

And now, because of him, she and Joe had found that elusive something, that thing that for a while seemed lost for all time.

And maybe somewhere down the road, they would even find ever after.

A NOTE FROM THE AUTHOR

Dear Friends,

Thanks so much for journeying with me through the pages of *Ever After*. I learned much about myself and about love as I wrote this book. I learned about sacrifice and patriotism. Without a doubt, I learned that I have a deep-seated respect and gratitude toward the men and women who serve our country through the armed forces, and for their families—all who sacrifice some, and some who sacrifice all.

My family often teases me when I write a novel. They sneak into my writing room with a cup of tea or a bowl of grapes or a sandwich, and they wonder at the tears in my eyes. "They're make-believe people," my husband tells me.

But not to me.

In my heart, they live and breathe and move, and when I write, I feel like a reader. The story is always entirely a gift from God, and me, the humbly grateful soul who gets a first peak at it. But this story was different. I wept more than ever before while writing *Ever After*. For the first time since I started writing books, I had to keep a box of tissues on the table beside me. One morning Kelsey walked in.

"Hi, Mom. Do you need anything?"

"Hi." I turned to her, a tissue in one hand, tears streaming down my face.

"Oh. Sorry for interrupting." She gave me a strange look. "But ... uh, can I get you anything?"

"Yes." I looked at her through clouded eyes. "Counseling."

And that's how I felt through the writing of this book. I was happy and joyful with my kids and family one minute, and then five minutes later I'd be at my laptop weeping over the loss of Justin Baker and the complexities of war. My emotions were so strong, and the story so vivid, that one day after breaking my personal record for words written in a given day, I found my husband and told him, "I love writing more than breathing. I just have to tell you. I absolutely believe this is where God wants me, and I love what I'm doing more today than ever in all my life."

Which is a good thing, since I've got lots more books ahead, God willing.

But the depth of my emotions made me sit back and ask myself where the feelings were coming from. And that's when I realized that they came from my gratitude for the men and women who fight for and defend our country. The story of Justin and Emily is all too real for thousands of people across our great land. Sacrifice is very much a part of living life as an American — and a story like *Ever After* lets us take time to remember that, to acknowledge it.

This book so completely filled my heart that I wrote it faster than any other. Like a living picture, it poured out of me in just five days. Five days. I was gripped by the story, and all I could picture was that in many ways, there was nothing fictional about Justin Baker's story. Like all of you, we know young men and women serving our country, people who need our utmost respect and support. People who lay down everything out of devotion to America.

If there was a point, a message I pray you received from *Ever After*, it was this: Love is not possible without sacrifice, and sacrifice is not possible without love. Isn't that what Jesus taught? He died on the cross as the greatest sacrifice, the greatest gift of love, and it's through His grace and salvation that we can do anything good and lasting.

Regardless of our differing political views, we must—as Americans—agree to pray and be grateful for the people who put their lives on the line so the United States can remain a free nation. I found myself loving Justin for who he was and for all the tens of thousands of young people he represented. These people are the heartbeat of America.

The cost of freedom is great.

Our family heard that message on Memorial Day this year, just as I was finishing the story of *Ever After*. At a quiet military cemetery in our town, I stood in dark sunglasses next to my husband and kids, crying silently through the entire ceremony. I was struck by the pride in the hunched over World War II Veterans, and the deep pain still in the eyes of the Vietnam Vets. I watched the flag being raised over the cemetery at the end of the service, and I clutched tightly to my family, thanking God for the privilege of living in America.

I pray that you might understand love and sacrifice a little better for having read *Ever After*. If you aren't familiar with Jesus Christ and His sacrifice on the cross, or if you'd like to know more about how you could receive His gift of salvation, please contact your local Bible-believing church. You could also write to me and put the words, "NEW LIFE" in the subject line. I'll be happy to send you a Bible and pray for you, that you'll find salvation in the only One who can give it.

The gift is free to you, but it was never really free. Jesus paid the price.

In the same way, living in the U.S. is free to all of us, but freedom is never really free either. A cost is being paid every day by the military men and women and families in our midst. Let's not forget that.

If you are among those serving our country, I thank you. With all that I am, I pray you will know how grateful I am, how grateful our family is, and how often we pray for your safety and success. Likewise, if you are among the hundreds of thousands of family and friends of those serving, my heart goes out to you. Thank you for allowing your loved one to serve and to sacrifice.

The price you are paying has not gone unnoticed.

You see, my little Austin—eight years old—is a kid like Justin Baker was. He plays army games and talks about "trying out" for the army one day—so that he can be among the best soldiers fighting for the United States. "I wanna keep America safe," he'll tell me.

He's just a kid, and I'm sure his interests could change over the coming years. But today, I see his tender heart and his great conviction, and I know—already I know—the great sacrifice it would be to take him to a recruiting office and let him begin a soldier's journey.

So for now I hold on a little longer to all my kids, and I remain grateful. Grateful to a God who would give us a land called America where we can live and serve Him and exist in freedom. And grateful to this country's military families. I pray for God's hand of protection and blessing on you all.

One more thing. You might remember at the front of this book, I dedicated *Ever After* to the memory of soldier Joshua Dingler. I learned about Joshua long after I finished writing this book. But the more I found out about Joshua, the more I discovered that his life had an uncanny resemblance to my fictional character, Justin Baker.

Like Justin, Joshua left behind a girl he planned to marry. He went into battle proud to help a nation find freedom, and in his brief life he was known for the way he helped other people. Like Justin Baker, the real-life Joshua Dingler was remembered by an entire city at his funeral. The day of his memorial service, thousands of people lined Highway 92 from the Pickett's Mill Baptist Church to the cemetery. People holding flags, men saluting from the bed of a truck, and endless rows of men and women with their hands over their hearts.

But Joshua Dingler is not a fictional character. He is real, and I pray that this book brings honor to his memory. What defined Joshua was not his death in Al Mahmudiyah, Iraq, south of Baghdad, August 15, 2005. For that reason, please visit my website at *www.KarenKingsbury.com* and pray for the military members represented there. Also, please send in your photos and bios of your loved ones serving our country. Check my website for details.

Finally, as always, I'd love to hear from you. My website is growing constantly and has become a community of readers and people like yourself. There is a link where you can post a prayer request or pray for others in need, and there are links for book clubs and readers looking to connect with each other. I've also included a blog with constant journal updates and a look into the writer's life, as well as my life as a wife and mother. It's my way of helping us all feel like friends.

There are also contests all the time. One ongoing contest is this: When you finish reading this book, lend it to someone who hasn't read one of my novels. Then email me and write, "SHARED A BOOK" in the subject line. In the message, tell me the first name of the person you shared with and why you shared the book. You will be automatically entered into a drawing that will take place each spring. The winner will bring a friend and spend a day in the Northwest with me and my family. Check my website for details, updates, or changes to this or any contest.

In the meantime, know that I am praying for you and yours. May God's face shine upon you. Until next time,

In His light and love,
Karen Kingsbury

ACKNOWLEDGMENTS

As always, this book couldn't have come together without the help of many people. First, a special thanks to my great friends at Zondervan, who believe in this sequel and have enormous dreams and prayers for the way it will touch people and change lives. Thank you!

Also, thanks to my amazing agent, Rick Christian, president of Alive Communications. I am amazed more as every day passes at your integrity, your brilliant talent, and your commitment to the Lord and to getting my Life-Changing Fiction™ out to readers all over the world. You are a strong man of God, Rick. You care for my career as if you were personally responsible for the souls God touches through these books. Thank you for looking out for my personal time—the hours I have with my husband and kids. I couldn't do this without you.

As always, this book wouldn't be possible without the help of my husband and kids, who will eat just about anything when I'm on deadline and who understand and love me anyway. I thank God I'm still able to spend more time with you than with my pretend people—as Austin calls them. Thanks for understanding the sometimes crazy life I lead and for always being my greatest support.

Also, thanks to my mother and assistant, Anne Kingsbury, for her great sensitivity and love for my readers. You are a reflection of my own heart, Mom, or maybe I'm a reflection of yours. Either way, we are a great team, and I appreciate you more than you know. I'm grateful, also, for my dad, Ted Kingsbury, who is and always has been my greatest encourager. I remember when I was a little girl, Dad, and you would say, "One day, honey, everyone will read your books and know what a wonderful writer you are." Thank you for believing in me long before anyone else ever did. Thanks also to my sisters, Tricia and Susan and Lynne, who help out with my business when the workload is too large to see around. I appreciate you!

And a thanks to Katie Johnson, who runs a large part of my business life—everything from my accounting to my calendar. God brought you to me, Katie, and I'll be grateful as long as I'm writing for Him. Don't ever leave, okay? And to Olga Kalachik, whose hard work helping me prepare for events allows me to operate a significant part of my business from my home. The personal touch you both bring to my ministry is precious to me, priceless to me … thank you with all my heart.

And thanks to my friends and family who continue to surround me with love and prayer and support. I could list you by name, but you know who you are. Thank you for believing in me and for seeing who I really am. A true friend stands by through the changing seasons of life and cheers you on, not for your successes, but for staying true to what matters most. You are the ones who know me that way, and I'm grateful for every one of you. Please keep praying for me, since I can't do a page of this, not even a word, without God's strength and gift.

Of course, the greatest thanks goes to God Almighty, the most wonderful Author of all—the Author of life (Hebrews 12:2). The gift is Yours. I pray I might have the incredible opportunity and responsibility to use it for You all the days of my life.

READING GROUP GUIDE

1. Explain Lauren Gibbs's feelings toward the war at the beginning of *Ever After*. What had shaped her viewpoints?

2. Do you think it would've been possible for Lauren to continue living in Fallon without spending additional time in the Middle East? Why or why not?

3. Discuss Shane Galanter's feelings toward war and the military at the beginning of *Ever After*. What had led to his viewpoints?

4. What are some of the differing opinions in the United States today regarding war in the Middle East or the defense of the country? Discuss.

5. Share an opinion that is different from yours regarding this issue. What do you think might lead someone to have this opinion? How can you better understand that person?

6. Explain how it is possible to have differing opinions and still be like-minded on the bigger issues. How did Shane see this as a possibility for him and Lauren early in the book?

7. Describe the character Justin Baker. What made him such an amazing young man? Why would a young man like Justin want to join the armed services? What characteristics do you see as common in the men and women you know who serve this country?

8. Give examples of Justin's character, and how Lauren, Shane, and Emily could see that character in action during the summer when he and Emily were dating.

9. Why did Justin feel strongly about serving in Operation Enduring Freedom, and the war in Iraq?

10. Why did Lauren feel she had to return to reporting on the war? What did she expect to find when she returned, and what did she pray for?

11. What was the epiphany for Lauren, the turning point that broadened her viewpoint on the war? Explain that scene and the emotions Lauren felt.

12. What emotions and feelings did Lauren have when she witnessed Yusef killed by a sniper? How did she feel about the war then, and her prior reporting on it?

13. Based on Justin's emails, photos, and firsthand accounts, what were his feelings toward the war? What were his feelings toward the Iraqi people?

14. How did Emily react to the news that Justin had been killed? Did it change her opinions on the validity of the war? How did Lauren react?

15. Explain Shane's feelings as he received word about Justin's death. What did he feel was the one enemy that could threaten a soldier? Why?

16. How did Shane find his way back to having purpose in his position as an officer in the military? Explain his feelings when Justin's body returned home in a flag-covered casket.

17. Explain the support Justin and his family received during the memorial service and graveside service. When have you seen that sort of outpouring of support for a member of the military? Describe the time.

18. The lasting message of *Ever After* deals with love and sacrifice. Explain how those two are intertwined, and how they model the greatest sacrifice of all—the one Christ made on the cross.

19. Tell about a soldier in your family or circle of friends. What price did he or she pay in the fight for freedom?

20. What can you do to support the troops in your area? How can you involve your family or church, your friends or co-workers?

KAREN KINGSBURY
NEW YORK TIMES
BESTSELLING AUTHOR
Leaving
BAILEY FLANIGAN
SERIES

An excerpt
from Karen Kingsbury's
Leaving

One

GOODBYES WERE ONE OF THE HARDEST THINGS ABOUT LIFE ...
one way or another people were always leaving. Always moving
on. That was the point the pastor was making, and Bailey Flanigan blinked back tears as she shifted in the pew beside her family.
Like Cody Coleman, she told herself. *Always leaving.*

"Life changes. People come and go, and seasons never last."
Pastor Mark Atteberry's voice rang with passionate emotion.
"Nothing stays the same. We can count on that. Good times come
and go ... finances are ever changing ... our health will eventually
fail us. And through death or decision, everyone we know will
someday leave us." He paused, his eyes searching the congregation. "All except for Jesus Christ. Jesus will never leave you nor
forsake you. And because of that we have the strength to love
with all our hearts ... even unaware of what tomorrow brings." He
smiled. "That's what I want you to take away from today's service.
Jesus stays."

Pastor Mark asked them to turn their Bibles to the book of
Deuteronomy. Bailey did as she was told, but the rest of the ser-
mon she struggled to stay focused. Cody hadn't talked to her since
that day on her parents' porch, the day he tried to convince her
it was finally and absolutely time to move on. Now, two months
later, the pain and silence of the passing time was just about killing her.

When the hour was almost over, Bailey's mom, Jenny, turned

to her. "Powerful message." Her voice was barely a whisper, only loud enough for Bailey.

Bailey nodded and managed a slight smile. She'd tell her mom later how much her heart hurt, how Pastor Mark's talk about goodbyes stirred up all the missing she'd ever felt for Cody. Never mind the days when she seemed over him, when she didn't look for a text every hour or catch the phone ringing at night and hope it was him. Today, even with her mom and dad and five brothers seated along the pew beside her, there was no way around her feelings.

She missed Cody with every aching breath.

The service ended with a song Bailey loved — a Chris Tomlin song called "Our God" that always stirred her love for the Lord and her belief in His promises. She stood next to her mom and glanced down the row at her family. How great that they could be here together, worshipping and praising God, and sharing everything they believed. How amazing to celebrate Sundays with them always. She smiled, ignoring the sting of fresh tears in her eyes. Wasn't that the point Pastor Mark was making? This picture of the Flanigan family wouldn't last either. They were all growing up. And some Sunday not far down the road they'd be spread out to other churches, other places where they would begin their own lives.

Because only Jesus stayed.

But God in all His goodness still allowed moments like this, and no matter how far they might someday be from each other, they would hold tight to the memory of this: what it felt like to be a family who loved each other deeply and cared for the people around the dining room table like they were each other's best friends. The sort of family other people only dreamed about.

Bailey closed her eyes and let the music fill her soul. "Our God is greater … our God is stronger … God you are higher than any other …"

The beauty of the moment mixed with the sweet sadness of losing Cody, of not knowing where he was or what he was doing. The idea seemed outrageous, really. He hadn't felt this far away when he was fighting in Iraq. Now he was only an hour away in Indianapolis, but it seemed like he'd fallen off the planet. At least that was where she assumed he was — the place he'd been the last time they saw each other.

Pastor Mark dismissed them, and Bailey felt her mother give her a side hug. "You were thinking about him." She pressed her cheek against Bailey's.

Bailey had nothing to hide where her mom was concerned. She looked straight at her. "How could I not?"

"We'll talk later."

"Okay." Bailey returned the hug and they moved into the aisle with the rest of the family. The knowing in her mother's eyes made Bailey grateful. Bailey kept no secrets from her mom and, because of that, they would always be close.

Anyway, the conversation would have to come later. Ashley Baxter Blake and her husband, Landon, had invited them over for dinner, which meant a house full of people. It was a Baxter family tradition, and at least once a month the Baxters invited Bailey's family too. The more people the better — that was Ashley's theory. She and Landon bought the old farmhouse from John Baxter, Ashley's father. Bailey was sure she saw a wistfulness in John's eyes whenever they gathered for dinner. A longing for days gone by maybe. Days that hadn't lasted any more than the ones now would last for the Flanigan family.

Bailey couldn't imagine raising a family for decades in a house and then coming back only as a visitor. But it was better than having strangers live in the place. Especially with all the memories that still lived between the walls and windows.

On the drive to the Baxter house, Bailey caught herself more aware than usual that even this — all eight of them traveling somewhere after church — wouldn't last. She was almost twenty-one, after all, in her third year at Indiana University. She leaned against the car door and listened to her brothers' conversations around her. Connor was seventeen and closest to Bailey in age. This was his junior year, and he was about to begin his final football season as starting quarterback — throwing for more than 200 yards a game, the way Cody had taught him.

Connor was class president and debating themes for the Spring Fling dance — an annual costume event at Clear Creek High. "I'm thinking 'Meant to Be.'" Connor glanced back at his brothers Shawn and Justin — both sophomores — and BJ, a freshman. "I mean, I kinda like it. What do you think? 'Meant to Be.'"

"Meant to be what?" Justin frowned.

In the seat beside Bailey, the youngest Flanigan boy — tow-headed twelve-year-old Ricky — giggled. "Like, you come as Batman, but you tell everyone you *meant to be* Robin?"

A round of laughter filled the Suburban. Bailey chuckled to herself and gave Connor a helpless look. The younger boys had a point.

Connor flashed a patient, crooked grin. "Not like that." He waited until he had their attention again. "Meant to be, like Batman and Cat Woman — two characters who were meant to be together."

"Or maybe just sort of 'Meant to *Bee*.'" Ricky let loose another few delightful bouts of laughter. "Like a bumblebee. Then everyone could dress in yellow and black."

"Yeah, or maybe Meant to *B*." Shawn's laugh was always louder than the others. "You know ... the letter *B*. That way everyone could dress as something that started with a *B*."

"Okay ... you're all comedians." Connor gave a mock surrender. "I'll ask the leadership class."

From the front passenger seat, their mom looked over her shoulder. "I like it." Her smile was kind, her eyes thoughtful. "A cowboy and a cowgirl … a doctor and a nurse … that sort of thing."

"Yeah, only if Justin goes with Kayla, he'll have to be the nurse." Shawn was working to keep his laughter down, but he was losing the battle. "Because she's a whiz kid at science. She wants to be a surgeon."

The conversation soothed the rough edges of Bailey's soul, helping her find perspective after an hour of being flooded with memories of Cody. This was her reality now. And though Pastor Mark was right — this season wouldn't last — for now it was exactly where she wanted to be.

"Have you heard from Brandon?" Her dad caught Bailey's attention in the rearview mirror. "Since they pulled the movie?"

"He texted me yesterday." The memory warmed her heart. "He's so different from the guy he used to be. His faith means everything to him."

"And the media knows it." He looked happy about the fact. "I'm proud of that young man. Very proud."

Bailey's mom angled herself so she could see Bailey. "His manager knows it, too. That's why they shelved the movie, I'm sure."

"Of course … I agree, definitely."

The boys still chattered about the upcoming dance, but the family could easily hold more than one conversation at a time. Bailey slid forward so her parents could hear her. "Brandon knows that's the reason. Everyone loved us in *Unlocked*, but his manager doesn't want Brandon to seem soft to the Hollywood crowd."

"Casting him in a movie about a NASCAR driver will definitely keep that from happening." Her dad raised his brow. "And Brandon's doing his own stunts, is that true?"

"It is." Bailey wasn't happy about that part. "I'm still trying to talk him out of it."

"Next time you two chat, tell him we said hi." Her dad kept his eyes on the road. "I pray for him every day." He caught her eye one more time. "The same way I pray for Cody." He hesitated. "Which reminds me ... Matt Keagan asked about you the other day. He figured out you were my daughter about a week after the season ended. Every time he stops in the weight room he doesn't let up."

Bailey laughed under her breath. "That's nice dad." She shared a look with her mom. "Matt Keagan has a million girls in love with him. I'll pass."

"He is cute, though." Her mom's eyes twinkled — proof that she was only having fun.

"Of course he's cute." Bailey shook her head, enjoying the lighthearted silliness of the discussion. "He's the strongest Christian in sports, he wears a wristband with Philippians 4:13 on it, and he takes mission trips to Ethiopia whenever he has a spare weekend. He's perfect." She laughed, and the feeling lifted her heart. "I heard he's dating the daughter of a pastor in South Africa."

"Last week everyone on Facebook and Twitter said Matt's hanging out with a finalist from *Dancing with the Stars*."

"Exactly." Bailey laughed. An icon like Matt Keagan? The line of girls would be longer than ten football fields. "I'm not interested."

The three of them fell quiet again, leaving just the boys' conversation the rest of the way to the Baxter house. Bailey stared out the window. The countryside in Bloomington, Indiana, the rolling snow-covered hills, and the crisp, blue sky that spread out forever around them spoke peace to her soul. February brought a mix of weather, but always snow clung to the ground somewhere. This year more than most.

Bailey thought about her life and the guys God had brought across her path. The last year was so crazy amazing she almost felt like the whole thing had happened to someone else. Brandon Paul — the nation's most popular young actor — had singled her out to star in his blockbuster movie *Unlocked*. The film was set to release in April, but it was still being edited. Bailey had never worked harder, and in the end she was satisfied with her performance.

But Bailey's was nothing to Brandon's. He played a teenager whose beautiful soul was locked in a prison of autism. She played his friend, the girl who believed she could draw him out and find a way for God to work a miracle in his life. She couldn't wait to see what critics would say about the movie, about Brandon's stunning portrayal of Holden Harris. The story was riveting — just like the bestselling novel by the same name.

Brandon had done the story justice, for sure. But, along the way, God had given him more than a key performance for his resume. During the shoot Bailey had talked to Brandon about the Lord, and the Bible, and God's plan for him. Last New Year's Eve Brandon came to the Flanigan house and had prayed to ask Jesus into his heart. Later that night, Bailey's dad even baptized Brandon in their Jacuzzi.

Never mind that Brandon had a crush on Bailey. She didn't see him that way — not with his past and the throngs of girls screaming his name. Brandon was a friend, nothing more. But in the wake of filming *Unlocked*, talk had immediately turned to the two of them starring in a love story.

"The chemistry between you is too strong to stop with *Unlocked*," the producer told them. He wanted to film this spring. But in late January the movie was shelved so Brandon could focus on a NASCAR story about a guy living fast and dangerously, a guy in conflict with his racecar driver father. The story was called *Chasing Sunsets*, and Brandon had already signed on to play the part.

Bailey had been offered roles in other films, but nothing she would take. Agents and producers in Hollywood didn't understand. She didn't want to move to LA and spend her days auditioning. She was two years from finishing her theater degree at IU. After that, she still dreamed about performing on Broadway in New York City. But no matter where she did or didn't act in the future her friendship with Brandon Paul would remain — she was sure of that.

She blinked, and lifted her eyes to the sky over Bloomington. The boys were talking about basketball, how Justin would be the fastest guard in the league.

"Cody Coleman was the fastest guy ever at Clear Creek High — football or hoops," Ricky made the pronouncement proudly. "But Justin, you never know ... maybe you'll be faster."

Cody Coleman. The boys' voices faded as Bailey pictured Cody and the way he'd looked the last time they saw each other. She had just wrapped up the shoot with Brandon, and Cody seemed distracted. Different. Maybe the movie had something to do with his distance. Or maybe he pulled away because of Bailey's closeness with Brandon Paul. A quiet sigh slipped from her throat.

Brandon could never be Cody Coleman.

She heard the slightest buzzing sound from her purse and realized she still had her phone on mute from church. She dug around, but by the time she found it the call was gone. She pressed a button at the top of the phone and a number flashed across the screen — one she didn't recognize. The area code was 212. New York City.

Strange, she thought. Tim Reed was the only person she knew living in New York. But she had his number programmed into her contacts, so unless he used a different phone, the call couldn't be from him. She was still staring at the number when her phone flashed that a voicemail had come in. At the same time, her dad pulled into the Baxters' driveway. The place looked beautiful, surrounded by snow and barren trees. A thin ribbon of smoke came from the chimney, and already six cars packed the area adjacent to the garage.

"I can smell the barbecue sauce from here." Ricky took a long whiff as they stepped out of the SUV. "Best barbecue in Bloomington." He grinned at the others, but then his expression changed sharply as he caught a teasing look from their mother. "Except for yours, of course. Second best. That's what I meant to say."

The air was cold against Bailey's cheeks as they walked across the cleared sidewalk and into the house. For the next two hours the warmth from the fire and the Baxters was enough to keep Bailey distracted. They heard about Ashley's paintings being discovered by a new gallery in New York City — one much larger than any gallery that had ever carried her work — and about how well the Baxter grandkids were doing in school and sports.

Bailey sat near her dad and keyed into a conversation between him and Ryan Taylor, the head football coach at Clear Creek High. Ryan was married to the oldest Baxter daughter, Kari. Until this school year, Cody had always been connected to Clear Creek High. Like Ricky said, he was the fastest football player there when he was a student and then, after returning from the war, he coached at Clear Creek.

Her dad and Ryan talked about how off-season training was going, and then Ryan set down his fork. "You hear much from Cody Coleman?"

A shadow fell over her father's expression. "No." He shook his head and wiped a napkin across his mouth. "Not for a couple months. I'm a little worried about him."

For a few seconds Ryan didn't say anything. "Rumor has it he's going for the assistant job at Lyle — that small Christian school outside Indianapolis."

Bailey felt her heart slide into a strange and unrecognizable rhythm. Cody was going for a job? Already? He still had another year of school left, two if he wanted a teaching credential. She looked at the food on her plate, but she wasn't hungry.

"Hmm. I didn't know." Her dad's expression remained flat, his tone even. "Maybe that's better for him."

"I'm not sure. Cody needs accountability." Ryan squinted, his concern obvious. "Your family has always meant so much to that kid." He hesitated. "I don't like that he hasn't called. We should pray ... that he isn't drinking again."

Bailey had to keep herself from blurting out that of course Cody wasn't drinking. He wouldn't go back to that, even if he never contacted them again. But she kept quiet.

It wasn't until later as they were headed home along the dark country roads, and the Suburban was quiet, that Bailey remembered her father's expression when Ryan Taylor brought up Cody's name. He almost looked angry, and suddenly in the silence of the ride she understood. Cody might be someone they all cared for, and he might have been a part of their family for many years. But now his silence hurt Bailey. It hurt all of them. And for that, her dad would only have so much patience.

Which explained the way her father teased about Matt Keagan. He was ready for Bailey to let go of Cody and get on with life. With someone more like her — someone like Matt.

Bailey stifled a quiet laugh. *Matt Keagan.* As if that were even a possibility ...

Not until they were home and she and her mom were in the kitchen making hot tea did Bailey remember the phone call from the 212 area code and the message she still hadn't heard. "Hey ..." She ran lightly to the other side of the kitchen bar where her purse hung on one of the stools. "I got a call from New York."

"New York?"

"Yeah." She dug around her purse again and after half a minute finally found her phone. "Listen." She pushed a few buttons and put the phone on speaker so they could both hear.

"Hello, this is Francesca Tilly, producer for the Broadway production of *Hairspray*. I was given your name by a friend of mine, a producer with the show *Wicked*." The woman's Italian accent was thick. She talked very fast and sounded quite serious. "We've lost members of our cast for various reasons, so we'll host a limited audition in three weeks. We know about your role in the Brandon Paul film, and we'd like you to attend." Another pause.

What in the world Bailey locked eyes with her mom. She covered her mouth with her hand and kept listening.

"I apologize for calling you on a Sunday, but our schedule is crazy tomorrow. If you're interested, contact me at my office number. You'll be given details then. Thank you for your time. I hope to hear from you."

The woman left her number twice, and the message came to an end. Bailey set her phone down and let out a brief scream. "Did you hear that?"

Her mom grinned big. "I knew it …" She laughed out loud and reached for Bailey's hands. "I knew someone would notice you after your last audition."

Bailey danced her way closer and took hold of her mom's fingers. "Can you believe it? *Hairspray?*" She screamed again. "That's my all-time favorite show! And they want me to audition!!"

"What's the commotion?" Her dad had been in the garage. He looked happy, but bewildered as he came closer. "Whatever it is, you're sure smiling big." He came to her and kissed the top of her head. "So I'm sure I'll like it too."

"I'm going back to New York!" Bailey's heart was still grasping the reality of the voicemail. "This producer wants me to audition for *Hairspray*! Isn't that the craziest thing?"

He smiled as he searched her eyes. "That surprises you?"

"Yes!" She squealed, dancing in place. "Of course it surprises me. I can't believe I'm still standing!"

They laughed and for the next half hour they talked about the songs Bailey could sing for the audition, and how she was more prepared now, and the fact that her dance lessons would definitely pay off because she was a better dancer than before.

Bailey thought about something Francesca Tilly had said on the message and for a moment her happiness dropped off. "You don't think they only want me because of my role in *Unlocked*, do you?"

"Of course not." Her mom's answer was quick, her tone convincing. "You have to be more than well known to survive on Broadway." She smiled. "They called you because of your skills, honey."

She nodded slowly. "I hope so." The last thing she would want was a role handed to her because of her visibility. On Broadway a person needed to earn their place — it was that simple. They talked more about the logistics of what lay ahead, and what the producers would look for during the upcoming audition. Bailey was exhausted in every possible way by the time she went to bed, and even then she wasn't sure she could ever find her way to sleep. She thought about Cody and how tomorrow was Valentine's Day. Not only would she go another February fourteenth alone, but he wasn't even part of her life to share in the excitement that had just happened. She rolled onto her side and stared at the moonlight splashed across the wall.

She was going back to New York for another audition! She'd asked God for this every day since her last one, when the producers of *Wicked* had cut her and offered her former boyfriend Tim Reed a part in the show. Now ... now it was finally her turn to show a different set of producers she had what it took to win a part.

She breathed out. *Calm down, Bailey ... you need sleep.* She smiled in the darkness but as she did, she remembered Pastor Mark's message from earlier. *Everyone says goodbye eventually ... people come and go ... nothing stays except for Jesus.* And suddenly amidst her very great joy came a flash of sadness. Grief, almost. Because if God allowed this, she might actually win a part on Broadway. All of which would mean one very certain thing. Despite everything she loved about Bloomington and her family and her classes at IU, this wouldn't be a time to think about Brandon Paul or to meet Matt Keagan or to wonder about Cody.

It would be her time to leave.

BAILEY FLANIGAN SERIES

Featuring members from Karen Kingsbury's popular Baxter family, the Bailey Flanigan Series completes he stories of Bailey and Cody— the finale readers all over the world have been waiting for.

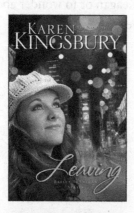
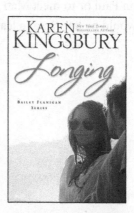
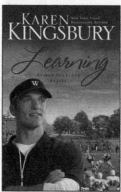

Available in stores and online!

About the Author

KAREN KINGSBURY is America's favorite inspirational novelist. There are more than 25 million copies of her award-winning books in print, including several million copies sold in the past year. Karen's recent dozen titles have all debuted at or near the top of *The New York Times* bestseller's list. She is also a public speaker, reaching more than 100,000 women annually through various national events. Karen lives and works outside Nashville, Tenn., with her husband, Don, and their five sons, three of whom were adopted from Haiti. Also living nearby is their only daughter, Kelsey, an actress in inspirational films and married to Christian recording artist Kyle Kupecky. For more information visit www.karenkingsbury.com. Karen is also on Facebook and Twitter, where she regularly interacts with nearly half a million reader friends.